The Spirit of Care

The Spirit of Care

The eight-hundred-year story of St John's Hospital, Bath

Jean Manco

Published by St John's Hospital, Bath

First published in 1998 by
The Hospital of St John the Baptist with
the Chapel of St Michael Annexed with
St Catherine's Hospital
Bath
BA1 2HQ
01225 448494

ISBN 0 9534652 0 9

Designed by Niall Allsop
Illustrations by Christine Molan
Cartography by Catherine Horton
Reprographics by Black Cat Graphics
Printed by Harlequin Colourprint

Typeset in Nueva, Goudy and Gill Sans

The archway leading into St John's Hospital

Contents

Foreword

When, some two years ago, the Trustees decided to commission a new history of St John's Hospital and its associated charities they had two matters chiefly in mind. First, that it was more than a century since the last account, by R. E. M. Peach, was published and much had happened since then. Moreover, recent research had revealed inaccuracies in earlier works and these needed to be put right.

The Trustees' second reason was rather more complex. It has always been – and remains – their policy not to seek publicity for the Hospital or themselves and, consequently, few people in Bath, unless directly connected with it, have more than the vaguest idea of what the Hospital does or is. This book may therefore serve to lift the veil a little, particularly in respect of St John's' current activities and the substantial future developments now in train.

As the present Chairman of the Trustees, it is my privilege to write this short foreword. In doing so, I echo Jean Manco's tribute in her preface to all those whom she mentions, for the valuable work that they have all put into this project. Our thanks must also go to designer Niall Allsop, illustrator Chris Molan, cartographer Catherine Horton, photographers Woodley & Quick and Simon Doling and, of course, to Jean Manco herself without whose scholarship, enthusiasm and gentle nagging of all concerned, this book would never have appeared.

We hope that readers will come to share our belief that St John's is much more than a collection of handsome buildings and gardens in the centre of Bath. It is a living entity which – imperfectly at times – has served the needy and infirm in and around the city for over eight centuries. There has been incessant change, of course: buildings, almspeople, staff, Masters, Clerks and Trustees have come and gone, but one thing has remained constant – the benign spirit of the place which touches everyone who comes to know it.

Richard Millar
Chairman of the Trustees, St John's Hospital

Preface and acknowledgements

This book was commissioned by the Trustees of St John's Hospital in 1996. It was a delight to undertake a project so close to my heart. For years I had been fascinated by the early hospitals of Bath and their survival and adaptation to each passing age. In 1991 Bath City Council commissioned research from me on the Georgian windows of St John's Hospital. Meanwhile, research for my own pleasure on St John's and the other hospitals found its way into lectures and publications.

It was a far from untrodden path. The Revd. William Luckman, Master of St John's 1877-92, requested a history of St John's from R. E. M. Peach, published in 1886. It relied heavily on previous published histories of Bath and Somerset and was more notable for its colourful invective than its depth of scholarship. The Revd. Charles Shickle, Master of St John's 1899-1927, was less easily satisfied. He worked tirelessly to uncover original sources for the history of St John's and the other municipal charities of Bath. Drawing on Revd. Shickle's notes and his own scouring of the minute books, Commander Arthur Day, Chairman of the Trustees 1969-72, produced booklets on the history of all the charities in 1970. Christopher Couchman, Clerk to the Trustees 1971-93, has done much to promote this present project, while the enthusiasm and support of his successor, Quentin Elston, and also of the Revd. Frederick Harte, Master of St John's, Derek Jones, Surveyor to St John's and Kay Bowen, Administrative Assistant, has been invaluable in carrying it to fruition.

I am grateful to those who have commented on the book in draft, most particularly Dr Robert Dunning, who read it all with scrupulous care. Others commented on their areas of special interest: Dr Peter Carpenter on the Magdalen and Leper's Hospitals, Peter Davenport on the archaeology, Elizabeth Holland on the Chapmans, Dr Roger Rolls on Bellott's Hospital and the Mineral Water Hospital and Timothy Tatton-Brown on the early hospitals of Canterbury. Others who have kindly supplied references are acknowledged in my footnotes. Any remaining errors are my own.

I am indebted to a number of individuals and bodies for illustrations.

Images are reproduced by kind permission of the Dean and Chapter of Wells (1), the Archbishop of Canterbury and the Trustees of Lambeth Palace Library (3), the British Library (4, 7, 70), the Master and Fellows of Trinity College, Cambridge (5), Bath and North East Somerset Heritage Services (8, 13, 15, 17-8, 26, 28, 33, 35, 39), Victoria Art Gallery, Bath and North East Somerset (10, 25, 31, 36, 48, 54, 56, 80, 85, 87), Archivio Segreto Vaticano (16), Bath and North East Somerset Library and Archive Service (Bath Central Library) (20, 29, 65, 71, 79, 83-4, 95-6), Bath and North East Somerset Record Office (21, 47, 81-2), the Governors of King Edward's School, Bath (27), Society of Antiquaries of London (30), Godfrey Laurence (45, 72), St John's College, Oxford (46), RCHME (51, 107-10), the National Portrait Gallery, London (60), Anthony Trollope-Bellew (75), the Trustees of the Holburne Museum (76), the Royal National Hospital of Rheumatic Diseases, National Health Service Trust (77), the Courtauld Institute of Art (80), Mrs Joan Fear (93, 106), The Bath Chronicle (96), Bath and North East Somerset Council (116). Historical items not otherwise acknowledged are the property of the Trustees of St John's Hospital.

Original artwork by Christine Molan (9, 11, 32). Original cartography by Catherine Horton (endpapers, pages 17, 31, 49, 65, 102, 103, 143). Photography by Woodley & Quick (frontispiece, 2, 6, 10, 12, 14, 19, 21-3, 24, 31, 34, 36, 38, 40-4, 47-50, 52-3, 56-60, 63, 67-9, 74, 79, 86, 88, 90-2, 94, 97, 105, 111, 115, 117-8, 121), Clive Quinnell (29, 75, 77), Dr John Wroughton (37), Simon Doling (62, 67, 69, 73, 104, 113, 119-20), Prof. R. A. Buchanan (112). Photographs were kindly loaned or donated by Tim Mowl (60), The Building of Bath Museum (70), Dr Peter Carpenter (89), Dr Brenda Buchanan (112).

Note: For the sake of consistency, the modern spellings of personal and place-names have been used throughout. Quotations are rendered in modern English, except words in italics. Until 1754, the English practice was to begin the year on Lady Day, 25 March. Dates before that from 1 January to 24 March are given in old and new style e.g. 14 February 1423/4.

Jean Manco
Bristol, August 1998

The Middle Ages

The foundation of St John's Hospital

The Hospital of St Mary Magdalen

The medieval Hospital of St John the Baptist

St Michael by the Baths

The Hospital of St Catherine or Black Almshouse

Rebuilding by Bath Priory

The foundation of St John's Hospital

St John's Hospital is a remarkable institution. Through centuries of change, it has remained true to its purpose. Founded in the twelfth century, it is still providing comfort in old age for those in need. Only a handful of hospitals in the country have so long a history.[1]

Modern hospitals are designed for surgery and treatment of medical emergencies. Medieval hospitals were quite different. They were places of refuge for the needy, usually run by religious men and women. In England and Wales about 10% were hostels for pilgrims and other wayfarers. About a quarter were leperhouses. Most of the rest were almshouses. Only about 8% were intended specifically for the infirm. However, the distinction between the almshouse and the infirmary is not clear-cut. Both cared for the poor, and poverty often sprang from a physical handicap. The blind, deaf, maimed or elderly would fare less well in the labour market and faced destitution if their families could not care for them. Then again a hospital for the local poor might also have a guest-house for wayfarers and facilities for pregnant women. All those functions were covered by the general term *hospital*, sometimes shortened to *spital*.[2]

While some hospitals had royal or aristocratic founders, the major source of charity in the Middle Ages was the Church. The clergy were bound by their vows to give alms to the poor and many bishops built hospitals. About 1180 Bishop Reginald Fitzjocelyn founded the Hospital of St John the Baptist for the poor of Bath, which in practice seemed to mean the infirm.[3]

Bishop Reginald's appointment to the Diocese of Bath came after a long period of vacancy. Robert of Lewes, third Bishop of Bath, died in 1166,[4] two years after the quarrel began between Henry II and his erstwhile friend Archbishop Thomas Becket. The ensuing struggle for power between Crown and Church kept vacant sees unfilled. Reginald Fitzjocelyn was unhappily drawn into the strife. He was a cosmopolitan and accomplished young man, a protégé of Becket and the son of Jocelyn de Bohun, Bishop of Salisbury. His natural inclination was to support the archbishop, but Becket's excommunication of his father in 1166 pushed Reginald into the king's camp.

1 There are about 20 others. Among those founded earlier than St John's and still functioning are St John the Baptist, Canterbury (*c*.1080), St Nicholas, Harbledown, Canterbury (*c*.1080), St John the Evangelist, Cirencester (by 1135), St Giles, Wilton (*c*.1135), St Cross, Winchester (1136), St Mary Magdalene, Gloucester (by 1160) and St Margaret, Gloucester (by 1163). St Bartholomew's, London (*c*.1123) is now a medical hospital.

2 Orme and Webster, chap.3; Gilchrist, 9-11, 28.

3 Early deeds of St John's refer to the inmates as poor or infirm or both. *Med Deeds* 1/18, 51, 61-2, 81, 124, 138, 154, 156-9.

4 *Ecclesiastical Documents*, 28.

The seal of Bishop Reginald Fitzjocelyn. The bishop is wearing mitre and stole. His right hand is raised in blessing, his left hand holding a crozier. From C. M. Church, *Chapters in the Early History of the Church of Wells* (1894)

5 *Materials for the History of Thomas Becket*, **3**, 524.

6 Church, 297-9; *Dictionary of National Biography*.

7 *Materials for the History of Thomas Becket*, **7**, 181.

8 Church, 300-3; *Dictionary of National Biography*.

9 *MSS of Wells*, **2**, charter 39.

10 *Collectanea I*, 63; *Radulfi de Diceto* 391. Peach described Reginald as the second bishop of Bath and Wells, from a misunderstanding in Le Neve and Hardy. A more modern history of the see appears in the *VCH Somerset* **2**.

11 *Dictionary of National Biography*.

12 *Radulfi de Diceto*, **1**, 398.

13 Manco, 'Bath Priory', 80, 84-5, fig.2.

14 *Med Deeds*, 1/1, 170.

15 *Collectanea I*, 63.

Though the de Bohuns were Norman-French in origin, Reginald was nicknamed the Lombard, from his education in Northern Italy.[5] His facility in Italian made him particularly useful to Henry II at a time when the king needed a persuasive voice in Rome. Reginald was among Henry's ambassadors to Pope Alexander III in 1167 and 1169.[6] He was so effective in the king's cause that Becket in fury described him as 'that bastard, that enemy of the peace of the church, that son of a priest'.[7]

After the murder of the archbishop in December 1170, Reginald was sent to the Pope to plead the king's innocence. Naturally Henry wanted to reward so faithful a servant. In April 1173 he procured the election of Reginald to the See of Bath. However, in the absence of an archbishop, the appointment had to be confirmed by the Pope, who might well hesitate. He had just canonised Becket. So Reginald travelled to Rome again, this time to plead his own cause. It took time. He needed to clear himself of complicity in Becket's death and bring witnesses to swear that he had been conceived before his father became a priest.[8] However, by 18 April 1174, Pope Alexander was prepared to ratify his election.[9] On his way back from Rome Reginald Fitzjocelyn was consecrated as the fourth bishop of Bath in the church at St.-Jean-de-Maurienne on 23 June 1174. He was 33 years old.[10] After a diversion to Grand Chartreuse, he met Henry II at Barfleur on 8 August.[11] It was not until 24 November 1174 that Bishop Reginald Fitzjocelyn was solemnly enthroned by the new Archbishop of Canterbury, who was touring his province.[12]

The ceremony would have taken place in the new cathedral in Bath (PLAN 1), started by the first Bishop of Bath, John of Tours, and completed by Robert of Lewes. Although Bishop Reginald continued to travel on State and Church business, his chief residence was his palace in Bath.[13] The needy of the city would have clustered at his gates and the bishop looked no further for a worthy object of his charity.

John of Tours had been granted the city and abbey of Bath in order to move his see from Wells to Bath, so Bishop Reginald was the city's lord and abbot. His duties made it impossible for him to be an active abbot, so the monastery was run by his deputy, the prior. Still if the bishop wished to found a hospital, one might expect him have a free choice of site. In practice his tenants might need some persuasion to move from the property he wanted. About 1180 Bishop Reginald confirmed a grant of land by his tenant Roger son of Algar to the hospital of the baths (3).[14] The location is not mentioned, but the fact that this is the earliest of the hospital deeds tells its own story. The bishop would have been anxious firstly to secure a suitable site. He, not Roger, was the driving force here. A medieval history of the see records Reginald as the founder of St John's Hospital.[15] In any case that is clear from what followed.

About 1190 Bishop Reginald placed the hospital under the control of the monastery in Bath. His deed describes it as the hospital of St John the Baptist for the support of the poor of Bath. The bishop endowed it with a sheaf of corn annually from each acre of the episcopal demesnes, while the

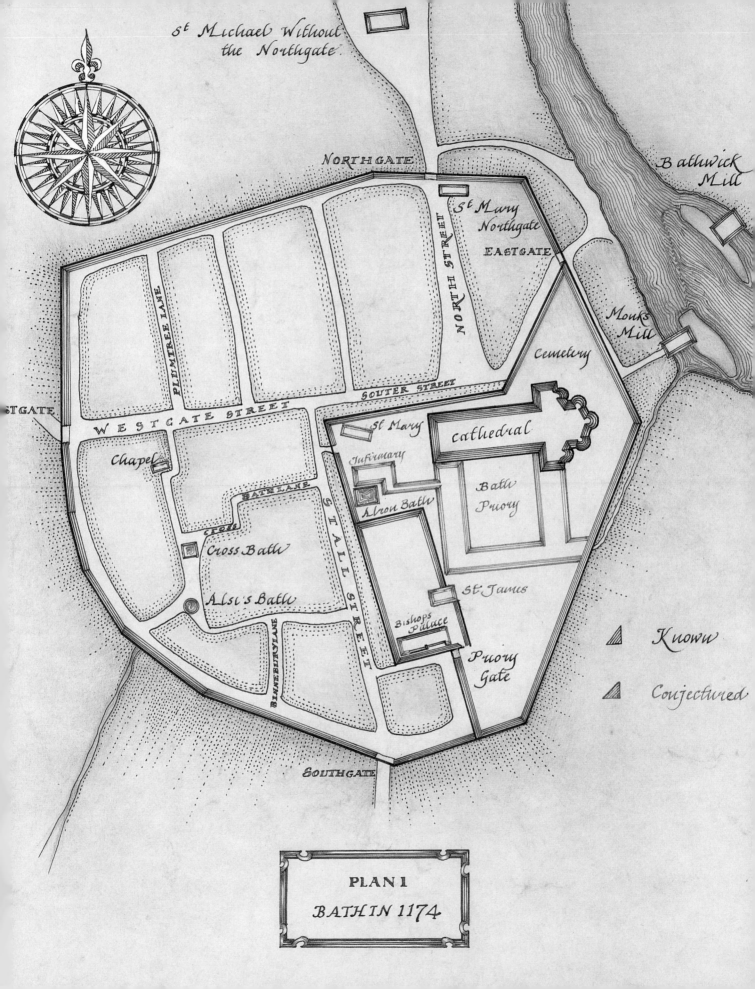

St Michael Without
the Northgate.

Bathwick
Mill

NORTHGATE

St Mary
Northgate

EASTGATE

NORTH STREET

Monks
Mill

Cemetery

SOUTER STREET

STGATE

WESTGATE STREET

PLUMTREE LANE

Cathedral

St Mary

Infirmary

Chapel

BATH LANE

Alron Bath

Bath
Priory

CROSS

Cross Bath

STALL STREET

St James

Alsi's Bath

Bishops
Palace

Priory
Gate

BINNEBURY LANE

Known

Conjectured

SOUTHGATE

PLAN 1

BATH IN 1174

2

The seal of the Hospital of St John the
Baptist. St John is baptising Jesus in the
River Jordan. The Holy Spirit is shown as a
dove. Below are the arms of the See of
Bath and Wells: St Andrew's Cross
surmounted by a mitre

16 *Med Deeds*, 1/5, 174.

17 *Ibid*, 1/3, 172.

18 *Ibid*, 1/6, 175.

19 The chapel is now dedicated to St Michael.
See the section 'St Michael by the Baths'.

20 Manco, 'Bath Priory', 92.

21 Gilchrist, 38 and fig. 16.

22 Miller, *The Birth of the Hospital*, 93, 126;
Miller, 'The Knights of St John, 728-9.

23 Riley-Smith, 37-41; Miller, 'Knights of St
John', 709, 718-9.

24 Henderson, 68.

25 Orme and Webster, 20-2.

prior and monks donated the same from their demesne, and a tithe of their
bread and salted meat.[16] At around the same time, the bishop granted to the
hospital a meadow outside the western city wall.[17] He also gave four marks
of silver (£2 13s 4d) annually, two loads of dead wood from his park each
week and the right to pasture 100 sheep on Lansdown and two horses and
two cows with the bishop's animals. The chaplain serving the hospital was
to be exempt from diocesan taxation.[18] Clearly the hospital had been built
and its chapel dedicated to St John the Baptist,[19] so the bishop was intent
on its organisation and provision.

Bath offered a hospital site like no other in the country. The city was
famous for its thermal waters. The hospital was built beside its two smaller
baths, while the cathedral priory's own infirmary was probably by the main
spring.[20] The mystery of the hot, bubbling springs had aroused religious awe
long before the Christian era. The Celts had worshipped Sulis as the goddess
of the springs. The Romans built a temple of Sulis Minerva beside their great
baths complex. By Reginald's time Christianity had replaced it with a cathedral,
but the principle remained the same: thanks should be given to a munificent
deity for these healing waters. Modern medicine is more sceptical than medieval
about the powers of spa water, but bathing must have soothed aches and pains
then as now.

The natural patron saint for the 'hospital of the baths' was St John the
Baptist, who plunged his followers in the Jordan in a ritual rebirth. The saint
is shown on the seal of St John's in the act of baptising Christ (2). At least
one other hospital of St John the Baptist was linked with baths; that in Oxford
was beside the Cherwell and a culvert from the river served baths in the
infirmary chapel.[21]

The dedication was in any case a popular one for hospitals, probably because
an early hospital of St John had so much influence on the development of
hospitals in the West. Care for the sick and helpless was advanced in the
Byzantine Empire. The Empress Eudocia founded houses for the aged in
Jerusalem c.443, so she may have been responsible for that attached to the
Church of St John the Baptist, which survived at least until the sack of
Jerusalem in 614.[22] Around 1070 a hospice for pilgrims was built beside the
same church. After crusaders captured Jerusalem in 1099, the Hospital of
St John assumed a new importance. Generous gifts enabled it to expand. By
1113 it had daughter hospices in France and Italy. At its height, the hospital
in Jerusalem had four physicians and four surgeons, serving around 1,000
patients. Until the loss of Jerusalem to Saladin in 1187, it was the most famous
hospital in the Christian world.[23] Two early hospitals in the West were also
dedicated to St John the Baptist. One had been established in Florence by
1040 for pilgrims and the poor.[24] The other was the first hospital for the infirm
in England, built on the outskirts of Canterbury by Lanfranc, Archbishop
of Canterbury (1070-1089).[25]

Bishop Reginald Fitzjocelyn had in his service two brothers, Hugh and
Jocelyn of Wells. At the time St John's was founded, they were in the humble

3

The earliest charter of St John's Hospital *c.*1180 (LPL MS 940, no.2). Bishop Reginald
Fitzjocelyn confirmed the grant of land by Roger son of Algar to the 'hospital of the baths'

positions of clerk and chaplain, and it was as such that they witnessed the earliest deeds of St John's.[26] The bishop's purpose evidently made a profound impression upon them. Both rose high in the Church. Jocelyn became Bishop of Bath and Glastonbury in 1206. Hugh was Archdeacon of Wells, then from 1209 Bishop of Lincoln. However, he clashed with King John as soon as he was consecrated and both brothers were in exile from 1209 to 1213. While abroad Hugh drafted a will in which he remembered 'the hospital of Bath', and left a much larger bequest to found a Hospital of St John the Baptist at Wells.[27] On their return Bishop Jocelyn supported the project and also the foundation by a layman of a hospital of St John the Baptist at Bridgwater.[28]

Bishop Jocelyn devised a set of rules for the Bridgwater hospital, probably based on Fitzjocelyn's rules for his foundation in Bath. While those for Bath do not survive, those for Bridgwater do. Bishop Jocelyn decreed that St John's Bridgwater should be run by a master elected from among the brethren. The brethren were to live by a monastic rule and wear a monastic garb with a black cross on their cloaks. A suitable brother should be given charge of the poor, infirm and needy persons in the infirmary, with the help of 'two or three women, not noble but suitable … who are willing and able to serve the infirm poor'.[29] Early deeds of St John's, Bath refer to the master, brethren and sisters serving God there [staff], and the poor and infirm [almsfolk].[30]

Bishop Reginald himself died an honoured man. He had remained a trusted advisor of Henry II and on 3 September 1189 he escorted Richard I at his coronation (4).[31] On 27 November 1191 he was elected to the highest position in the English Church, Archbishop of Canterbury. He had not sought the honour, but the monks of Canterbury were anxious to secure this 'devout, learned, discreet and provident man'. However, it was not to be. Reginald, having been present at the election, returned to Bath, 'to settle the affairs of his church there, which he dearly loved and by whom he was even more dearly loved.' On his way back to Canterbury he was seized with a sudden paralysis at his manor of Dogmersfield in Hampshire on Christmas Eve. Two days later he died. His body was taken to Bath for burial near the high altar of his cathedral.[32] A chronicler of the time, playing on the name Reginald (ruler), gave him this epitaph:

> WHILE REGINALD LIVED, HE RULED HIMSELF AND HIS SUBJECTS WELL.
> WHATEVER HE TAUGHT, HE DID; LET NO ONE SEEK FOR MORE.[33]

The Hospital of St Mary Magdalen

Although St John's was the first hospital within Bath, there was almost certainly another already operating close by. In the 1170s Elias, a leprous monk of Reading, came to Bath in search of a cure. He bathed in the hot waters for 40 days to no avail.[34] Still the hope was there, and no doubt the reputation of Bath waters drew other lepers. What provision was there for them? There has been a good deal of confusion on this point.

The idea that King Athelstan founded a leper hospital at Bath is a

26 *Med Deeds*, 1/1, 2, 3, 5, 110, 121.

27 *MSS of Wells*, **1**, 431-2.

28 *VCH Soms*, **2**, 154,158-9.

29 *The Register of Thomas Bekynton*, no.1062.

30 *Med Deeds*, 1/18, 51, 61, 62, 81, 124, 137, 138, 154.

31 *Dictionary of National Biography*.

32 *Epistolae Cantuarienses*, **2**, 352-5, 360, 554; *Ralph de Diceto*, **2**, 103-4; *Chronicle of Richard of Devizes*, 55-6.

33 *Chronicle of Richard of Devizes*, 56.

34 *Materials for the History of Thomas Becket*, **1**, 416; **2**, 242.

Cy deuise les ordonances du sa
cre au roy richard dangleterre ·

et autres en chappes de draps dor
brodees de perles deuant lesquelz

4
The coronation procession of Richard I in 1189 (BL Royal MS 15 E IV, vol.1, f.257v). Bishop Reginald Fitzjocelyn
walks on the king's left hand. The fifteenth-century Flemish artist has set the scene in his own period

5

The examination of a leper by a medieval physician. A marginal sketch in a medical manuscript (Trinity MS 0.1.20, f.264r)

35 *Valor Ecclesiasticus*, **1**, 177.

36 *Two Chartularies*, 2/808.

37 Orme and Webster, 19-20.

38 Collinson, **1**, 42, repeated in Warner, 278-9.

39 Manco, 'Bath Priory', 87.

40 Orme and Webster, 22.

41 Richards, 4; Gilchrist, 38.

42 Orme and Webster, 27.

43 Rawcliffe, *Medicine and Society*, 14-7; Orme and Webster, 24-5.

44 Kiple, 274.

45 The charter is undated. It cannot be earlier than 1088, when John of Tours became Bishop of Bath, or later than 1100, when William II died, since it describes him as king. The name Hussey derives from Old French *Hosed*, rendered as *Hosatus* in the Latin deed. The charter survives in a late fifteenth-century copy in the back of the Saxon gospels from Bath priory: Corpus Christi College Cambridge MS 140; facsimile with transcript in Stokes Shaw, 98, 100.

46 *Domesday Book* **8** *Somerset*, 7/4, 10; p.384.

47 *Domesday Book* **6** *Wiltshire*, B5, 34/1 and note.

48 The advowson of St Mary Northgate in Bath was owned by later lords of Wilmington, indicating that the church had been founded by a predecessor, presumably as the domestic chapel of his town house. *Pedes Finum*, SRS **6**, 253-4, SRS **12**, 137.

misunderstanding. The monastery of Bath distributed alms to the poor and lepers 'from the endowment of Athelstan' and later benefactors,[35] but this was to feed 100 poor people on the donors' anniversaries. Athelstan made no stipulation that his alms should go to lepers or to a particular institution.[36] Claims of an Anglo-Saxon foundation for hospitals elsewhere are based on similar misconceptions. In fact there is no evidence for any free-standing, independent hospital in England before the Norman conquest.[37]

In another muddle Bishop Robert of Lewes has been credited with building a hospital for the leprous poor c.1138, dedicated to St Lazarus and provided with a bath fed from the Hot Bath.[38] In fact Bishop Robert rebuilt the infirmary of Bath Priory after a disastrous fire in 1137.[39] The Lepers' or Lazars' Bath with its tiny hospital beside the Hot Bath belongs to a much later period. Bath's medieval leper hospital was outside the city limits, as *leprosaria* invariably were.

Archbishop Lanfranc founded the first English leper hospital at Harbledown near Canterbury.[40] Soon others were following Lanfranc's lead. Leper hospitals sprang up on the outskirts of towns all over the country. Most were founded in the twelfth and thirteenth centuries, so leprosy must have been widespread then. The growth of towns would help spread the disease. Leprosy thrives on close human contact.[41] Whether or not this was fully understood, the Church acted to isolate lepers. In 1175 the English Church Council ordered that lepers should not live among the healthy. In 1179 the Lateran Council at Rome decreed that leper communities should have their own priests, churches and cemeteries.[42]

This dreadful disease produced a welter of emotions in the medieval mind. Pity vied with horror. Those ravaged by leprosy were shunned not only through fear of contagion, but because they were so hideously disfigured. It was widely seen as a divine punishment for sin. However, the more compassionate felt that such suffering must bring lepers closer to God and revered those with the courage to care for them.[43] It has often been said that other ailments were confused with leprosy in the Middle Ages. Certainly the disease can be hard to recognise in the early stages. However, medieval physicians were well versed in the works of Galen, who gave clear and precise descriptions of leprosy. No doubt mistakes were made, particularly where physicians were not involved, but there is evidence of considerable caution in diagnosis.[44] This is understandable. Committal to a lazar house was a death sentence.

Sometime between 1088 and 1100 Walter Hussey gave his house in Holloway outside Bath, with the adjoining chapel of St Mary Magdalen, to Bishop John and the cathedral at Bath.[45] Walter was a tenant of the cathedral priory, holding its manors of Wilmington (in Priston) and St Catherine (then part of Batheaston), and one tenth of its manor of Lyncombe.[46] He also had property in Wiltshire.[47] It seems that Walter had chosen to live on his land in Lyncombe, close to the security of the walled city of Bath, where he probably had a town house.[48] In Lyncombe he had built his house and chapel at a spot where the road to Bath lay conveniently close to one of the springs of Beechen

Cliff. The deeply-cut old road was known as the 'hollow way', like others of the type elsewhere. The modern misconception that the name meant 'holy way' has been linked with the belief that the chapel was built for pilgrims. That idea probably arose in the eighteenth century, when the true origins of the hospital had been forgotten.[49] St Mary Magdalen was clearly Walter's own domestic chapel. From about 1094 Walter became the Sheriff of Wiltshire[50] and would have had quarters in the castle of Salisbury, which could explain why he gave up his house in Holloway.

Walter made the gift for the good of his soul and those of his family, on condition that the chapel of St Mary Magdalen would be rebuilt and 'exalted' by Bath Priory. Presumably he wanted it to become monastic. (There was a similar clause in a grant to Bath Priory of a chapel at Dunster, which was converted into a daughter priory.[51]) Monks were seen as especially close to God, well placed to intercede on behalf of sinners. The medieval mind in fear of purgatory craved monastic prayers for the swift passage of their souls to heaven.[52]

Bishop John of Tours had been the king's physician.[53] One can imagine him seizing the opportunity to create a refuge for lepers. The isolation of the house – across the river from the city – would have made it ideal for the purpose. It was also beside a main road, a popular position for hospitals, so that the occupants could beg for alms from passers-by.[54] However, the first mention of the 'house of lepers in the suburb of Bath' comes in 1212 in the draft will of Hugh of Wells, Bishop of Lincoln.[55] Then on 16 July 1256 royal protection was issued to the Master and brethren of the hospital of lepers of St Mary Magdalen outside Bath.[56] In the same year the Master appeared in a legal case, in which the hospital was described as being in Holloway.[57] So clearly the hospital had been created from Walter Hussey's gift, but at what date?

If Bishop John did immediately convert Walter's house into a leper hospital, then it would have been among the earliest in the country. The reputation of the Bath house might then explain why St Mary Magdalen became overwhelmingly the most common dedication for leper hospitals in England, unlike France where St Lazarus reigned supreme.[58] St Lazarus was the obvious choice: a conflation of Lazarus of Bethany, whom Jesus raised from the dead (John 11:1-44) and the allegorical Lazarus full of sores who lay at the rich man's gate (Luke 16:19-31). It was from the latter that lepers were known as lazars. However, by the medieval period St Mary Magdalen was identified with Mary the sister of Lazarus of Bethany,[59] and so could be seen as an appropriate patron. There were 55 English leperhouses dedicated to her.

The hospital of St Mary Magdalen has been much changed over the centuries, so we can only guess at its original form. At Harbledown the lepers lived in small wooden huts, while other *leprosaria*, like that of St Mary Magdalene at Glastonbury, had communal infirmaries.[60] Since the main element of Walter Hussey's house was probably a timber hall,[61] it would have been easily converted to an infirmary. The present Magdalen House attached

6
Seal of the Hospital of St Mary Magdalen. The saint is shown with flowing hair, kneeling before the cross

49 A claim of pilgrim use was made in 1836: BaRO Acc 59, bundle 2, nos.49/50, p.26.

50 *Regista Regum Anglo-Normanum*, **1**, nos. 347, 593, 811, **2**, nos. 494, 673, 874, 883-4; *Two Chartularies*, 1/53.

51 Manco, 'Bath Priory', 84.

52 Rosenthal.

53 *Willelmi Malmesbiriensis*, 195; Orderic Vitalis, **5**, 204-5.

54 Orme and Webster, 45-47.

55 *MSS of Wells*, **1**, 431-2.

56 *Calendar of Patent Rolls 1247-58*, 488.

57 *Somersetshire Pleas*, no.1525.

58 Clay, 252.

59 Haskins, 1-32.

60 Orme and Webster, 22; Gilchrist, 45.

61 Grenville, 66, 71-2.

to the west end of the chapel is probably on or close to the site. Farm buildings would have been part of the complex. Walter had also granted the land that belonged to the house, with the stock, listed as six oxen, four cows, 60 sheep and 30 rams.[62] The hospital would be largely self-sufficient. The sheep would supply wool for clothing and for sale, though Bath Priory took a tithe.[63] Able-bodied lepers would help to work the fields and gardens.

The rules for St Mary Magdalen have not survived, but probably resembled those for the leper hospitals of St Mary Magdalene in Exeter and Gloucester. The Gloucester rules decreed that the lepers should observe the disciplines of obedience, patience and charity, and hold all their property in common – the principles of monasticism. Meat could be eaten on three days of the week and feast days, but not on other days. Men and women were to be strictly segregated in and outside the house. At Exeter the lepers were expected to live chaste and honest lives and they were not to enter the city without the permission of the warden.[64]

Under monastic rule the spiritual welfare of the inmates took priority. There was a constant round of prayer, with special thanks to benefactors. In 1263 Brother Nicholas, Master of St Mary Magdalen, promised prayers to a couple who had granted a 10s rent in Beckington to the hospital.[65] Benefactors might also claim burial rights. In 1525 Robert Gibbs and his wife chose to be buried in St Mary Magdalen. Their memorial stone, decorated with a coat of arms, was prominently set in the middle of the chapel floor, with a plea for prayers for their souls.[66] Nursing was probably left to lay sisters. A grant of c.1270 to St Mary Magdalen mentions the brothers and sisters serving God there.

That grant was the interesting gift by John Wissy of his land in Berewick (in Lyncombe) for the souls of himself, his family and the commonalties of Bristol and Bath. John stipulated that prayers for them were to be said by the hospital chaplains in what had been his own chapel at Bath.[67] This was clearly a device to set up a chantry cheaply. The rents from the Berewick land amounted to only 2s 6d annually, not enough to support a chaplain, but by granting it to an established institution, Wissy could have prayers in his family chapel. John Wissy was a burgess of both Bath and Bristol, who served as mayor of Bristol in 1272-3.[68] Among his Bath properties was a tavern in Westgate Street, on the western corner of Parsonage Lane.[69] His chapel may have been behind the tavern.[70]

However, St Mary Magdalen attracted few benefactors, and known bequests were small, such as the 5s left to the hospital in 1286 by Sir Anselm de Gournay, lord of Englishcombe.[71] Since Walter Hussey and John Wissy were vague about the amount of land they were donating and no other early deeds have survived, we cannot be certain how much property was given to the hospital. The lack of documentation led to suspicions in the eighteenth century that the charity had been embezzled and property spirited away.[72] But the indications are that the endowment was never large. Where properties can be traced from the medieval period, they were generally still in hospital hands at the time of

62 Stokes Shaw, 98, 100.

63 MSS of Wells, 1, 386; Warner, appendix 75.

64 Orme and Webster, 69, 226.

65 Pedes Finum, SRS 6, 197.

66 A. à Wood, 19.

67 Two Chartularies, 2/345.

68 Great Red Book of Bristol: Text, 1, 111. Dated by the mayoralty of William FitzNicholas; see Cartulary of St Mark's, appendix II, 283 for revised date; Two Chartularies, 2/380; Cartulary of St Mark's, 64, 148; appendix II, 284.

69 Two Chartularies, 2/373, 376. Described as being between Serlo's Lane and the property of the Abbot of Keynsham. The Abbot of Keynsham had a plot on Plumtree (now Bridewell) Lane (SRO DD/WH6 Box 60/2), so Serlo's Lane must be Parsonage Lane.

70 Parsonage Lane was sometimes called All Saints Lane (Ancient Deeds, 5/83), which suggests a chapel. In 1585 a ruined chapel was rented to Thomas Turner, whose properties included a house in Parsonage Lane. The chapel was subsequently leased to William Chapman, who held the corner property once John Wissy's tavern: Accounts of the Chamberlains, 36; BaRO TS P. R. James (ed), 'Documents of the City of Bath' TS, 2, nos. 36, 37, 41; BaRO 1641 Survey of Bath f.89, no.3.

71 Episcopal Registers Worcs: Giffard, 296

72 BaRO, Enquiry into Somerset Charities, 1734-5, 1, 21, 80-85.

7

A female leper begging for alms: 'Some good my gentle master, for God's sake'.
The bell warns passers-by of her disease. (BL Lans. MS 451, f.127)

these allegations. For example, a house in Bath owned by St Mary Magdalen from at least 1292 was incorporated in 1806 into the White Hart Inn. Only when the inn was transferred to Bath Corporation for demolition did the property leave the ownership of the Magdalen charity.[73] An exception was a stall in Stall Street which the Master of St Mary Magdalen had sold by 1339.[74] The sale might have been a property exchange or an act of desperation.

The royal protection issued in 1256 presumably allowed hospital personnel to beg.[75] Certainly a royal protection was granted in 1348 for the master and brethren and their attorneys and messengers collecting alms.[76] Another potential source of income was the sale of indulgences – the forgiveness of sins. On 23 May 1332 Ralph of Shrewsbury, Bishop of Bath and Wells, granted an indulgence of 20 days for all those giving alms to the Hospital of the Holy Cross and St Mary Magdalen at Bath.[77] The addition of 'Holy Cross' to the name never reappears and can be dismissed as a clerical error – perhaps a confusion with Lyncombe fair, which was held on the Feast of the Invention of the Cross.[78] The fairground was above St Mary Magdalen on what is now Bear Flat. The yearly influx of people would have provided the ideal opportunity to beg for alms, as the master may have mentioned in seeking the indulgence.

The medieval Hospital of St John the Baptist

Masters and management

Soon after its foundation St John's Hospital was led by one Nicholas, who described himself as the 'Prior and Master'.[79] Later heads settled on 'master' as their title. Still, like priors, they were in charge of a group of brothers who followed a monastic rule. The Rule of St Augustine was a common choice for hospitals, being the most adaptable.[80] It was in force at the Hospitals of St John the Baptist in Wells and Bridgwater.[81] One postulant wished to join the brothers at Wells when the hospital happened to be without a master. A proxy was needed to accept his profession. The bishop selected the Master of St John's in Bath.[82] So was the same rule operating there? It would certainly have been appropriate. It emphasised that care should be taken of the sick and recognised that bathing might be necessary to health, although bathing simply for pleasure was frowned on.[83] The Augustinian habit was a black or brown robe, cloak and hood, with a cross on the cloak.

All monastic rules required services at fixed hours through the day. St John's also functioned as a chantry. In the twelfth century there were several grants to St John's in return for prayers. Richard of Combe and his wife Alice gave a meadow in Frome, for which the chaplains of St John's would celebrate mass annually for their souls.[84] William, Vicar of Locking, bought property to donate to the hospital; in return the brothers and sisters were to find a chaplain to serve his soul.[85] A generous bequest to the hospital by William de Wethamsted, Canon of Wells, was intended partly to maintain a secular chaplain, or one of the brethren, to perform a special daily service for his soul in the chapel or infirmary. His name was to be recited daily among the

73 *Two Chartularies*, 2/481; *MSS of Wells*, **2**, 623; SRO DD/WH6 Box 60/2; BaRO Enquiry into Somerset Charities 1734-5, 1, 81, 85; BMCA BMC/3, 1855, 1862; Manco, 'The History of Binbury', plot 2.

74 *Ancient Deeds*, 4/42.

75 *Calendar of Patent Rolls 1247-58*, 488.

76 *Calendar of Patent Rolls 1348-50*, 181.

77 *Register of Ralph of Shrewsbury*, 95 (no.401).

78 *Calendar of Charter Rolls 1300-26*, 47.

79 *Cartulary of Cirencester Abbey*, **2**, nos. 602-3.

80 Orme and Webster, 70.

81 *Registers of Thomas Wolsey et al*, 178.

82 *Register of John Stafford*, 233-4.

83 *Rule of Saint Augustine*, 14-5, 20-1.

84 *Med Deeds*, 1/82.

85 *Ibid*, 1/37.

brethren and sisters and the poor in the infirmary. Also each year there was to be a solemn service on the anniversary of his death, at which his gift to the hospital was to be read out, and the brethren and sisters present were to receive 2s.[86] (That would ensure full attendance.) William did not intend to be forgotten. He founded another chantry in the Priory of Woodspring.[87] In 1348 Henry Marshal of Bath left 6s 8d to St John's 'for celebrating my soul'.[88] Even where a grant did not specify prayers in return, they still might be expected. Prayers for the souls of founders and patrons were customary. For example St John's offered up masses and prayers for the bishops of the see in return for their sheaves of corn.[89]

Bishop Reginald Fitzjocelyn had unequivocally granted control of the hospital to Bath Priory, but that did not prevent some of his successors from contesting the matter. Those who built a church had the right of patronage for themselves and their heirs; they could select the incumbent. So one can see the logic for later bishops. Since Reginald had founded St John's Hospital, his successors should have the right to appoint its master. The Priors of Bath were equally certain that the right belonged to them. There is a hint of battles resolved by compromise in 1343. Thomas Gosmale, a professed brother in St John's, was appointed master in September that year both by Prior John de Iford and the bishop, Ralph of Shrewsbury. The bishop declared that the appointment had devolved upon him 'this turn', as though the bishop and prior alternated the patronage.[90]

Trouble arose in 1399. On 5 March Bishop Ralph Erghum granted permission to the brothers of St John's 'of which the bishop is founder and patron' to elect a master to succeed John Ashwick. Their choice fell upon John Shaftesbury, a brother of the hospital. He was inducted into the post by one of the other brethren, rather than the prior. This declaration of independence naturally affronted the prior. However, Shaftesbury enjoyed the confidence of the bishop. After the Prior of the Hospital of St John the Baptist in Redcliffe (Bristol) was deposed by the bishop for mismanagement in 1413, Shaftesbury took his place and managed both hospitals until 1424, when he resigned from Redcliffe. Finally in May 1428 Shaftesbury resigned as master of the Bath hospital.

Bishop John Stafford then placed St John's, Bath in the guardianship of Peter Buryman, a chaplain and brother of the hospital, pending a decision on the question of patronage. On 28 September Prior William Southbroke conveniently appointed Peter Buryman master. Still this was not the end of the matter. As Peter Buryman grew old, the question of his successor loomed large. In 1451 Buryman sent a brother of the hospital to Bishop Thomas Beckington with documents laying out the dispute over the patronage at the time of his appointment and its resolution in favour of the priory.[91] The bishop was unmoved. In January 1457/8 he decided that Peter Buryman was 'so broken with age and blindness' as to be unable to run the hospital, so he appointed John Philips, Vicar of Weston, to act with him. Philips made such a success of it that the bishop kept him in the post after the death of Buryman in June

86   MSS of Wells, 1, 144.

87   Ibid, 1, 153.

88   Ancient Deeds, 6/31.

89   Register of John de Drokensford, 99.

90   Register of Ralph of Shrewsbury, 493; Two Chartularies, 2/49.

91   Register of Nicholas Bubwith, lx-lxi, 337, 455; Register of Thomas Bekynton, 440-1; Two Chartularies, 2/279. The latter is a memo in a later hand, probably made in pursuit of the priory's claim to appoint the master.

1459. However, he replaced Philips a year later with 'brother John Vobe, priest, professed in the order of St John the Baptist'. Once again this was pending a decision between the bishop and prior as to the patronage. But once again a bishop had neatly pre-empted the selection. On 9 January 1460/1 John Vobe was appointed master, on the presentation of Bath Priory.[92]

In practice the choice of candidates for the mastership must have been so limited that the end result might be the same whoever made the selection. In 1377, a list of religious in the deanery of Bath includes John Ashwick, Master of St. John's Hospital. Brothers Peter Harding, John Dunster, John Brewton and John Wedmore are listed after him and were presumably of the hospital.[93] They were a small band. St John's was not large enough to require or support a great number. Of those few brethren, not all would be qualified for the mastership. The master would need to be a priest as well as a monk, in order to serve the chapel. There were four stages of ordination and it might take years to progress through them. Brother Richard Williams of St John's (Welsh in origin) managed it rather more quickly. On 12 March 1434/5 he was ordained acolyte and also subdeacon. Just weeks later he was ordained deacon. However, it was not until 22 September 1436 that he travelled to St Mary Redcliffe (Bristol) to be ordained priest.[94]

10
St John's Chapel in 1694 from Gilmore's map of Bath. The clock on the east gable was Elizabethan, but otherwise the chapel looks unchanged from when it was built

The site and buildings

The standard plan for a medieval hospital was a hall with beds on either side, like a modern hospital ward. This was the infirmary. It was often divided into three aisles, so that the beds could be screened off. At the east end was a chapel. Ideally the inmates should be able to see the altar from their beds and so have the comfort of religion in their worst hours.[95] Medieval deeds of St John's mention the chapel and infirmary.[96]

Where the hospital had inmates of both sexes, there had to be some means of segregation. Men and women could be housed in parallel halls or on two storeys. At the fifteenth-century hospital of SS John the Baptist and John the Evangelist in Sherborne, Dorset, women occupied the upper hall and men the lower. Alternatively, one long hall could be divided across the middle, with doors either side of the division leading into a chapel at right angles, forming a T.[97] We cannot be sure of the arrangement at Bath. All that is certain is that the present chapel is on the site of its twelfth-century predecessor. However, since the land north of the chapel was not initially owned by St John's, the T-plan can be ruled out. This means that the infirmary almost certainly ran west from the chapel. There is a clue that it was two-storeyed. At Sherborne the women had their own gallery in the chapel, where they sat during services. In Bath a 'room over the body of the chapel' is mentioned in 1581.[98]

That suggests a large gallery. Possibly the whole nave was two-storeyed, as shown here (9). The thirteenth-century Templar Chapel at South Witham was arranged in that way,[99] and the Knights Hospitaller favoured two-story chapels, like that at Chibburn.[100] In two seventeenth-century views St John's

92 *Register of Thomas Bekynton*, 297, 310, 323, 346-7, 354.

93 E. Green, 'A Bath poll tax', 298.

94 *The Register of John Stafford*, 344-5, 347, 355.

95 Gilchrist, 17.

96 *MSS of Wells*, 1, 144.

97 Gilchrist, 21 and fig. 9.

98 BaRO account roll 12, St John's.

99 Gilchrist, 81 and fig. 47.

100 M. E. Wood, fig.71; Gilchrist, 90-2.

Chapel seems largely unchanged from when it was built (8, 10). Although by 1180, the Gothic pointed arch was beginning to emerge elsewhere, St John's Chapel looks Romanesque.

The infirmary and chapel formed the core of St John's, but other buildings would have been needed (PLAN 2). Early medieval houses tended to be simple structures; people would eat, sleep and cook all in the same room. However, a separate kitchen had obvious advantages. At first this would be a detached building. A thirteenth-century manor house, for example, might have a hall, chapel, kitchen, brewhouse and other outbuildings grouped around a courtyard.[101] Hospitals too could be arranged as a quadrangle, with the infirmary forming one side. Kitchens, stables, latrines and staff quarters could be on the others.[102] So it seems to have been at St John's, with the infirmary and chapel on the north side of a court. The chapel's southern door would have led out to the courtyard. A small building attached to the south-eastern corner of the chapel (8) was described in 1626 as the gate to the court.[103]

At Bridgwater the sisters were initially expected to sleep in their own room within the infirmary.[104] Probably at Bath too the brethren and sisters at first slept in the infirmary with the poor. Monks were committed to an austere life. In the early days of monasticism, the head of the house slept and ate with the other monks, but gradually abbots and priors drew apart, building their own separate lodgings. The Prior of Bath had his own quarters by the mid-thirteenth century above the cellarium, the great storage building that formed the west range of the priory.[105] In hospitals too the master tended to gain his own accommodation.[106] The evidence at St John's points to a small-scale version of the Bath Priory arrangement. The present Abbey Church House incorporates a medieval cellar (12), which could have been a ground-floor store originally, and the remains of a storey above it.[107] Both floors had doors facing south. Presumably the courtyard had a back gate in its south-west corner, through which provisions were brought in from the farm to the store-house. The first floor could have been used by the master both as living quarters and to conduct the business of the hospital. Certainly in the Elizabethan period the quadrangle south of the chapel range was described as the house formerly that of the Master of St John's.[108]

Water draining from the Hot and Cross Baths passed through the city wall and down a ditch to the River Avon (13).[109] It formed the natural southern boundary of the St John's Hospital site. That outflow could have been easily diverted for the use of St John's. Monastic plumbing was advanced. In 1598 it was claimed that in the house formerly used by the Master of St John's 'there hath been always, time out of mind, a bath … for the proper and peculiar use of the Master …, derived … from … the Hot Bath.'[110] The most convenient place for this bath would have been on the east side of the court, close to the Hot Bath. The remains of a bath were discovered in that area by workmen c.1718.[111] This convenient source of water could also have been used to flush latrines. Sanitation was given a high priority in hospitals.[112] The diverted water presumably ran out of St John's courtyard at its south-west corner to

101   Grenville, 101-5, 118-9.

102   Gilchrist, 21-2; Orme and Webster 86-7.

103   BaRO 1641 Survey f.131, no.1.

104   *Register of Thomas Bekynton*, no.1062.

105   Manco, 'Bath Priory', 89.

106   Orme and Webster, 90.

107   Davenport, 123-8.

108   BaRO 1641 Survey f.182, no.1; *Acts of the Privy Council 1597-31*, 373-5.

109   *Med Deeds*, 1/38; *Ancient Deeds*, 3/26-28.

110   *Acts of the Privy Council 1597-8*, 373-4.

111   J. Wood, *Description of Bath*, 119. Wood's speculation on the origin of this bath was romantic, rather than scholarly.

112   Gilchrist, 37-8.

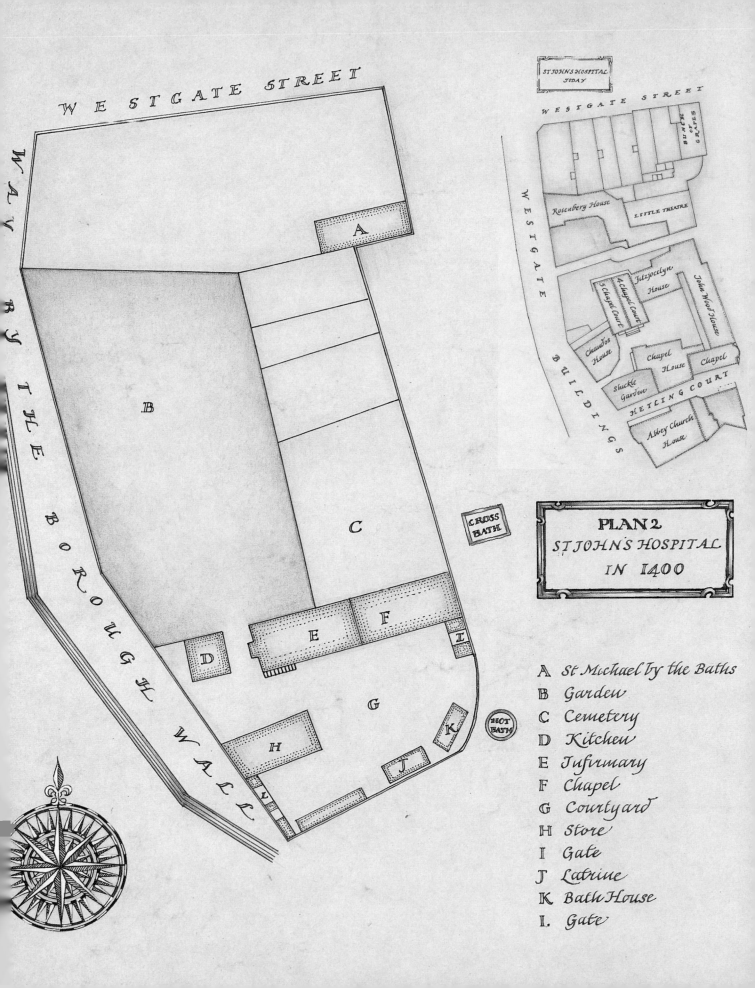

WESTGATE STREET

WAY BY THE BOROUGH WALL

A

B

C

CROSS BATH

D

E

F

I

G

H

J

K

HOT BATH

I

WESTGATE STREET

BUNCH OF GRAPES

Rosenberg House

LITTLE THEATRE

Fitzjocelyn House

4 Chapel Court

5 Chapel Court

John Wood House

Chandos House

Chapel House

Chapel

Shickle Garden

HETLING COURT

Abbey Church House

WESTGATE BUILDINGS

PLAN 2
ST JOHN'S HOSPITAL
IN 1400

A St Michael by the Baths
B Garden
C Cemetery
D Kitchen
E Infirmary
F Chapel
G Courtyard
H Store
I Gate
J Latrine
K Bath House
I. Gate

Chris Molan

12.
The medieval cellar in Abbey Church House. The wide doorway once led out into the hospital courtyard. The corbel on the right of the doorway supported an original ceiling beam

113   *PSANHS Bath Branch* 1914-18, 225; 1924-8, 65-7.

114   Manco, 'Bath Priory', 94.

115   BaRO Enquiry into Somerset Charities 1734-5, **1**, 53-9.

116   *Med Deeds*, 1/2, 171.

117   *Ibid*, 1/26-29; excavation on the site of Rosenberg House showed no occupation from the mid-thirteenth to the mid-seventeenth century: Greene, 14.

118   *Med Deeds*, 1/30; *Ancient Deeds* 1/3.

119   *Register of Ralph of Shrewsbury*, 286-7.

120   Wedlake, 84-6.

121   Baker and Baker, 328, note 1; BaRO Enquiry into Somerset Charities 1734-5, **1**, 53-59.

122   *Med Deeds*, 1/3, 172.

123   *Med Deeds*, 1/31-2.

124   *Ancient Deeds*, 6/71

125   *Med Deeds*, 1/38; *Ancient Deeds* 3/26-9.

126   *Med Deeds*, 1/23-5, 31-7, 40-3, 45-59.

127   *Ibid*, 1/98-100, 111-5, 124-41, 154-5.

128   *Ibid*, 1/15-16, 67-79, 88-92, 101-5, 116, 142-53.

129   *Ibid*, 1/17-22, 82-7, 106-9, 117-20, 123, 156-9, 164-8.

join the main drain, which may explain nineteenth-century claims that a tunnel once ran from the Abbey Church House to beyond the city wall.[113]

Fresh drinking water would have been available to St John's from its foundation. Bath Priory had water piped from springs on Beacon Hill and Beechen Cliff. The water from Beechen Cliff crossed the river in pipes attached to the bridge and fed a cistern just inside the South Gate, which came to be known as St James's pipe, from the nearby church of St James.[114] When St John's Hospital was rebuilt in the 1720s, there were complaints that the alterations had disrupted the piped water supply from St James's.[115]

St John's was clearly seen as a deserving charity, attracting donations of property in Bath and places round about. Gradually the hospital site was extended. An early benefactor granted land by the West Gate. That was then exchanged for more convenient land by the baths,[116] which may have formed part of the original quadrangle. In the first half of the thirteenth century two houses in sizeable plots were donated north of the hospital beside the city wall. Together they created a large area, which was cleared for cultivation.[117] The hospital gardens would produce fruit and vegetables, so a convenient place for the kitchen would have been between the gardens and the cellar. In the mid-thirteenth century St John's acquired vacant land immediately north of the chapel; there was apparently a herb-garden on part of it.[118] It was the ideal site for a cemetery. On 9 June 1336 the burial ground of St John's Hospital was consecrated by Ralph of Shrewsbury, Bishop of Bath and Wells.[119] Two burials were discovered during rebuilding in 1954 on the north side of Chapel Court.[120] Others must lie beneath the present courtyard, still described as the burial-ground in 1734.[121]

Beyond the city wall, St John's had two meadows (13). A strip of land alongside the wall had been given to the hospital by Bishop Reginald. It lay between the wall and 'the old ditch' which formed part of the city's defences, and ran south from the West Gate to the drain from the smaller baths.[122] Beyond that was a larger meadow, granted to St John's in the thirteenth century,[123] which became known as St John's Mead. The corner of it nearest to the West Gate was a convenient place for the hospital's barn. Bath was almost ringed with meadows belonging either to Bath Priory or St John's, which created no little frustration in Bath citizens wanting to pasture their animals.[124] In 1438 the then mayor, Walter Rich, managed to obtain from St John's the strip by the wall (later known as Butthays) for a 2s rent.[125]

The estate and other income
Meanwhile lands had been granted for the support of the hospital in Bath,[126] and places around it: Langridge, Newton St Loe, Swainswick, Tadwick and Twerton.[127] There was a cluster of property to the south-west of Bath at Ashwick, Chilcompton, Hallatrow, High Littleton, Midsomer Norton and Timsbury.[128] To the south-east there was another cluster in and around Frome: Berkley, Lullington, Rodden, Standerwick and Woodman's Hill.[129] Further south there had been grants and purchases at (Higher) Alham and Chesterblade

near Evercreech,[130] and at Wells and Ilchester.[131] To the west of Bath, St John's had properties in Bristol and Keynsham,[132] while in Gloucestershire there had been grants in Cold Ashton, Cirencester, Foxcote and Gossington.[133] Generally the properties were small parcels, an acre or two here or a house there. If a benefactor granted cash, then the master could select suitable land to invest in, but even so, he would be restricted by what was available for purchase. In 1259 William de Wethamsted bequeathed £35 8s 8d to St John's, with which the master bought lands in Timsbury, (High) Littleton, Hallatrow and Chesterblade.[134] It must have been difficult to run such a scattered estate.

Land could be farmed directly by the master of the hospital, using local labour. However, liberties might be taken with a distant landlord. In 1329 the Master and brethren of St John's Hospital complained that 'certain sons of iniquity unmindful of the safety of their souls' had damaged crops in some of their fields.[135] The bishop threatened the guilty parties with excommunication if they did not desist, but one wonders if they were ever caught. At least the sheaves of corn granted by Bishop Reginald would simply have to be collected, or delivered. The same was true of the crannock of corn from Foxcote and crannock of beans from Gossington granted to the hospital by another benefactor.[136] Even so there was the problem of transporting bulky crops over many miles. From 1315 successive bishops chose to pay St John's £5 a year in lieu of the corn,[137] which was no doubt more convenient.

Bath Priory could easily have delivered its dole of corn, bread and salted meat, but the amounts would vary over the years. The priory gave one sheaf to St John's per acre of demesne, so a decision to lease manors to tenants could radically cut the obligation to St John's. The priory had promised St John's a tithe of its bread and meat, which would depend on how many mouths there were to feed in the priory. In 1206 there were 41 monks. There would also have been servants and guests to consider. But when the number of monks was halved by the Black Death,[138] food quotas would have fallen too. By the end of its history the priory was giving St John's nine loaves of the better sort, eleven inferior loaves and seven gallons of convent ale each week, as well as 30s worth of meat a year and fish, cheese and other victuals.[139]

Urban properties of St John's would simply be leased. Nonetheless rents could take days to collect on horseback. In 1286 St John's leased a house in Redcliffe St, Bristol, with the proviso that if any brother or servant spent more than one day at Bristol collecting rent, it would be at the expense of the lessee.[140] Inevitably some tenants defaulted. In 1268 Robert, Master of St John's, was obliged to sue Adam le Deneys for 40s arrears of rent for a house in Wells.[141] By the Tudor period the hospital employed a bailiff or steward, who was responsible for the administration of the estate and collection of rents. The more distant lands were probably leased to locals, with the hospital retaining a cluster of lands near Bath in demesne, known as St John's Farm. Even the demesne farm was leased by c.1530.[142]

By the late thirteenth century the Crown was becoming concerned about loss of revenue as a result of grants of land to religious houses. In 1279 the

13
The meadows of St John's outside the West Gate on Savile's map of Bath. Butthays ran beside the city wall. At its southern end was the ditch carrying the overflow of hot water from the Hot and Cross Baths. Part of St John's barn can be seen on the corner of St John's Mead

130 *Ibid*, 1/9-13.
131 *Ibid*, 1/93-5, 160-3.
132 *Ibid*, 1/60-66, 96-7; *Ancient Deeds*, 6/64.
133 *Med Deeds*, 1/14, 80-1.
134 *MSS of Wells*, 1, 144.
135 *Register of Ralph of Shrewsbury*, 42 (no.160).
136 *Med Deeds*, 1/81.
137 *Register of John de Drokensford*, 99.
138 Manco, 'Bath Priory', 87.
139 PRO E368/384, m.37.
140 *Med Deeds*, 1/64.
141 *Pedes Finum*, SRS 6, 221.
142 *Star Chamber*, 131.

Statute of Mortmain prohibited religious houses or other corporate bodies from receiving land without royal licence.[143] Although there are a few grants to St John's Hospital after this, its medieval estate was largely formed in the first century after its foundation. Although considerably better-endowed than the Hospital of St Mary Magdalen, St John's was a modest institution by comparison with Bath Priory. At the Dissolution the hospital's regular income was £22 16s 9d a year, while Bath Priory had an income of over £617 a year.[144] Few English hospitals were really wealthy.[145]

Other sources of income were needed, particularly when the upkeep of buildings stretched resources. When Bishop Ralph consecrated St John's burial ground in 1336, he granted an indulgence of 40 days to those who made offerings to the hospital.[146] Then on 13 April 1400 the Pope granted remission of sins to those who visited St John's on certain days with donations towards repairs. The designated days were Holy Thursday and the three following days, and the feast of the Nativity of St John the Baptist (24 June) and the two days before. The Master of St John's could deputise four or six priests, monastic or other, to assist in hearing the confessions.[147] Clearly quite a crowd was expected.

Despite its charitable status, the hospital did not altogether escape taxation. In 1297 the Master of St John's was exempt from an ecclesiastical taxation, since he was not holding an ecclesiastical benefice,[148] but in 1377 the master and brothers of the hospital paid 12d each in a clerical poll tax.[149] The hospital was free of taxation for some time before 1428, when it paid a tax of 2s, and then exempt again in 1450, on account of its poverty.[150]

Care of the infirm

The whole purpose of the hospital was to care for those in need. How were they selected? Early deeds of St John's refer to the inmates as poor or infirm or both.[151] A fourteenth-century bishop described the inmates as weak and infirm.[152] Bishop Reginald Fitzjocelyn intended the hospital for 'the poor of Bath', but did this include those attracted to the city by its waters? Surely it did. Bath was a magnet for the desperately ill from far and wide. Sick and infirm Bathonians would mainly be cared for in their own homes, with the waters close at hand. Still there must always have been some who could not be cared for by their families. They would probably be long-stay patients, especially the elderly, leaving fewer beds for visitors. From the Elizabethan period, as Bath's reputation as a spa town grew, other hospitals were provided specifically for the visiting sick and St John's concentrated on local needs.

In general the master would select inmates, although each Prior of Bath when he was first appointed had the right to nominate one person to St John's. Priors would probably use this opportunity to provide for aged priory servants. Robert de Sutton was elected prior in 1332. On 7 July the Master of St John's granted a corrody and a chamber within the precinct of the hospital to John of Glastonbury, at the nomination of Prior Robert, 'which right pertains to the prior at first on his election as prior and which his predecessors anciently

143 Plucknett, 94-102, 109.

144 *Valor Ecclesiasticus*, **1**, 177-8. Both figures are net.

145 Orme and Webster, 84.

146 *Register of Ralph of Shrewsbury*, 286-7.

147 *Calendar of … Papal Letters*, **5**, 286.

148 *Calendar of Various Chancery Rolls*, 20-1.

149 E. Green, 'A Bath poll tax', 298.

150 *Feudal Aids* **4**, 411; *Register of Thomas Bekynton*, 150.

151 *Med Deeds*, 1/18, 51, 61, 62, 81, 124, 138, 154, 156-9.

152 *Register of Ralph of Shrewsbury*, 286.

14
Alham Farm in the parish of Evercreech, which has
been in the ownership of St John's Hospital since c.1200

15
The Church of St Michael by the Baths on Savile's map of Bath. This is the only view of it by an eye-witness

had.'[153] A corrody was the means of existence – food and clothing. The details are spelled out when the next prior made his choice. As it chanced that was less than a year later, since Prior Robert of Sutton stepped down in October 1332 in favour of Thomas Christy. On 1 May 1333 Prior Thomas granted a lodging in St John's to Clement at Appeldore, along with half a pound of wool yearly and a daily ration: a loaf of bread from St John's and a gallon of ale from Bath Priory's own cellar. Clement was also to have a plate of meat and a pittance from the kitchen, presumably of the priory, since St John's is not specified.[154] The division of maintenance between the priory and St John's may have been special to this case. Prior Thomas may have been reluctant to overburden the hospital with two priory nominations following so close upon each other.

At Bridgwater the rules were that:

> No lepers, lunatics, or persons having the falling sickness or other contagious disease, and no pregnant women, or sucking infants, and no intolerable persons, even though they be poor and infirm, are to be admitted to the house; and if any such be admitted by mistake, they are to be expelled as soon as possible. And when the other poor and infirm persons have recovered they are to be let out without delay.[155]

This last rule seems optimistic. Treatment was limited and many who entered a hospital would leave it only for the grave. Nonetheless the helpless infirm could be made more comfortable in a warm, clean hospital than they might be in the hovels of the poor.[156] In Bath the medical resources of the priory could be shared with the hospital. The monastic library contained some works of Galen, the renowned second-century Greek medical writer, and a book on fevers, translated from Arabic to Latin by a monk of Monte Cassino.[157] Those books contained some of the best understanding of disease that the medieval world had to offer, but alongside them was a guide to the use of bleeding as a treatment.[158] Presumably the priory physician attended St John's. Master Roger, medicus, witnessed a grant by Bishop Reginald to the hospital.[159] He could have been either of the bishop's household or the priory. A grant by Bishop Savaric to St John's was witnessed by Master Arnold of Bath,[160] the priory physician.[161] However given the limitations of medieval medicine, the inmates might benefit more from good nursing. At Bridgwater the sisters were to be 'watchful and ready, night and day, to help the infirm and to minister to them in all things'.[162]

St Michael by the Baths

Early hospitals had chapels dedicated to a particular saint, from whom the hospital took its name. So it was with St John's in Bath. The hospital chapel was dedicated to St John the Baptist. Surprisingly it is now dedicated to St Michael. The change was made in the nineteenth century, but the reasons for it stretch back into the more distant past. St John's Hospital was long linked to a parochial chapel of St Michael nearby (PLAN 2). Since there was a larger Churches of St Michael outside the city's North Gate (PLAN 1), the

153   *Two Chartularies*, 2/716.
154   *Ibid*, 2/738.
155   *Register of Thomas Bekynton*, no.1062.
156   Orme and Webster, 59-60; Gilchrist, 34-6.
157   Williams, 34-40.
158   Warner, appendix 51, 45-6.
159   *Med Deeds*, 1/3.
160   *Ibid*, 1/7.
161   *Two Chartularies*, 2/3, 4, 8, 33, 78, 84.
162   *Register of Thomas Bekynton*, no.1062.

16
The Vatican's copy of the letter sent by Pope Boniface IX on 15 April 1400 to St John's (Lateran Regesta 80, f.70d).
It granted permission for the parishioners of St Michael's by the Baths to be buried in the hospital chapel and cemetery

smaller St Michael's was known as St Michael by the Baths, Little St Michael's or St Michael Within. It was a simple, unadorned building, with a round-headed, probably Norman, door (15). It is first mentioned by name c.1285.[163]

What were its origins? St Michael's had no cemetery, suggesting that it started life as a domestic chapel. Both in town and country, many such chapels evolved into parish churches. A man who owned a block of urban land might have a chapel attended by his tenants as well as his own family and servants, forming a loyal enclave that was eventually given parochial status. In the 1180s Master Eustace of Bath granted land to Bath Priory between the northern city wall and the Chapel of St John's Hospital. That would have included the site of the Chapel of St Michael. The chapel itself is not mentioned, but we would not expect it to be, if it was just a private chapel at the time, belonging to a house on Westgate Street. St Michael's could have been built by Eustace's father Master Martin of Stalls, from whom he inherited property in Bath, Berewick and Widcombe,[164] or one of their ancestors.

Eustace and his brother Nicholas were in holy orders. Gilbert, Prior of Bath, employed Nicholas as a clerk and had found Bath benefices for both brothers.[165] It was generally younger sons who went into the Church, so we may guess that Eustace inherited unexpectedly. With no son to follow him, we can understand his decision to grant all his property to Bath Priory, keeping a life interest for himself and his sisters.[166] On their deaths Bath Priory could have acquired not only land, but one or more family chapels. Is it simply a coincidence that around 1210 we first hear of Bath Priory possessing chapels in Berewick and Widcombe and the 'parochial chapel of St John the Baptist'?[167] The 'parochial chapel' might have been the hospital chapel acquiring an additional function. A few hospital chapels were also parochial.[168] It seems more likely though that priests from St John's had been privately serving St Michael's, and that when it came into priory hands, the bishop designated it as parochial. Certainly the parish of St Michael covered the same area that had belonged to Master Eustace.

On 15 April 1400 a papal licence was granted to the Master and brethren of St John's to bury in the cemetery or church of their hospital, in addition to their inmates, the parishioners of the nearby chapel with cure of St Michael, held by the hospital, as well as any others who so desired (16). Previously the parishioners had been buried in the cemetery of St Mary of Stalls.[169] Stalls Church (as it was generally known to Bathonians) belonged to the cathedral priory; indeed it stood within the priory precinct and its cemetery was part of the cathedral cemetery (17). For centuries all Bath's citizens within the city walls were buried there.[170] Around 1300 Eva, widow of Richard the knight, was buried in the churchyard of the cathedral, but she provided for weekly masses in St Michael by the Baths,[171] presumably her parish church. Burial fees would have gone to the priory. Because of the income involved, burial rights were jealously guarded. Normally a church wanting to acquire burial rights would petition the bishop of its diocese, but the Bishop of Bath and Wells was the abbot of Bath Priory. St John's appealed direct to the Pope.

163 *Ancient Deeds*, 5/41, 61.
164 *Two Chartularies*, 2/11, 14, 81; *Med Deeds* 1/54. I am indebted to Alan Keevil for clarifying Eustace's ancestry.
165 *Two Chartularies*, 2/1, 2, 3.
166 *Ibid*, 2/11 14.
167 *Ibid*, 2/76 96.
168 Orme and Webster, 55
169 *Calendar of … Papal Letters* **5**, 313.
170 Manco, 'Bath Priory', 80.
171 *Ancient Deeds*, 1/61.

The parish of St Michael by the Baths encompassed the city block containing St John's Hospital, the block north of Westgate Street bounded by the city wall and Bridewell Lane, and houses on the east side of St Michael's Place.[172] It was a small parish in a poor district. Apart from the houses fronting Westgate Street, the properties were not on prime city sites. In 1379 the inhabitants of 'By the Bath Street' were all labourers, paying the minimum 4d in tax, while Westgate Street had only three citizens paying more.[173] In 1524 the parish of St Michael by the Baths was easily the poorest in Bath.[174] It is not surprising that St Michael's remained a small and simple church. The income from tithes would have been low and there were few parishioners wealthy enough to endow their church. Only one rent of 6d was donated to it, and even this was forfeit to the Crown in 1548 as chantry income.[175]

The difficulty of maintenance may explain why St Michael's ceased to function as a church soon after that and came into the hands of Bath Corporation. In 1548 the Master of St John's was still the Parson of St Michael's, but by the time the Corporation accounts start in 1568, the 'church and procession way' was being rented to William Chapman for 2s.[176] In November 1572 Queen Elizabeth granted to the Corporation the patronage of St John's with the annexed St Michael's, in Crown hands since the Dissolution.[177] From then on the Corporation accounts show various outgoings for St Michael's by the Baths including procurations to the archdeacon and the Archbishop of Canterbury,[178] which in theory were payments to cover their expenses in visiting operating churches. However St Michael's continued to be leased and was ruinous by 1610.[179] It was never restored as a church.

St John's Hospital is still officially described as 'with the chapel of St Michael annexed'. For centuries this was just a meaningless archaism, but around 1860 the hospital Chapel of St John the Baptist was rededicated to St Michael.[180]

The Hospital of St Catherine or Black Almshouse

By 1608 Bath had gained another three hospitals. In the later Middle Ages, it became more common for almshouses or hospitals to be lay institutions, founded perhaps by a wealthy burgess and run by a guild or the municipality.[181] Like the earlier hospitals, they might incorporate a chapel, but the open-hall infirmary had lost favour. Individual rooms provided greater privacy, so new almshouses were built as a range of separate dwellings, or ranges around a quadrangle.[182]

Bath's first municipal charity was St Catherine's Hospital in Bimbury Lane (18). The founder was William Philips, a wealthy clothier of Broad Street.[183] He was one of Bath's two Members of Parliament in 1420[184] and served as mayor at least four times.[185] On 23 June 1435 Philips bought five cottages and a yard in Bimbury Lane.[186] It seems that he started building on the site

17
The ornate Church of St Mary of Stalls, demolished in the seventeenth century. Medieval burgesses maintained the Chapel of St Catherine in this church

172 Modern street names used.

173 E. Green, 'A Bath poll tax', 301, 304.

174 E. Green, 'Bath lay subsidies', 388-95.

175 *Valor Ecclesiasticus* 1, 178; *The Survey ... of the Chantries*, 148, 328; BaRO St Michael's parish v Corporation, bdle 77: Parcel of the possessions which came into the hands of the late King Edward VI under the Act of Parliament for dissolved colleges, chantries, etc.

176 In later years this church is named as St Michael's. *Accounts of the Chamberlains*, 1, 14, 23, 37, 42, 74, 93, 102, 108-9, 115, 119, 120-1, 124, 131, 138.

177 *Calendar of ... Patent Rolls 1572-5*, 383.

178 *Accounts of the Chamberlains*, 15, 24, 30, 34, 49, 70, 75, 80, 93, 95, 103, 106, 111.

179 BaRO 1641 survey of Bath f.130, no.1.

180 *Bath Directories* 1858 (St John's), 1864 (St Michael's).

181 Orme and Webster 142.

182 Orme and Webster 136-9; Gilchrist 54-5.

183 *Somerset Medieval Wills 1501-1530*, 338-9; *Ancient Deeds*, 4/104: his widow Agnes lived in Broad St.

184 Clark et al, 1, 590-1.

185 *Ancient Deeds*, 1/24, 49, 53, 5/59, 87.

186 *Ibid*, 4/102.

18
The Hospital of St Catherine on its original site at the southern end of Bimbury (now Bilbury) Lane

shortly afterwards, for in 1444 he was said to have built four almshouses 'long ago'. He created a trust for the new foundation. The trustees were his son-in-law John Shipward, who was a merchant of Bristol, and Roger Haines of Bath. Philips gave them the newly-built almshouses, together with three houses, a barn and a chamber (to endow the charity).[187]

Philips died in March or April 1444 and his will reveals that he had recently begun rebuilding the 'Chapel of St Catherine at Bath.' He ordered his executors to 'finish this with all possible haste'.[188] In his time burgesses of Bath took a solemn oath to maintain St Catherine's Chapel and observe St Catherine's day (25 November).[189] The symbol of St Catherine of Alexandria was the wheel, so she had become the patroness of spinning – a suitable heavenly guardian for a cloth-making town like Bath. She had other attributes which made her a general favourite. Her legend claimed that she was of royal birth, and that at the age of about 18 she confounded 50 pagan philosophers, burst the wheel on which her persecutor tried to break her, but was then beheaded. So she was depicted as a beautiful young martyr, frail in frame but strong in faith and wisdom (19). She was also the patroness of education.

The popularity of St Catherine made her widely honoured in Bath. There were altars dedicated to her in several Bath churches.[190] Stalls Church (17) contained the Chapel of St Catherine, used as a chantry for the commonalty of Bath.[191] Communal chantries were popular with those who could not afford the luxury of their own personal chaplain. By banding together, they could maintain one who would pray for them all. Like other mutual aid groups of the time, they were known as guilds or fraternities. Burgesses of Bath contributed to the Fraternity or Guild of St Catherine.[192] Clearly this was the chapel rebuilt by William Philips and his executors made detailed arrangements for an annual service there for his soul.[193]

The executors were the same John Shipward and Roger Haines who had been holding the almshouses and other property in trust. On 1 August 1444 the trust was conveyed to the mayor and commonalty, with stipulations on the use of the income. Each year 5s 1d was to be spent on the service for William and his wife Agnes in the Chapel of St Catherine in Easter week. On the same day, 100 poor people were to be given a farthing loaf and a peck of beans each at the Guildhall. The remainder of the income was to be spent as William Philips had directed in his lifetime. There was a careful penalty clause. If the mayor and commonalty failed in any of these duties, then all the properties were to go to the wardens of St Michael Without,[194] the donor's parish.[195]

The four almshouses were to house eight poor people, including the bedeman (warden) and his wife, who should pray for the current mayor and all the brethren and sisters in 'the chapel of the said foundation.'[196] In the eighteenth century it was claimed that there was anciently a chapel attached to the almshouse, which had perished long since.[197] However, Philips had made no provision for a chaplain. Nor was a new chapel licensed by the bishop. It would appear therefore that the 'chapel of the foundation' was St Catherine's

187   *Ibid*, 4/104. For the legal benefits of creating a trust for charitable purpose in this period see G. Jones, 6-7.

188   *Somerset Medieval Wills 1501-1530*, 338-9.

189   Warner, appendix 51.

190   *Two Chartularies*, 1/3; Greening; *Somerset Medieval Wills 1501-1530*, 326; Manco, 'Bath Priory', 86.

191   *Ancient Deeds*, 3/82, 4/75, 5/59; *Somerset Medieval Wills 1383-1500*, 166-7.

192   *Somerset Medieval Wills 1383-1500*, 214, 343; 1501-1530, 354-5; 355-6; 1531-1558, 24-5.

193   *Ancient Deeds*, 4/104. The church is not named, but it was the clerk of Stalls who was to light the candles and ring the knell.

194   *Ancient Deeds*, 4/104.

195   *Somerset Medieval Wills 1501-1530*, 338-9.

196   *Ancient Deeds*, 4/104.

197   Collinson, 1, 44.

19
St Catherine depicted in old stained glass in the Church of St Catherine, near Batheaston.
The chancel was built by Prior John Cantlow, who also rebuilt the Chapel of St Mary Magdalen in Holloway

Chapel in Stalls Church. The link with the chapel gave the charity its name, although for centuries it was more commonly known as the almshouse in Bimbury or 'the Black Alms', from the colour of the gowns worn by the almsfolk.

'St Katherine's Hospital' was depicted *c.*1600 as a two-storey range with tall chimneys (18). The building scarcely changed between then and its nineteenth-century demolition (20-1). However it seems to have gone through several phases of development before 1600. At the north end of the hospital were four rooms with thin partitions between them, but massive exterior walls. Clearly they were built as a range. Their doors and windows had medieval pointed arches. So those were probably the original four almshouses built by Philips, which had a garden behind. Three larger rooms were added to the south, probably before 1500, to judge by the style of the doors and the two-light window on the ground floor. The square-headed windows above suggest that the top storey was an Elizabethan afterthought. A slice of one room was sacrificed to create a passage through to a staircase at the rear, while a second staircase was awkwardly fitted into the centre front of the hospital. St Catherine's had 14 rooms in 1749,[198] so the extra room at the rear was presumably added later.

Rebuilding by Bath Priory

By the end of the fourteenth century, leprosy was dying out in England and many leper hospitals gradually emptied. It was not difficult to find a new use for them. Former *leprosaria* lent themselves to the care of another group shunned by society – the mentally ill – or they could become almshouses.[199] Sad to say, leper hospitals in Somerset were not falling into disuse. In the sixteenth century bequests were still being made to the poor lazar people in the hospitals of Langport and Taunton,[200] while the Bath waters were still attracting lepers.[201] So St Mary Magdalen continued to serve its original purpose until after the Dissolution.

Up to the time of the Black Death documents referred to the brethren of the hospital, but in 1377 Edward, Master of St Mary Magdalen, appeared alone in a clerical poll tax.[202] By 1486 the hospital was ruinous, impoverished and in debt. No brothers were living there and only two or three poor people. John Cantlow, Prior of Bath (1483-99), rather unfairly blamed the negligence of past masters. The mastership being vacant, he petitioned the Pope to unite the hospital of St Mary Magdalen with Bath Priory. The prior had always selected the master, but once in office the master was in charge. Prior Cantlow wanted to abolish the mastership and run the hospital directly. He promised that he would repair its buildings and relieve it from debt. The Pope granted permission, although with the proviso that the revenues should be used for the maintenance of the poor and infirm or other approved hospital uses.[203] Prior Cantlow kept his word on rebuilding, as a verse inscription records (23).

His pride in his work is obvious. 'Flourished with foremost spectable' means

198   J. Wood, *Description of Bath*, 306.

199   Gilchrist, 38, but see Orme and Webster 139 for exceptions.

200   *Somerset Medieval Wills 1531-1558*, 14, 39, 79, 108.

201   *Itinerary of John Leland*, 1, 141-2.

202   E. Green, 'A Bath poll tax', 298.

203   *Calendar of … Papal Letters* 15, no.168. For Cantlow's dates see *Star Chamber* 38-49; *Registers of Oliver King and Hadrian de Castello*, 518-9.

The Black Alms as they stood previous to the Building of the United Hospital. 1825.

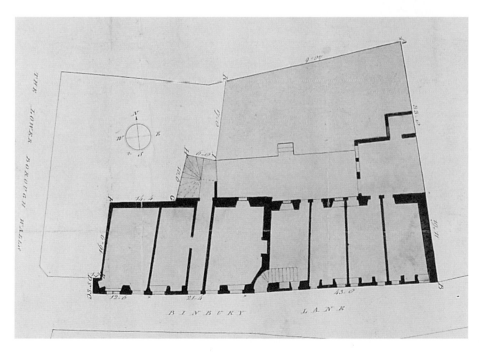

20-21
TOP St Catherine's Hospital in 1825, just before its demolition. The four chimneys on the right
probably belong to the original four almshouses built c.1436 by William Philips, Mayor and M.P. for Bath
BOTTOM Plan of St Catherine's Hospital c.1820; red = rooms of almswomen, brown = paved court, green = garden

22
Some of Prior Cantlow's work remains in St Mary Magdalen. This niche on the north side of the chapel once held a statue, probably that of St John the Evangelist, Cantlow's patron saint

splendidly embellished. Cantlow had not stinted on the ornamentation. There was lavish stained glass. The east window had three compartments. As usual Christ crucified was in the central panel. The Virgin Mary was in her customary place at Christ's right hand, while St Mary Magdalen was on his other side. Other elements of the scheme are more obscure. There was a large figure of St Bartholomew beneath Christ, identified by name. His prominence here is hard to explain. Other windows depicted SS Peter, Philip and James, so Bartholemew may have been part of a series of apostles. Two unnamed monks above the two Marys were probably SS Leonard and Benedict, suitable choices for a hospital run by Benedictine monks. Either side of the east window were niches (now moved to the south wall) which would have held statues, probably of the two Marys to echo the window. We know from an inventory that there was a statue of St Mary Magdalen somewhere in the chapel, clothed in velvet. A niche on the north wall (22) presumably held the statue of St John in 'a coat of tissue'.[204] St John the Evangelist was Cantlow's patron saint,[205] so the tissue may have been silk shot through with gold or silver. There are two more niches on the porch: one over the inner and one over the outer door.

The chapel had a gallery, which was eventually pulled down in 1878. Before the changes then made, there were Tudor doors and windows related to the gallery, proving that it was original to Cantlow's building.[206] Possibly women sat in the gallery, as at St John's Hospital.

Cantlow seems to have kept his word to the Pope and rebuilt the hospital of St Mary Magdalen too. It would be no hardship to a man who clearly enjoyed building and expected to reap rewards from it in heaven. We know that 'poor lazar people' lived in a 'house adjoining' the chapel in 1536.[207] The earliest view of the chapel (25) shows a house adjoining with a mullioned window which could be Tudor. Cantlow went on to build the Church of St Thomas à Becket in Widcombe and the chancel of St Catherine's, north of Batheaston. He also renovated part of the priory.[208]

Even the better-endowed St John's began to struggle under the burden of maintenance. By 1527 the problems had reached such an intolerable level that the master himself recommended amalgamation with Bath Priory, which had far greater resources. The master, James Horton, was prepared to sacrifice his post to make this possible. He reported that the income of the hospital was insufficient to maintain himself and the poor of the hospital, which had caused great suffering. Many parts of the fabric had perished and the remnant was threatened with irreparable ruin. This time it was the bishop who was petitioned and responded favourably, after satisfying himself that the facts were as stated. Bishop John Clerk issued the decree of amalgamation on 8 February 1526/7, with the proviso that the hospital income should continue to be used for the benefit of the poor. Prior William Holloway then spent over £100 (over four times the annual income of St John's) on rebuilding the hospital and its properties.[209] This was all the more remarkable since Bath Priory had been building a new cathedral (now Bath Abbey) since 1500, a

204 Appendix 10; A. à Wood, 19; Collinson, **1**, 173-4; Woodforde, 40.

205 The stained glass in the Church of St Catherine, near Batheaston, includes and eagle, the symbol of St John the Evangelist, holding Cantlow's name.

206 BMCA MH/2/1; Stokes Shaw, 104-5.

207 PRO REQ2/8/217.

208 Manco, 'Bath Priory', 91.

209 *Star Chamber*, 136, 154-6.

23
The verse inscription in the porch of St Mary Magdalen. Put into modern spelling it reads:
THIS CHAPEL FLOURISHED WITH FOREMOST SPECTABLE
IN THE HONOUR OF MARY MAGDALEN PRIOR CANTLOW HATH EDIFIED
DESIRING YOU TO PRAY FOR HIM WITH YOUR PRAYERS DELECTABLE
THAT SUCH WILL INHABIT HIM IN HEAVEN THERE EVER TO ABIDE

24
This blocked Tudor doorway in Abbey Church House once led into the storehouse of St John's Hospital.

huge project which was still absorbing a great deal of the priory income in Prior Holloway's time.[210]

It seems that he decided to replace the old infirmary with a range of six rooms on a new site north of the chapel (PLAN 3). A survey in 1548 reported that St John's Hospital was for six poor men, living in.[211] The present John Wood House rests on Norman rubble, mixed with medieval pottery, and similar material is incorporated into the base of the west wall.[212] Norman rubble would have been in plentiful supply in 1527 from the demolished Norman cathedral. Prior Holloway used Walter Simon as the master mason on St John's, supported by two other masons and a crew of labourers.[213] So the new hospital was of stone. The roof was evidently leaded, since lead was stripped from it during the Elizabethan rebuilding.[214] The old infirmary, repaired or rebuilt, could have been put to other uses. To judge from stylistic details, the store-house was enlarged at this time and given doors (24) on each floor facing east.[215]

It was while the hospital was being rebuilt that the scheming William Crouch came on the scene. Crouch was a quarrelsome, grasping, ruthless man, who rode roughshod over others. He became the Crown bailiff of Sherston (Wilts.) in 1524 and served as MP for Calne (Wilts.) in 1529.[216] But by then he had settled at Englishcombe, probably as steward to the lord of the manor,[217] and was taken into the service of Prior Holloway. Here he cast an acquisitive eye over priory property. He particularly coveted the hospital. The mastership had been abolished and Crouch, as a layman, would not have been eligible for it anyway, but this did not deter him. By first dwelling on the possibility that a subsequent bishop might revoke the amalgamation and then offering money to reimburse the prior for his building costs, he persuaded Prior Holloway c.1532 to give the mastership to a clerical kinsman of his – John Simons.[218] Simons then made Crouch his steward.[219]

But this was not enough for him. Crouch also wanted the right to choose the next master of the hospital, which he claimed the prior had promised him, and he resorted to the law. Tempers became frayed. When on 2 June 1533 a servant of Crouch's attempted to serve Prior Holloway with a subpoena in Bath Cathedral, he was frogmarched out by two of the priory servants, Thomas Horner and Thomas Batten. On 10 June Horner and an armed band waylaid Crouch and put him in the stocks. After three days of imprisonment, Crouch was brought to sign a £200 bond for his good behaviour. He retaliated in August, imprisoning Horner in his house at Englishcombe. A mass of priory servants and tenants then besieged the house and attacked the doors with hatchets. Crouch tried to hold them off with a shower of arrows, but released Horner when the mob threatened to burn the house down. It became clear at the trial that years of friction lay behind this explosion of local feeling. Crouch was habitually abusive and threatening. Two Mayors of Bath, both cloth-makers and major employers, had been so oppressed by him that they left for other cities, to the great impoverishment of Bath. A third former mayor testified to the difficulty of keeping the peace, with Crouch coming

210   Manco, 'Bath Priory', 95-8.

211   *Survey ... of the Chantries*, 148.

212   Wedlake, 84-5; Roman Baths Museum, Wedlake archive. There are discrepancies between the excavation drawings prepared by Wedlake and those which were published, but it seems that the western section of the building is resting on Norman rubble.

213   *Star Chamber*, 156-7.

214   *Accounts of the Chamberlains*, 58-9.

215   Davenport, 124.

216   *Letters and Papers of Henry VIII* 4(1), no.86 (22); Bindoff, 735-6.

217   Manco, *The Parish of Englishcombe*, 12.

218   *Star Chamber*, 129-161.

219   *Valor Ecclesiasticus*, 1, 178.

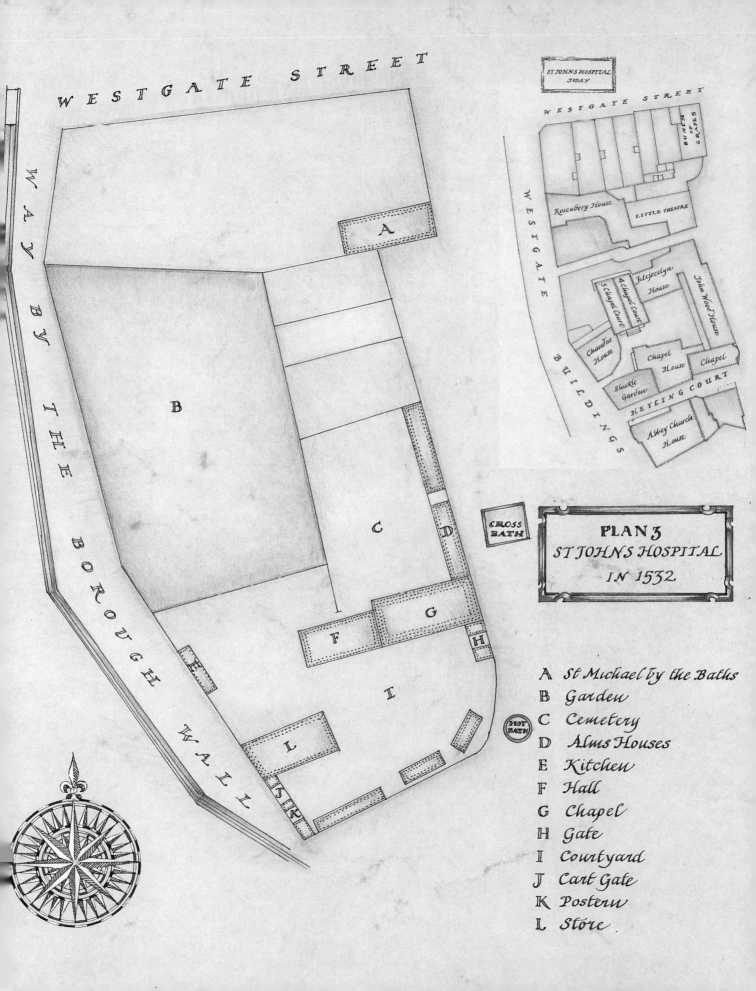

WESTGATE STREET

WAY BY THE BOROUGH WALL

A

B

C

D

E

F

G

H

I

J K

L

CROSS BATH

HOT BATH

PLAN 3
ST JOHNS HOSPITAL
IN 1532

A   St Michael by the Baths
B   Garden
C   Cemetery
D   Alms Houses
E   Kitchen
F   Hall
G   Chapel
H   Gate
I   Courtyard
J   Cart Gate
K   Postern
L   Store

to Bath night and day with a band of armed rowdies and causing constant quarrels and affrays.[220]

The case threw up the first balance sheet for St John's (appendix 9). Some interesting facts emerge. The income was from rents, tithes and the bishop's payment in lieu of sheaves. The hospital was in difficulties largely because of the decay of its properties. In theory it should have been receiving £22 8s 5d a year in rents, but £5 15s of this had to be written off, because the buildings were in ruins. The largest expense was the £14 6s 8d paid to two priests. This was in keeping with national trends. The percentage of hospital income spent on the clergy had risen over the years at the expense of the poor.[221] Only four persons were supported within the hospital, while a fifth was given a hospital property rent free. Their allowances were low. In this period £2 to £3 a year was given to the inmates of well-endowed hospitals.[222] St John's was spending only £1 6s 8d a year on its out-pensioner and 17s 4d a year each on inmates. However, these sums would not have to cover all their living expenses. St John's Farm had been let,[223] but the hospital gardens were large enough to provide fruit and vegetables, and some bread and meat was supplied by Bath Priory.

In 1535 'The Hospital of Bath with the chapel of St Michael annexed' was assessed at a net annual value of £22 16s 9½d, a dramatic improvement. Rents had recovered, presumably because of Prior Holloway's renovation of hospital properties. Instead of two priests there was just the master, John Simons. However, alms distributed to the poor had been reduced to 17s 4d, so there must have been only one almsperson left in the hospital. The fees to William Crouch as steward (26s 8d) and John Wikewike as bailiff (10s) added up to the total for the previous rent collector.[224] Wikewike was probably doing the work, while Crouch enjoyed the lion's share. This avaricious man continued to receive a fee as steward of St John's until his death in 1586.[225]

'The Hospital of the Blessed Mary Magdalen' was listed among the possessions of Bath Priory in 1535. It was valued at only £3 6s 3d a year, after the bailiff had been paid his 10s fee. The income was from both rents and demesne land.[226] The Master of St Mary Magdalen held one virgate (about 30 acres) of land in Lyncombe.[227] It made sense to lease out more distant property, such as *Mawdelens* ground in Laverton, which Bath Priory let to John Crouch of Laverton in 1530.[228]

Here again we see the influence of William Crouch on Prior Holloway. Crouch had the manor of Laverton on a lease from the Duchy of Cornwall, and had granted property there to his brother John.[229] Naturally John appeared on William's behalf in his case against Prior Holloway, as did John Simons.[230] It was fruitless. In May 1536 Prior Holloway granted the next presentation of the mastership of St John's to Nicholas FitzJames of Woolston, Somerset and his son and heir Robert.[231]

220 *Star Chamber*, 129-161.

221 Orme and Webster, 129.

222 *Ibid*, 123.

223 *Star Chamber*, 141.

224 *Valor Ecclesiasticus*, 1, 176, 178.

225 BaRO Account roll 15, 19, 21: St John's.

226 *Valor Ecclesiasticus*, 1, 176.

227 SRO DD/X/HY I, 130ff.

228 Bodleian Library Rawl B419, f.13v.

229 *Letters and Papers of Henry VIII* **4**(1), no.1533 (4); PRO C3/38/80: George Crouch v Mary Bamfield 7 May 1568.

230 *Star Chamber*, 141.

231 Warner, appendix 54. Probably both Nicholas and Robert FitzJames died before John Simons, for neither in fact presented.

25

The Chapel and Hospital of St Mary Magdalen in 1723, from a view of Bath by William Stukeley.
The chapel built by Prior John Cantlow was unchanged. The house adjoining had been the Tudor hospital, or part of it.
Stukeley does not show a building behind, but one could have been hidden from his view

Tudor and Stuart

The Reformation

Henry VIII's survey of ecclesiastical income in 1535 revealed the astonishing wealth of the monasteries. There was a groundswell of feeling that affluence had corrupted many religious, whose lives were no longer conspicuous for spiritual fervour. The pressure for reform was convenient for the Crown, whose depleted coffers could be filled by the confiscation of monastic estates.[232] At first only the smaller monasteries, with an income less than £200 a year, were suppressed by Act of Parliament in March 1536.[233] Bath Priory was not affected.

However, without a shred of legal justification Henry VIII appointed Simon Shepherd Master of St Mary Magdalen on 23 April 1536.[234] The appointment was successfully contested by Prior Holloway and Bath Priory continued to run St Mary Magdalen as before.[235] No monks lived at the hospital. An ordained brother simply visited to serve the chapel. Among the monks of Bath was John Beckington, whose family name was Romsey.[236] He was a trusted man. It was Beckington who kept the accounts for the rebuilding of St John's, and he had charge of the priory kitchen. He was also studious. The parson of Walcot left all his books to Master Beckington.[237] Holloway ordered Beckington to celebrate mass at the chapel of St Mary Magdalen about three times a week for the poor lazar people in the adjoining house. The prior supplied the chalice and other items needed.[238]

Between 1537 and 1539 the larger monasteries were gradually surrendered to the Crown. By 1540 the Dissolution was complete. Around half of the hospitals in England were closed as religious houses.[239] These included the Hospitals of St John the Baptist at Bridgwater and Wells. St John the Baptist at Redcliffe survived only four years longer.[240] Ironically, it was the unscrupulousness of Henry VIII and the scheming of William Crouch that saved St Mary Magdalen and St John's in Bath, by giving them secular masters. As clerics, rather than monks, John Simons and Simon Shepherd were in a similar position to those holding church benefices in the gift of monastic houses. They remained in office, while the patronage of their churches went to the Crown. So when Prior Holloway surrendered Bath Priory on 27 January

232 Smith, 27-8.

233 Youings, 42 and doc.10.

234 *Letters and Papers of Henry VIII* **10**, no.777(2).

235 PRO C1/903/30; PRO REQ2/8/217.

236 The Bath monks of this time apparently changed their surnames on entering the monastery, mainly taking their place of origin as their new surname.

237 *Star Chamber*, 157: he is described as the priory 'cosyner' [kitchener]; *Somerset Medieval Wills 1531-1558*, 11.

238 PRO REQ2/11/101; REQ2/8/217.

239 Gilchrist, 61.

240 *VCH Soms.* **2**, 152-61.

1538/9,[241] the Hospitals of St John the Baptist and St Mary Magdalen survived.

Still today there is a remnant of the monastic past in St John's. The residents are legally known as 'co-brethren and sisters'. Of course in the medieval period it was the religious serving the hospital who were 'brethren and sisters', while those they cared for were 'the poor and infirm'. For centuries afterwards the inmates were still called 'the poor' or 'the almsfolk', but they might become 'co-brethren and sisters' in a legal context.[242] Legal language tends to be conservative. Medieval grants to the hospital were made to the 'master and brethren and sisters', indicating a corporate body. Later lawyers would prefer to use the same terminology in deeds. So the usage goes on.

John Beckington was pensioned off, like the other monks, and went to Oxford University, so Simon Shepherd was finally able to take over as Master of St Mary Magdalen. In September that year the hospital rent-collector reported that the revenues were being paid to Shepherd.[243] Yet Shepherd was dissatisfied. He brought a case against Beckington in the Court of Requests, complaining that the former monk had kept him out of the mastership for three years and removed many of the books and ornaments from the hospital chapel. Beckington denied any culpability.[244] In fact the Crown Commissioners were almost certainly responsible. Treating St Mary Magdalen as a possession of Bath Priory, they would have confiscated its assets. An inventory of ornaments and livestock removed from the Chapel of Mary Magdalen (appendix 10) was probably compiled by them.

Shepherd also had to contend with demands from the Exchequer. Crown accountants, regarding the hospital as part of the former priory, expected to receive the rents of its properties, totalling £4 15s 8d a year. Although it was noted in 1539 that Shepherd was legally receiving the rents, the Crown account continued to show this sum as a rent due from Shepherd, which he never paid.[245] In 1560 the Exchequer launched an enquiry. Thomas Turner, Mayor of Bath, was commissioned to investigate. On 26 September a local jury declared that certain poor lepers resided, as poor lepers had from time immemorial resided, in a mansion house in the suburb of Bath called the Hospital of Mary *Mawdelyn*. The jury could not say by what right Simon Shepherd held the mastership, but he took the issues and profits of the estate, valued at £5 a year, for his own use and had nearly withdrawn support to the poor. He had also taken all the lead from the chapel roof and replaced it with tiles. However, Shepherd established his title in the Court of Exchequer. He claimed that the lead had been removed by robbers in the dead of a winter night. It might even have been true, but clearly Shepherd was unpopular locally.[246]

The Master of St John's was perhaps in better repute. It says something for John Simons that he retained the friendship of the scholarly and charitable former monk Nicholas Jobbyn BD, Vicar of Stalls.[247] However, Simons was hopelessly entangled with the Crouches. It was clearly an annoyance to the grasping William Crouch that the profitable St John's Farm had been let to Thomas West.[248] After West's death his lease apparently went through

241 *Letters and Papers of Henry VIII*, **14** (1), 148.

242 BaRO council minutes 27 July 1664; *Report of the Commissioners for Charities* **4**, 283.

243 SRO T/PH/VCH6 microfilm of PRO SC6/Henry VIII/3144.

244 PRO REQ2/11/101; PRO REQ2/8/217.

245 PRO SC6/Henry VIII/3144-3150.

246 *Report of the Commissioners for Charities*, **6**, 555-6, 743-5.

247 *Registers of Thomas Wolsey et al*, 167; *Ancient Deeds*, 5/45; *Somerset Medieval Wills 1531-1558*, 145-6.

248 *Star Chamber*, 141; E. Green, 'Bath lay subsidies', 388.

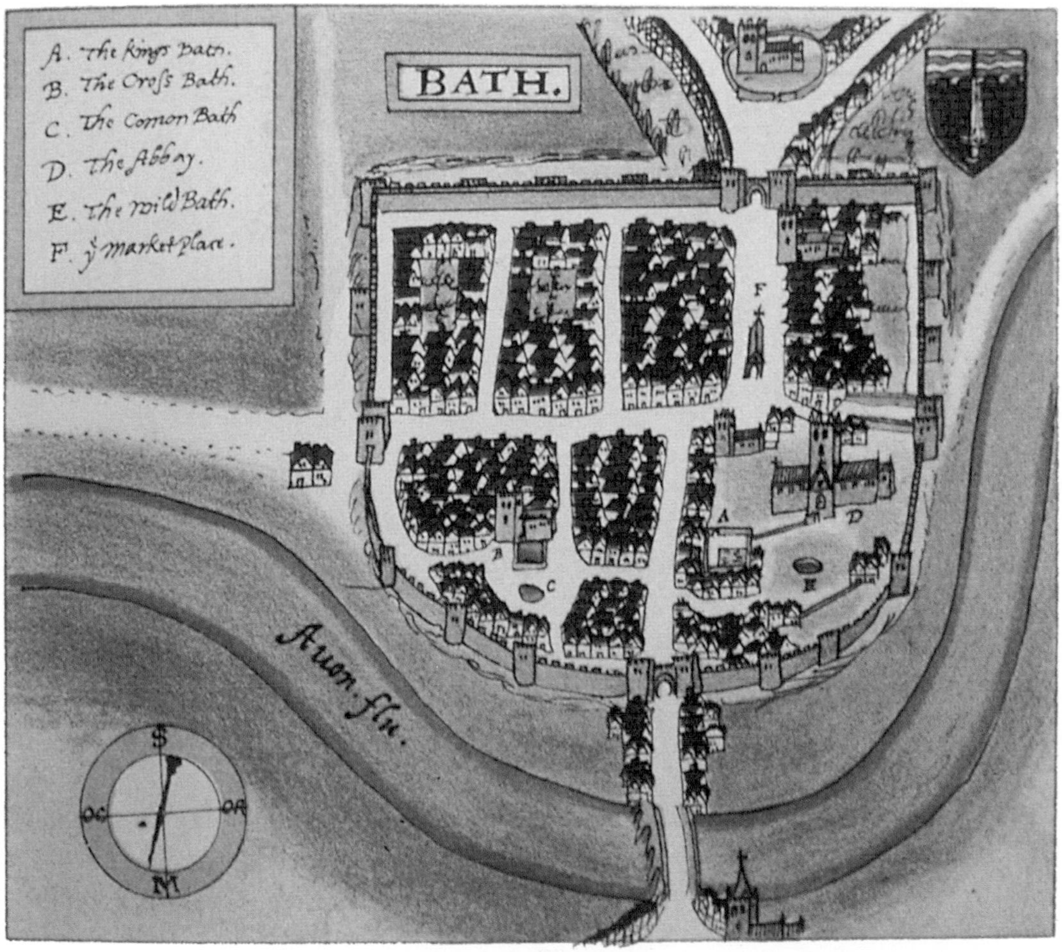
A. The kings Bath.
B. The Cross Bath.
C. The Comon Bath
D. The Abbay.
E. The wild Bath.
F. ye market place.
BATH.
Avon flu.

26
St John's Farm outside the West Gate can be seen on this crude bird's-eye view of Bath c. 1568 by William Smith.
From *The Particuler Description of England 1588* edited by H. B. Wheatley and E. W. Ashbee (1879)

other hands. It was not until 20 October 1551 that Simons could grant a 99-year lease of the farm to Crouch. It was a sizeable property: St John's barn outside the West Gate with an ox-shippon attached (13, 26), about 80 acres of land west and north of Bath, and the right to pasture 100 sheep on Lansdown and four oxen with the cattle of Barton Farm. Crouch initially sub-let the farm to his friend William Chapman. Then around 1562 Crouch sold the lease to his son Walter, who inherited his father's love of litigation. In 1571 Walter sued Peter Bewshin of Barton Farm over the pasturage rights and also a disputed acre of Kingsmead.[249]

Even with the farm and the stewardship of St John's, the Crouches were still not satisfied. On 14 July 1552, Simons granted a 99-year lease to John Crouch (the younger, nephew of William) of the 'Manor and Courtplace called the Hospital of St John the Baptist' together with all its property for £10 a year.[250] Simons thereby handed over to Crouch complete control of the whole hospital and estate of St John's. William Crouch rewarded Simons two years later with the rectory of Wellow.[251] It was an infamous exchange. In this cosy family arrangement, the hospital would be stripped of its assets for generations. William Crouch had long served the powerful Duke of Somerset, uncle of Edward VI. While Somerset ran the country as guardian to the young king, Crouch would have been difficult to oppose.

Somerset was intent on sweeping away the chantries. Since many hospitals had acted as chantries, this brought a new danger. Under the 1547 Chantries Act, the endowments of Church and lay corporations were to be surveyed. Those founded for superstitious uses, such as masses for the souls of the dead, or lights in churches, were confiscated. Endowments to support the poor were to be continued.[252] But how could the two uses be disentangled? St Catherine's Hospital was in part a chantry for William Philips. We have seen how much of the income of St John's and Magdalen's was given in exchange for prayers. However their masters were too wary to admit it. John Simons simply avoided giving evidence. When the chantry surveyors visited St John's he was conspicuous by his absence. 'No foundation deeds were shown', they reported, 'nor would the master appear'.[253] The Hospital of St Mary Magdalen also evaded direct attention. The Wissy chantry chapel attached to St Mary Magdalen was allowed quietly to decay. But once again Bath's hospitals survived.

Indeed St Catherine's was to benefit from Crown generosity. Edward Ludwell, a wealthy cloth-maker of Broad Street,[254] had become the Crown bailiff in Bath, collecting rents from the former priory properties.[255] Bath Priory had been the landlord of a large part of the city. As Mayor of Bath in 1552, Ludwell petitioned Edward VI to endow a grammar school and almshouse with that estate. This proposition was considered by the Privy Council on 1 February.[256] On 12 July Edward granted to the Mayor and Commonalty of Bath all the former priory property in the city for the foundation of a grammar school, to be named after the king, and the relief of ten poor people (27). There was a rent of £10 a year.[257] Even so the endowment was a generous one. The site of the priory itself had been sold

249   PRO REQ2/101/59; *Star Chamber*, 146.

250   BMCA StJH/7/263 (quoted in a lease of 1665); John Crouch the younger was the son of John Crouch of Laverton, brother of William. PRO C3/38/80; C3/45/84; REQ2/101/59.

251   *Somerset Incumbents*, 207.

252   G. Jones, 12-3.

253   *Survey ... of the Chantries*, 148.

254   Bindoff, 556; *Ancient Deeds*, 5/21.

255   Symons, 90-1

256   *Acts of the Privy Council 1550-2*, 471; *Report of the Commissioners for Charities* 4, 512.

257   *Calendar of Patent Rolls 1550-3*, 439-40; *Report of the Commissioners for Charities*, 4, 269-70.

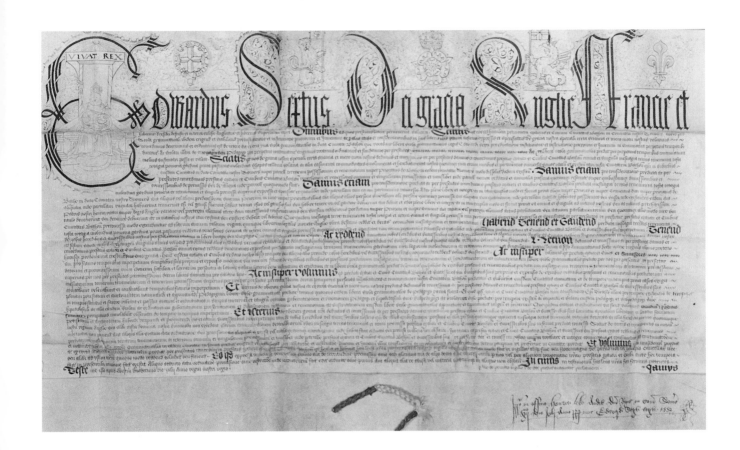

27
Edward VI's charter endowing a school and almshouse
in Bath is decorated with a portrait of the young king

28
A bird's-eye view of Bath c.1600, engraved from a drawing by physician Henry Savile. The city had become a fashionable spa and the map was intended as a guide for visitors. The text describes the city's history and the use of the baths

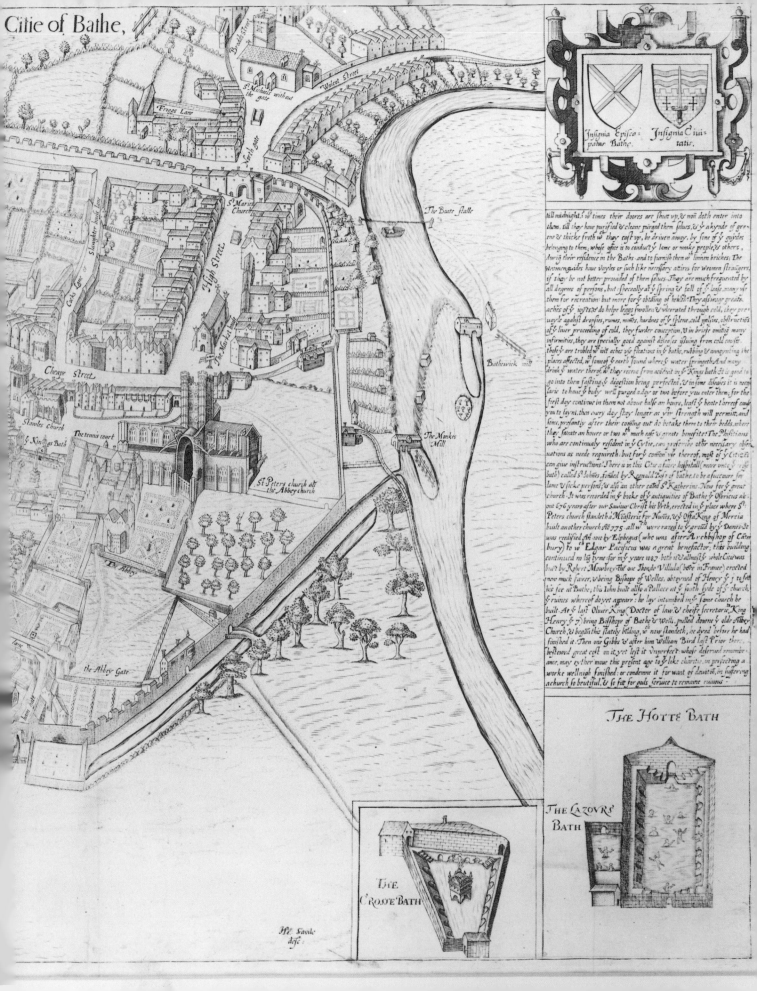

Citie of Bathe,

by the Crown, but the priory rental lists 80 properties and two fisheries in Bath. With the items on which the priory had not charged rent, the total was about 100 properties.[258]

What was the thinking behind the Edwardian charter? Had the bequest of William Phillips been depleted by confiscation of chantry property? Or was the Corporation simply anxious to expand its provision for the poor? The top storey of St Catherine's hospital could well have been added in this period. Also there was a new Corporation almshouse in Bridewell Lane by 1575.[259] However, the chamberlain's accounts made no distinction between the inmates of the Bridewell Lane and Bimbury almshouses; all were the 'almsfolk of the city'. There was no separate trust fund, supporting the school and a 'King Edward's Almshouse'. This was to lead to bitter recriminations and public scandal generations later.

The Leper's Hospital and Bath

Queen Mary (1553-58) did her best to reverse the Reformation, even re-founding Westminster Abbey, but when Elizabeth came to the throne the nation returned to the reformed religion. During the reign of this great queen, Bath emerged from the turmoil of the Reformation as a proud and confident city. The medieval cloth town dominated by its monastery was transformed into a thriving spa, controlled by its own citizens. That is the city we see in Henry Savile's bird's-eye view of Bath (28), drawn in the last years of Elizabeth and printed for spa visitors.[260]

As the cloth trade declined, some Bathonians had realised that the thermal waters, properly managed, could be a stream of gold. Dr William Turner, Dean of Wells and former physician to Protector Somerset, sounded the clarion call to recognise their glorious potential.[261] He had been in exile before the Reformation and under Mary, and had taken the opportunity to visit the great European spas. He was struck by the luxurious facilities which put Bath to shame. The baths of Bath had changed little since the medieval period and were simply open pools with seats in niches around the sides. They had no changing rooms and no system for draining the pools in order to clean them out. Turner's book on the baths in 1562 urged improvements. Commenting acidly that while there was money enough for cock-fighting, tennis, plays and other idle pleasures, 'I have not heard tell that any rich man hath spent upon these noble baths, being so profitable for the whole common wealth of England, one groat these twenty years.' He suggested the segregation of the sexes and of bathers with infectious skin diseases.[262]

It took time and a certain amount of pressure from national government, but in the 1570s the city was prepared to invest in improvements. Beside the King's Bath the Corporation built a new bath for women, later known as the Queen's Bath.[263] Other improvements were achieved by private donation, as Turner had hoped. Ironically his plea was heeded by one of his most fervent religious opponents. John de Feckenham, the son of peasants, had risen in

258 *Domesday Book* **8**: *Somerset* 7/1; SRO DD/X/HY1 (Bath Priory rental 1501-4); *Report of the Commissioners for Charities* **4**, 513-24.

259 Then known as Culverhouse Lane: *Accounts of the Chamberlains*, 26, 56, 71-2.

260 Manco, 'Henry Savile's map of Bath'.

261 *Dictionary of National Biography*; Bindoff **3**, 490-92.

262 Turner, *A Book of the ... Bathes* (Cologne 1562).

263 James, 48, 54.

the Church on his own abilities and remained true to the old faith at the Reformation. Queen Mary therefore appointed him Abbot of the re-founded monastery of Westminster. Naturally on the accession of Elizabeth, he lost that position and was shortly afterwards sent to the Tower for 'railing against the changes that had been made.' However in 1574 the leading Roman Catholic prisoners were released on bail and on 18 July 1575 Feckenham was given permission to go to Bath until September.[264] There he would have seen the inadequate provision for poor visitors to the baths and resolved to remedy matters. He 'relieved the poor wheresoever he came.'[265] In the city accounts for the twelve months to June 1576 we find three tons of timber and four hundred laths supplied free to Feckenham 'to build the house for the poor by the Hot Bath'.[266] Feckenham was probably also the builder of a small bath nearby. As John Wood later put it:

> A new cistern was made on the west side of [the Hot] Bath to receive the overflowing water of it, and to serve as a bath for the use of the lame and diseased poor people ...; it took the name of the Leper's Bath; and it was accommodated with a small room for the bather to strip and dress themselves in, which in process of time was called the Leper's Hospital ... The Leper's Hospital is a building of eight feet six inches in front, to the east, on the ground floor, fourteen feet in front above, and thirteen feet in depth; but yet it is furnished with seven beds, for the most miserable of objects, who fly to Bath for relief from the hot waters. This hovel stands at the corner of Nowhere Lane; and is so near the Leper's Bath, that the poor are under little or no difficulty of stepping from one place to the other.[267]

This we can see for ourselves in a wonderfully detailed plan of the Hot Bath, with the Leper's Bath adjoining and the tiny hospital beside it (29). Figures are shown sharing three beds of straw on the ground floor of the hospital, while a staircase leads to the upper floor. Wood's measurements show that the top floor was jettied out right over Nowhere Lane.

In June 1576 the Privy Council once again granted a licence to Dr Feckenham to go to Bath until September for the recovery of his health.[268] Perhaps it was in this season that Feckenham realised the need for medical advice for poor visitors who could not afford physicians. He compiled a recipe book of herbal medicines with advice on the use of the baths, though it was never published.[269] The following year Feckenham was committed to the custody of the Bishop of Ely and never returned to Bath. By coincidence the Bishop of Ely had by then married Dr Turner's widow.[270]

Rebuilding by Bath Corporation

The Mastership of St John's had become a sinecure. After the death of Simons, Elizabeth used the post to reward favoured clerics. Thomas Greenway was one of the Protestants who fled abroad for safety in the reign of Mary. Elizabeth recompensed him with the Mastership of St John's Hospital on 19 April 1561.[271] He promptly sued John Crouch and others for having possession of the hospital deeds and seals.[272] Meanwhile Crouch took action against the Mayor of Bath

264 *Dictionary of National Biography; Acts of the Privy Council 1575-7*, 8.

265 Fuller, **3**, 80.

266 *Accounts of the Chamberlains*, 32.

267 J. Wood, *Description of Bath*, 200, 306.

268 *Acts of the Privy Council 1575-7*, 142.

269 Gasquet, 257-8.

270 *Dictionary of National Biography*.

271 *Calendar of Patent Rolls 1560-63*, 25.

272 PRO REQ2/209/55.

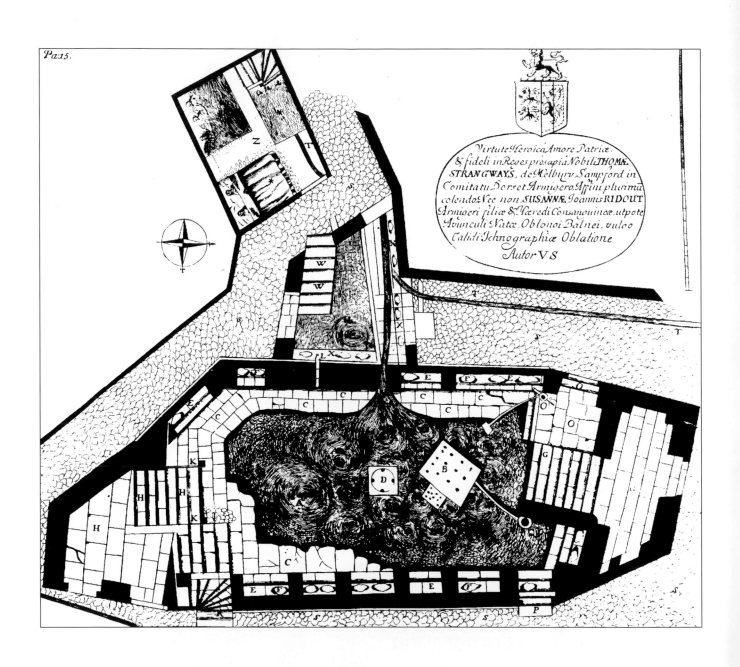

Pa:15.

Virtute Heroica Amore Patriæ
& fideli in Reges prosapia Nobili THOMÆ
STRANGWAYS, de Melbury Sampford in
Comitatu Dorset Armigero. Affini plurimu
colendo: Nec non SUSANNÆ, Joannis RIDOUT
Armigeri filiæ & Hæredi Consanguineæ, utpote
Avunculi Natæ, Oblonoi Balnei, vulgo
Calidi Ichnographiæ Oblatione
Autor V S

29

Plan of the Hot Bath from T. Guidott, *De Thermis Britannicis* (1691). The Lazars' Bath was built onto its west side, using the overflow. Figures are shown sharing three straw beds in the tiny Leper Hospital. A staircase led to the upper floor, where there were another four beds

ELIZABETH by the grace of God Queene of England, Fraunce, and Ireland, defendour of the fayth. &c. To all and singular Archbyshops, Byshops, Deanes, Archdeacons, & other Officials persōs Uicares, Curates, Ministers, and to all other spirituall persōs whatsoeuer they be, and also to all & singular Iustices of peace, Maiors, Shireffes, Baylyffes, Constables, Heddoroughes, Churchwardens, Tythyngmen, and all other our Officers ministers & subiectes, to whō these presentes shal come, greetyng. Wheras we vpō humble sute made vnto vs by diuers of our Nobilitie, and many others of great credite, & specially at the most humble desire and zealous sute of the Maior & Citizens of our Citie of Bathe, haue giuen licence to new builde and erect one Church, vpon the foundations of the late Abbey Church of the late dissolued Monastery of Bathe, for the receauyng of such of the Nobilitie, and other our subiectes as resort or shall from tyme to tyme haue occasions to resorte to that Citie, there to haue cōuenient place to heare Sermons, and other diuine seruice, which cannot cōueniently be in any other Church within our sayd Citie, for the smalenes of the rowmes & buildinges of the same. And heretofore for lacke of cōuenient rowmes within our sayd Citie, the Sermons haue ben made in the open market place there, beyng not mete nor conuenient for such purpose, which greater Church cannot be of new buylded and finished without greater sūmes of money thē the Citizēs there be able to beare or sustayne. And albeit they shew them selues very zealous, and do employ great trauayles and charges therin, yet are they not hable to finish the same, therfore haue made their further humble sute vnto vs to licence them and theyr assignes & deputies to receaue the gratuities of our subiectes within this our Realme of England and Wales for the finishyng of the sayd Church.

Know you therfore that we acceptyng very well of this zealous entent & good meanyng of the sayd Maior & Citizens & tendyng their ayde and helpe towardes the new buildyng of the sayd Church, & also towardes the enlargyng & betteryng of an Hospital within that Citie of Bathe called S. Ihones, there erected for the relefe and cōfort of certaine sicke & diseased poore persōs that resort thether, from diuers partes of this our Realme are pleased & contēted, and by these presentes for vs our heyres and successours do giue licēce & free libertie vnto the sayd Maior & Citizens of our sayd Citie of Bathe & their assigne or assignes, deputie or deputies bearers of this our licence & graūt or the duplicate, or true copy hereof duryng the space of vij. yeares, next commyng to aske gather receiue & take the gratuitie, gift, almes, and deuotion, of all and euery or any our louyng subiectes dwellers within this our Realme of England & Wales, aswell within the liberties as without for the buildyng & erecting of the sayd Church and Hospital.

Wherfore we will and commaunde you the sayd Parsons, Uicars, and Curates, & all other aforesayd that you and euery of you at such tyme and tymes, as the sayd Maior and Citizens or any of their assigne or assignes deputie or deputies, or any of them bearers or bearer hereof or the duplicate hereof, shall repayre vnto your Churches and other places to aske and gather the gratuities, giftes, almes, and deuotiō of our louyng subiectes or any of them, that ye permit and suffer the sayd Maior and Citizens & theyr assigne or assignes deputy or deputies so to do, without your let or interruption and to declare the tenor and effect of these our letters patentes vnto our louyng subiectes exhortyng them to extend to so honorable a worke their gratuities and charitable giftes and almes, redoundyng greatly to the glory of almighty God, and the great renowne of this our Realme, and the ease and commoditie of our louyng subiectes.

And we further straitly charge and cōmaunde all and euery hygh Constable of the hundredes Heddoroughes and other Constables, Churchwardens, and Tythyngmen that vpon the open readyng of these our letters patentes or the duplicate or true copy therof in any Church or other open place or places what soeuer, to collect and gather all the giftes and deuotiōs of all our louyng subiectes, where soeuer the same shalbe read or declared and what summe or summes, soeuer shalbe so leuied and receaued to be deliuered to the vse of the sayd Maior and Citizens for the purpose aforesayd, and cause the same summes to be endorced vpō these presentes or the duplicate or true copie hereof, to the entent it may playnly appeare what hath bene collected towardes the erectyng of the sayd Church and Hospitall, within this our Realme of Englād and Wales. In witnes wherof we haue caused these our letters to be made patentes, witnes our selfe at Westminster the xiij. day of Aprill, the xv. yeare of our raigne.

per breue de priuato Sigillo.   *Dupl.*   Powle.

God saue the Queene.

¶ Imprinted at London by Iohn Daye.

30

Proclamation by Queen Elizabeth granting permission for collections throughout the country for the rebuilding of Bath Abbey Church and the enlarging and improving of St John's Hospital

31
The architecture of civic pride. A view of St John's Hospital in 1694: inset from Joseph Gilmore's map of Bath. From columns to cupola, the centrepiece was intended to impress. The use of Classical details such as the pediment shows Renaissance ideas filtering into Elizabethan Bath

for discontinuing an annuity of £5, which he claimed was due to him under his lease of the hospital. (The annuity was that once paid to the hospital by the Bishop of Bath and Wells in lieu of sheaves of corn.[273]) The mayor was unimpressed. He had paid the £5 to the new master, as was proper.[274] Greenway was elected President of Corpus Christi College, Oxford on 3 January 1561/2, but he did not resign from St John's, so it is unclear why on 29 August 1562 the Crown presented John Louth LLB to the mastership.[275] (Louth was another strong Protestant, who had already been rewarded with two prebends.[276]) In any case Greenway continued as master. In April 1571, just a few months before his death, he successfully petitioned the Crown for the cash equivalent of the corrody granted to St John's Hospital by Bath Priory c.1190. This allowance of food had ceased at the Dissolution.[277]

Meanwhile Bath Council was grappling with another consequence of the Dissolution. The priory had given Bath a grand church. Now it was an empty shell. Elsewhere some former monastic churches had been converted to parochial use and an ambition rose in the breasts of the city fathers to take over the priory church (commonly called the Abbey Church). Edmund Colthurst, owner of the former priory site, was willing to give the church to the city. The creation of a new, united city parish would also remove the evil of Crown patronage of city churches.

The mayor and burgesses petitioned the Queen *via* Lord Burghley, her Secretary of State until July 1572, when he was appointed Lord Treasurer. The reasons they gave for wanting to rebuild the Abbey Church are revealing. 'There is in the spring time and at the fall of the leaf yearly great repair to the … city of noble men, men of worship and others for relief at the baths there and no convenient church … for any company to resort together.' Bath had always attracted visitors, but the city was now on the verge of a renaissance as a fashionable spa. It needed a great church, not simply for its own year-round population, but for the seasonal flood of visitors taking the waters. However, this ambitious project was beyond the city purse, so the city fathers also asked for permission to gather charitable donations for the purpose. In addition they wanted to take over the patronage of St John's Hospital and enlarge it. They pleaded:

> That whereas there is an hospital there for four poor people, whereof the patronage
> is in the Queen's majesty, that it would please her grace to grant … [us] licence
> to augment the same to the number of ten persons … towards the better relief
> of poor impotent persons resorting to the baths there.[278]

The Queen was prepared to be generous. On 21 November 1572 Elizabeth granted to the city the patronage of St John's Hospital with the annexed Church of St Michael, along with that of the other city churches. St John's Hospital had joined St Catherine's as a municipal charity. Edmund Colthurst was given permission to grant the ruined monastic church to the citizenry, and the latter had licence to restore it as a parish church.[279] There remained the problem of finance. On 13 April 1573 Elizabeth gave permission for collections to be made for seven years nation-wide towards the rebuilding

273 *Register of John de Drokensford*, 99. The bishop's estate in Bath was leased to the civic body by 1447 (King and Watts, 28 and appendix A, no.34), evidently with this charge upon it. In 1548 the bishop granted title to the Crown (*Calendar of Patent Rolls 1548-9*, 128), but the Mayor and Commonalty continued as lessee.

274 PRO C3/45/84.

275 *Calendar of Patent Rolls 1560-3*, 269

276 'Reminiscences of John Louthe', 7-14.

277 PRO E368/110, LR6/17/2.

278 PRO SP12/384, p.58 (no.24).

279 *Calendar of Patent Rolls 1562-5*, 383.

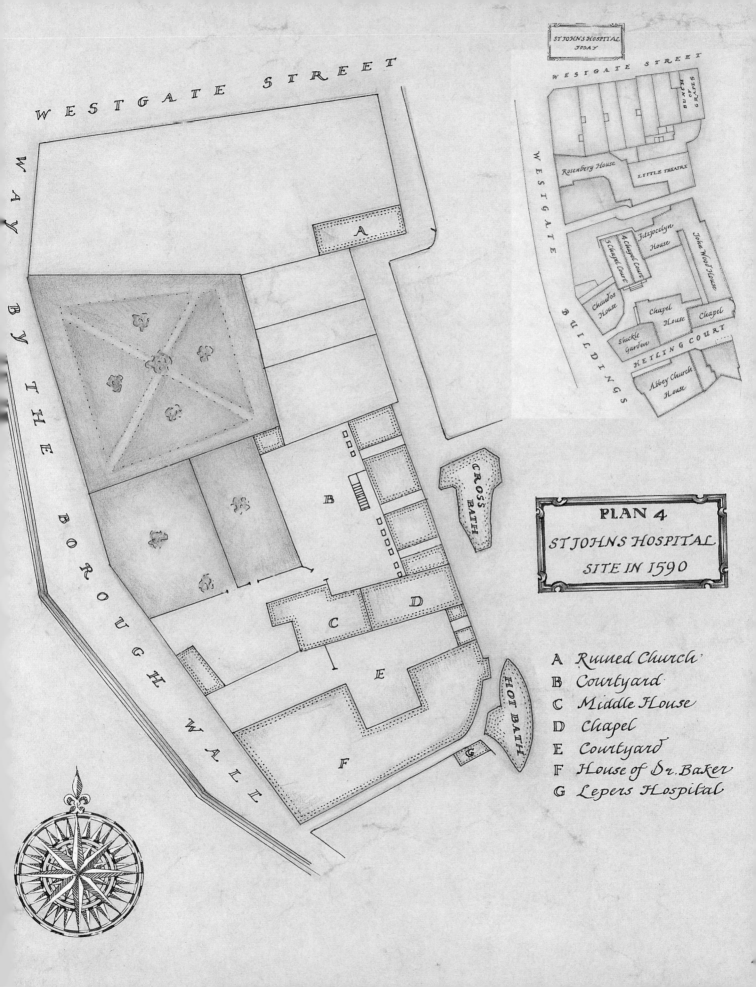

WESTGATE STREET

WAY BY THE BOROUGH WALL

A

B

C

D

E

F

G

CROSS BATH

HOT BATH

PLAN 4
ST JOHNS HOSPITAL
SITE IN 1590

A Ruined Church
B Courtyard
C Middle House
D Chapel
E Courtyard
F House of Dr. Baker
G Lepers Hospital

ST JOHNS HOSPITAL
TODAY

WESTGATE STREET

WESTGATE BUILDINGS

BUNCH OF GRAPES

Rosenberg House

LITTLE THEATRE

Fitzjocelyn House

4 Chapel Court

5 Chapel Court

John Wool House

Chandos House

Chapel House

Chapel

Shickle Garden

HETLING COURT

Abbey Church House

32
An imaginative reconstruction of St John's Hospital from the courtyard in 1590. In a development unique to Bath, wealthy spa visitors lodged over the heads of the almsfolk, who lived on the ground floor. Both almsmen and almswomen wore uniform blue gowns, from which St John's became known as the 'Blue Alms'. They were cared for by a washerwoman who also acted as a nurse. She is shown here chatting to a resident and a friend. Meanwhile a gentry family settles into lodgings, distracting a servant girl from her washing

33
The Middle House and its gardens c.1600

280 *Ibid*, 527; *Tudor and Stuart Proclamations* **1**, 680.

281 *Statutes of the Realm*, **4**, 590-98 (14th Eliz cap.5).

282 BaRO account roll 6: St John's.

283 BaRO account rolls 9, 12: St John's, *Accounts of the Chamberlains*, 58-9.

284 *Accounts of the Chamberlains*, 50-1, 58-9, 88.

285 J. Wood, *Description of Bath*, 303.

286 BaRO account rolls 12 onwards St John's; *Report of the Commissioners for Charities* **4**, 284.

287 BaRO account roll 12: St John's: Mr Bewshin paid 6s 8d for the seal of his lease; a payment was made for making a 'glychon' between Mr Fitch's chamber and the chamber of Mr Bewshin.

288 BaRO account roll 12: St John's; Fitch was mayor in 1586 (*Accounts of the Chamberlains*, 93.)

289 The gallery was leased with the rooms over the hospital in 1717: BMCA StJH/7/117. The staircase was mentioned in 1630 in a lease of rooms over the north side of the hospital: BaRO 1641 Survey of Bath, f.174, no.2; a rectangular projection shown on a plan of Bath in 1725 for the Duke of Kingston (BaL) presumably indicates the stair.

290 J. Wood, *Description of Bath*, 303.

of the Abbey Church and the enlarging and improving of St. John's Hospital. A printed proclamation of the grant was issued (30), to be read out in churches or open places up and down the land. It was designed to move the nation. Like the original appeal to the queen, it portrayed the country's ailing rich and poor converging on Bath. Supposedly both church and hospital would serve them.[280]

In reality St John's could not hope to provide for the influx of poor diseased people attracted to Bath, who were becoming a great burden to the city. This was just part of what was perceived as a rising national nuisance of beggars, rogues and vagabonds. Legislation addressed the problem in 1572 with a combination of ferocious punishment for begging and provision for the aged and genuinely disabled to be supported by the parish. The Poor Relief Act noted the particular problems of Bath and Buxton and stated that charity cases wishing to visit either spa should be licensed by two Justices of the Peace and provided for by their own parish.[281]

From 1577 the city chamberlain kept separate accounts for St John's Hospital.[282] By this time the Corporation had clearly managed to persuade John Crouch to hand over his lease of the hospital and its properties. Under this lease, the Corporation was entitled to collect St John's rents and pay the hospital only £10 a year. It did no such thing. The full rent income of £32 12s was paid into the hospital accounts. The Corporation was acting as an honest guardian and forgoing any profit.

The accounts show that the hospital was enlarged in 1580, when the national collection was complete. There are payments for building up the walls, a new floor, two pairs of stairs, a loft, a new roof and a great door in the entry.[283] The Corporation paid for tiles for the hospital roof, since it had melted down the old lead for pipes.[284] The dimensions of the building were the same as they are now. If there were only six rooms before the Dissolution, then another six must have been added at this time (PLAN 4). There were three passages through from east to west, into each of which four rooms opened.[285] It is not clear why there were 12 rooms. A maximum of ten almsfolk lived in St John's for many years after its rebuilding. However, it did create space for expansion and the number had increased to 12 by the early eighteenth century.[286]

Another storey and attic were added above the rooms of the almsfolk, partly to provide a lodging for the master (31-32).[287] The main aim, though, was to swell the hospital revenues. The potential of the site, so convenient for the smaller baths, had not been lost on the Corporation. Alderman Thomas Fitch bought the first lease of 'the chambers over the hospital'.[288] Access to the lodgings was provided in the fashion of inns of the time. From the courtyard an external staircase led up to a gallery.[289] Below was a colonnade, six feet broad including the width of the columns.[290] This hybrid structure, with wealthy spa visitors over the heads of poor almsfolk, was unique.

The new St John's had a hybrid architecture too. Classical features – columns, entablature, pediment – were pasted onto a gabled building with the carefree eclecticism of the time. Bath's Market House was rebuilt in 1626 along similar lines.[291] But the Classical influence on St John's was more startling. Before the Georgian period, we know of no other building in Bath with a pediment. Its tympanum was decorated with a head of St John the Baptist.[292] Even more extraordinary was the cupola. Such an architectural flourish might be expected on the palatial homes of Elizabethan grandees. For example Burghley House was bedecked with cupolas in 1577.[293] It was built by the Lord Treasurer, who accompanied Queen Elizabeth to Bath in August 1574.[294] Did he have a hand in the design of St John's? Whatever the inspiration, the new hospital was an expression of civic pride.

The new upper storeys of the hospital were built against the northern windows of St John's Chapel. It seems that these were left open, as windows between the lodgings and chapel (see p.92). The chapel itself was given a timber bell tower in 1580, the chancel was reroofed, the roodloft removed and seats fitted. However, this did not amount to a major rebuilding. The fabric was probably still largely Norman. The chapel was the same size as the present chapel and evidently had a gallery, leased out to Alderman Fitch as 'a room over the body of the chapel'.[295] There were no more leases of this room, but in 1659 there was work on the gallery.[296] An interesting feature was the clock on the eastern gable (10), which was one of the earliest public clocks in Bath. It may have been a private gift to St John's, since it is not mentioned in the accounts until it was mended in 1602.[297] The Corporation maintained only one other clock in this period, which was at the King's Bath. Since private clocks were rare, many Bathonians would have relied on St John's clock. A less pleasing addition was the shop built in 1626 against the south-east corner of the chapel.[298]

In 1580 Richard Bewshin MA became the first Master of St John's to be selected by the Corporation.[299] Richard was the son of Peter Bewshin, farmer of Barton Grange and other lands around Bath. It was an omen of things to come. In their selection of masters the Corporation consistently favoured the clerical sons of local families, but this did not necessarily produce closer attention to the hospital. Richard Bewshin was already Rector of Beckington and went on to become Rector of Standerwick, both in Somerset.[300] He probably made little use of his lodging at St John's. During his time Thomas Hill served as 'reader to the poor',[301] in other words as acting chaplain. Hill was the Parish Clerk of St Mary of Stalls (1569-1615).[302] Not surprisingly, the master's lodging over the hospital was let by 1622. Together with the other lodging there, it brought in £8 10s a year, the highest rent of all St John's city property.[303]

The Elizabethan rebuilding made the old hospital quadrangle redundant and so released more accommodation to let. West of the chapel, on the site of the old infirmary, was the 'Middle House' (33). This was leased to the Town Clerk, Robert Chambers, along with the gardens of the hospital.[304] It was a valuable property. The Middle House apparently had its own bath supplied from the Hot Bath.[305] The gardens were extensive for an urban house.

34
The ornate head of a fountain, found on the site of the seventeenth-century formal garden when the foundations were dug for Rosenberg House

291   Holland, 169 and cover picture.

292   J. Wood, *Description of Bath*, 305.

293   Girouard, 34 and fig.14.

294   *Acts of the Privy Council 1571-5*, 286.

295   BaRO account roll 12: St John's. The timber of the roodloft was sold to innkeeper Peter Chapman, a member of the family that was to produce so many Masters of St John's.

296   BaRO CA 102 St John's.

297   *Accounts of the Chamberlains*, 186, 188.

298   BaRO 1641 survey of Bath f.131, no.1.

299   *Accounts of the Chamberlains*, 49.

300   Foster, *Alumni Oxoniensis 1500-1714*, 120.

301   BaRO account rolls: St John's.

302   Bristol University Library, BaL and BaRO, P. R. James 'The Incorporation of the City of Bath: its origin and its working' (PhD thesis 1956), 656.

303   BaRO 1641 survey of Bath f.174, no.2, f.175, no.1.

304   Leases of adjoining properties give Chambers as the occupant of the Middle House and gardens from 1591 to 1620: BaRO 1641 survey of Bath f.130, no.1, f.176, no.2, f.182, no.1.

305   In 1583 the Corporation mended the pipes leading from the Hot Bath into Mr Chambers' bath: *Accounts of the Chamberlains*, 70-71.

35
Dr Baker's House (now the Abbey Church House) c.1600

Perhaps it was Chambers who created the formal garden at the northern end (33-4). The small building at its south-east corner may be a summer house. After the master gave up his lodgings over the hospital, it seems that a vestry was created in the Middle House. In 1665 a lease of the house excluded a chamber over dining room, to which the Master and his curate had free entry. It was on the first floor next to the chapel and facing the southern courtyard.[306]

From 1578 Mr Fulks (*Fowkes*) paid 40s a year for 'the house of St John's',[307] apparently the rest of the medieval quadrangle. His house too had a bath from the Hot Bath.[308] As the Elizabethan Court began to flock to Bath, houses close to the baths were snapped up by physicians to lodge and treat their noble patients. A private bath would be a particular asset. No wonder this house was rebuilt along grander lines by Dr Robert Baker around 1590 (35). It is now the Abbey Church House. Dr Baker had settled in Bath by 1587, when he paid 20s rent to St John's.[309] On 25 March 1591 St John's granted him a lease of the area from Hot Bath to the way by the city walls, with the new buildings erected on it by Baker, and the great pitched or paved court 'now divided into two courts'.[310] The great chamber of his house is still there, with some of its Elizabethan panelling and the elaborate chimney-piece (38). On the overmantle are the arms of his wife, Elizabeth, who was a Clarke of Wookey.[311] Before war-time damage, the panelling ran to the ceiling, with carved panels at the top forming a frieze similar to one at Montacute. This grand mansion was considered second only to the Abbey House among Bath's noble lodgings and later leases call it simply the Great House.

Dr Baker did not enjoy his new house for long. In November 1596, he was buried in Bath Abbey.[312] His widow then married another physician, Dr Reuben Sherwood, formerly the Head Master of Eton. He held the Great House in her right, but in February 1598, before he had even settled in Bath,

> Certain lewd and disordered persons of base sort and condition … did in tumultuous
>
> sort assemble themselves together and shutting the doors of the Hot Bath unto
>
> them did dig up the spring and head of [Sherwood's] private bath.[313]

Dr Sherwood complained to the Privy Council, who demanded swift action by Bath Corporation, since the Marchioness of Northampton was intending to visit Bath in April, especially to use this private bath. The Marchioness was a particular favourite with Queen Elizabeth. Helena Ulfsdotter Snakenborg came to England as a maid of honour to Princess Cecilia of Sweden and captured the heart of the much older William Parr, Marquis of Northampton. By the time of this visit to Bath she had long outlived him and no doubt developed the aches and pains of middle age. Perhaps the Bath waters did her good, for she came again at least seven times and was a generous benefactor to the city (see below p.78). Then in May 1599, Dr Reuben Sherwood entertained William, son of Sir Robert Cecil, the Queen's Principal Secretary of State.[314] All must have seemed set for a flourishing Court practice. But Dr Sherwood was buried in Bath Abbey that July.[315] By 1603, Elizabeth Sherwood had married a third husband, Jeremy Horton of Broughton Giffard,[316]

306   BMCA StJH/7/1(a), 114.

307   BaRO account rolls 8, 9, 15: St John's.

308   *Accounts of the Chamberlains*, 70-71.

309   BaRO account roll 24: St John's.

310   BaRO 1641 survey of Bath f.182, no.1.

311   The tomb of Thomas Clarke in Wookey Church shows his arms and those of his wife Anthoni. These are quartered on the shield in Abbey Church House, indicating a descendant of theirs. Thomas died in 1554, leaving a son Henry, who died in 1582. Among his children was Elizabeth, who by 1586 had become Elizabeth Baker. *Abs. Somerset Wills*, **2**, 89, **3**, 31-2.

312   *Registers of the Abbey Church*, **2**, 336.

313   *Acts of the Privy Council 1597-8*, 373-5.

314   MSS at Hatfield, **9**, 179.

315   *Registers of the Abbey Church*, **2**, 337.

316   *Visitation of Gloucestershire 1623*, 84; *Registers of the Abbey Church* **1**, 14.

36
The northern front of Mrs Savile's Lodging (now the Abbey Church House) in 1694, from
Gilmore's map of Bath. It was the second best lodging in Bath, patronised later by royalty

37
A rare glimpse of pre-Georgian Bath: a seventeenth-century ceiling in the Bunch of Grapes, Westgate Street

who seems to have been drawn into the dispute with Bath Corporation about the private bath.[317]

Later the 99-year lease to Robert Baker went through the hands of the Ward and Ivy families.[318] A few years before it was due to expire Sir Giles Hungerford (d.1685) seems to have bought a new lease. In 1691 his daughter and heir Mary married Lord Lexington, who gave the lease to Mary's cousin Mrs Honor Savile in lieu of a legacy. The Great House was therefore described by Gilmore as Mrs Savile's Lodgings near the Hot Bath (36). His view is of the north façade, which by this time had been extended east to form an impressive six-gable front. In 1697 Mrs Savile married the apothecary William Skrine, who took advantage of the pipe from the Hot Bath to draw water off for sale.[319]

With the rise of the spa, sites near the Hot and Cross Baths were in demand for lodgings, taverns and inns. The Hospitals of St John and St Mary Magdalen had properties in the area, some of which were sadly decayed in 1527 (appendix 9). Now there was a fever of rebuilding, with fine houses springing up.[320] The Bunch of Grapes on Westgate Street is the only example still standing. It seems Jacobean or Carolinian behind the Georgian façade. Some panelling of this period survives on the second floor, along with a small blocked-in window of the arch-headed type. But the most notable feature is the ceiling in the first floor drawing room (37). Its heavy strapwork is typical of the period. The centrepiece includes the double-headed eagle, famous as the symbol of the Holy Roman Empire. This has generated speculation that the house was used by Charles Granville, 2nd Earl of Bath, who became a Count of the Holy Roman Empire in 1684.[321] But that date is too late for the style of the ceiling. The house was leased in 1620 to Richard Gay, three times Mayor of Bath.[322] It seems that he sub-let it to Dr John Ostendorph, a physician from Germany who had settled in Bath by 1637.[323] Ostendorph's widow certainly lived there after his death.[324] The double-headed eagle could have been a patriotic gesture by a man far from the land of his birth.

The Corporation accounts provide glimpses into the daily life of the hospital after its rebuilding. Mother West was the hospital laundress. She was paid extra for looking after the almspeople when they fell ill. Mother Bird lay sick a long time, tended by West. No expense was spared. The considerable sum of 13s 4d was paid for a cure for Mother Bird's mouth. Still the inevitable end came; the cost of her shroud and grave is recorded. Mother West's own grave was paid for in 1598. Every few years blue broadcloth was bought and made up into gowns for the almsfolk. It was from these gowns that St John's was known as the 'Blue Alms'. The gowns were lined with durable white cotton and fastened with clasps. Occasionally other garments were bought; St John's was a flexible charity. For instance 5s was spent in 1581 on 'apparel to Joan Beckett's daughter to set her to a master.' Each of the almspeople was paid £1 a year,[325] and there were treats. Most of the rents of St John's country properties included one or two fat capons at Christmas, adding up to 14 birds for the festive table in St John's.[326] In February 1586/7 John Bewshin was

317   BaRO council minutes 4 Oct 1614.

318   A Mr Ward was in the house by 1626. He passed the lease to Thomas, eldest son of Sir George Ivy, who was holding it on the eve of the Civil War (BaRO 1641 survey of Bath f.131, no.1, f.182, no.1). By 1644 Thomas Ivy was dead. His widow Lettice left to her children Thomas, Ferdinando and Lettice the house in which she dwelt by the Cross Bath (BL MSS Harl. Ch.112 A 38).The Ivys then leased it for some years to Mrs Mary Burford, but in 1662 Ferdinando Ivy owed a 6s rent to St John's (BaRO CM 28 June and 4 October 1652; BaRO account roll 104). In 1678, a Mr Freeman was living in the large house built by Dr Robert Baker (A. à Wood, 16.)

319   *Complete Peerage* **7**, 628; *Registers of the Abbey Church* **1**, 230; J. Wood, *Description of Bath*, 85, 227; Walker, 100.

320   Manco, 'Bath and the Great Rebuilding'.

321   M. Green, 27; *The Complete Peerage*, **2**, 21.

322   BaRO 1641 Survey of Bath f.180, no.1.

323   Guidott, 213; *Registers of the Abbey Church* **1** , 33; BaRO chamberlain's account roll for 1658 mentions Mr Ostendorph's house in Westgate Street.

324   BMCA StJH/7/263

325   BaRO account rolls 1, 12, 15, 17, 24, 26, 30: St John's.

326   BaRO 1641 survey of Bath, ff.194, 196, 197, 201, 205, 207, 209.

38
The grand Elizabethan fireplace in Dr. Baker's House (now the Abbey Church House).
On the overmantle are the arms of his wife Elizabeth née Clarke

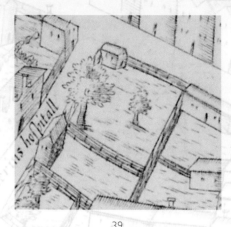

39
The site that Thomas Bellott chose for his almshouse: a house and garden leased by St John's to the Byam family. on Savile's map of Bath c.1600

appointed master of St John's on the death of his brother Richard.[327] John was notorious for his neglect of the almspeople, so they would scarcely have noticed the exchange of one Bewshin for another. Thomas Hill continued as their chaplain.[328]

Meanwhile at St Catherine's the almsfolk received less in cash than their counterparts in St John's, but they had wood or coal at Christmas and bread in Lent.[329] Their gowns were made of black cotton, with red cloth to protect the sleeves.[330] The number of shrouds bought for them suggests that they were mainly aged. In 1587 the Corporation 'gave to old Humphrey at times, being very sick 2s 7d, gave to George Cox's wife, being very sick 3d, gave to Butler, being very sick 6d, gave to Lovett, being very sick and towards a shroud 7d'.[331]

Bellott's Hospital

In the last decade of Elizabeth's reign concern rose nationally for the suffering of the poor and the possibility of social upheaval unless it was ameliorated. A series of statutes reshaped the system of community support. The Poor Relief Acts of 1572 and 1576 had been something of an experiment in social engineering. The latter was re-enacted in 1593, with a revision permitting charitable donors to grant land for the use of the poor.[332] By 1597 it was apparent that this was not enough. Potential donors were still deterred by the Statute of Mortmain. So the Act for Erecting Hospitals loosened the controls; for the following 20 years new charitable institutions could be founded simply by deed enrolled in Chancery.[333] This was the legislation of which Thomas Bellott took advantage. 1597 also saw the passing of the landmark Act 'to reform deceits and breaches of trust, touching lands given to charitable uses', which was re-enacted in amended form as the Charitable Uses Act of 1601. These statutes created a far more effective form of State supervision for charities, though it was dependent upon local people being able and willing to draw attention to abuses. These would be investigated by county commissioners through local juries.[334] We shall see the procedure in action in the eighteenth century.

Thomas Bellott was an extraordinary man, whose charitable impulses were lavished upon Bath, a city he must have loved, though he came to it as a stranger. He was a member of a Cheshire family which produced a number of able and devout sons. Thomas's brother Hugh was the Bishop of Chester. Thomas himself was born in 1534 and at 14 entered the household of Sir William Cecil, later Lord Burghley. When Elizabeth came to the throne, her first act was to make Cecil her Secretary of State and he remained her trusted advisor until his death in 1598. Thomas Bellott was the steward of this powerful man from 1566-98 and then his executor. Subsequently he served Burghley's son Robert Cecil, also a Secretary of State, and was a servant of James I.[335]

Burghley made several visits to Bath and perhaps brought Bellott. All that is certain is that Bellott was in Bath without his master in 1595.[336] His

327 BaRO quoted in council minutes 22 May 1617.

328 BaRO account rolls 1, 24, 26.

329 *Accounts of the Chamberlains*, 38, 39, 43, 47-8, 71, 76.

330 *Ibid*, 86-7, 104, 117, 121, 126, 144, 150.

331 *Ibid*, 97.

332 *Statutes of the Realm*, **4**, 854-6 (35 Eliz cap. 7).

333 *Ibid*, 902-3 (39 Eliz cap. 5).

334 *Ibid*, 903-4 (39 Eliz cap 6); G. Jones, 22-56.

335 Bush and Hatton.

336 *Letters…of Sir John Harington*, 64.

40-43
Bellott's Hospital: These four water-colours by Henry Venn Lansdown were made before the hospital was rebuilt in 1859.
They were purchased jointly by a number of Bath citizens and presented to the hospital trustees in 1862:
TOP The front facing Beau Street, with its ornate doorway.
Through the arch one can see into the central courtyard and the garden beyond
CENTRE LEFT The courtyard looking west, with the archway to the street on the right
CENTRE RIGHT The courtyard looking east
BOTTOM The back of the hospital from the garden

44

The coat of arms and motto of William Cecil, Lord Burghley was transferred from the old Bellott's Hospital to the present building. The belt around the arms shows that he was a Knight of the Garter

first concern was Bath Abbey. The national collection had not yielded enough money to complete the restoration, which had gone no further than roofing the choir and north transept. From the money Burghley left for pious uses and from his own, Bellott paid for the lengthening and glazing of the east window and fitting up of the choir so that it could be brought into use.[337] This work was probably done *c.*1600 since the Corporation supplied panelling and benches at that time.[338] Bellott went on to contribute £200 to the restoration of the south transept.[339]

He then turned to the poor and sick. In March 1605 he promised £800 towards the building and endowment of an almshouse on Robert Cecil's estate at Enfield.[340] In Bath he saw a need, like Feckenham before him, to provide for poor spa visitors. In 1598 St John's Hospital had leased a property on Bell Tree Lane to members of the Byam family.[341] It was an almost square plot which was largely garden (39). Bellott bought the lease from the Byams and built an almshouse, which he then handed over to the Corporation. The precise date is unknown. However, the chamberlain's accounts for 1606 include a gift to Bellott, perhaps in thanks.[342] 'Saint' Bellott's 'new hospital for lame pilgrims' is mentioned on 5 September 1608 by his admirer Sir John Harington.[343] Bellott then purchased an estate in Wiltshire in November 1608 to endow his charity. This was granted to the Corporation on 5 January 1610/1. The deed sets out Bellott's actions and intentions for the foundation; he had 'bestowed much costs and charges on repairing, amending and making said tenement fit for the harbouring and relieving' of poor diseased persons coming to Bath.[344] A copy was enrolled in Chancery.

This almshouse survived largely unchanged until its rebuilding in the nineteenth century and some delightful water-colours of it hang in the present Bellott's Hospital (40-43). More space was available to Bellott than Feckenham, which resulted in a completely different structure. Instead of a tiny timber building, mushrooming out on top, Bellott's Hospital was a single-storey quadrangle in stone, typical of almshouses of the period. Fourteen rooms were arranged around a courtyard.[345] The ornate street entrance from Bell Tree Lane (now Beau Street) led into the quadrangle and from there another passage led through into the garden beyond. Over the door was Lord Burghley's coat of arms and his motto *Cor unum via una* (one heart one way) (44). Below that was inscribed *Ne dormiat in thesauris tuis quod pauperis prodesse potest. Dormis securus paupertas est tibi mutua.* (Do not leave dormant in your store that which would relieve the poor. If the poor sleep soundly, so will you.)

The hospital was open only in the bathing season: two months in the spring and one in the autumn. Those with contagious diseases were excluded, which may explain why Feckenham's became known as the Leper Hospital. Those denied access to Bellott's would resort to the smaller hospital. In line with the current legislation, patients had to bring with them a certificate from some neighbouring justice, or by the minister, constable or churchwarden of their parish, as proof that they were genuinely poor and needed to use the baths. Bellott's could house 12 at a time, each person staying no more

337 Warner, appendix 73.

338 *Accounts of the Chamberlains*, 180.

339 Warner, appendix 73.

340 *MSS at Hatfield*, **17**, 97.

341 BMCA BH 6/1.

342 BaRO account roll 47, 2.

343 *Letters…of Sir John Harington*, 135.

344 BMCA BH/1; BH/6/1; *Report of the Commissioners for Charities* **4**, 292; BaRO Furman bdle 18, item 7.

345 J. Wood, *Description of Bath*, 305.

than 28 days in any year. They were paid 4d a day, along with their gowns, room and bed. The patients were to be cared for by a keeper and his wife, who would have a room in the almshouse and 40s a year to welcome and courteously treat the poor, keep the house clean, make the beds and look after the furniture. A surgeon would visit to examine the patients before admission. He too had a room in the house, along with a salary of 20s a year. The Corporation was required to receive the rents (£22 10s yearly), pay the charges and keep the almshouse in repair.[346]

The Corporation was faithful to its responsibilities, keeping accounts for the hospital in a special book. Most interesting is the section started 28 March 1616 to record the details of patients. They came from far afield. The intake that year included William Dellward from Leicester, 'troubled with swelling in both his legs', Mark Gay from Drewsteignton, Devon, who had aching legs, and similar cases from Berkshire, Devon, Gloucestershire, London, Northamptonshire, Pembrokeshire, Somerset and Wiltshire. All were men. In each case, a note was made of the number of days the patient stayed, the amount he was paid and his progress. For example in April 1618 Thomas Nightingale of Twyford in Dorset was admitted, being lame in one knee. He 'received some comfort' and was allowed 9s 4d. Ailments included aching limbs, neck, back and joint pains, sciatica, dropsy, lameness and paralysis, and patients reported anything between 'great comfort' and 'no ease'. In April 1620 an amazing case was prosaically recorded: 'William Powell of London, lame in all his lower part, was admitted into the house for the whole 28 days. Was wholly recovered.' From these few tantalising details, it is impossible to guess what wrought this miracle cure. A similar case in May had no such outcome. Arthur Jackson, also from London, was admitted with a numbness in his lower part and found small help. Occasionally, we are given a clue to the cause of the trouble. For example Ralph Evly of London had fallen from a pigeon house; happily his pains were greatly eased by the Bath waters.[347] From 1626 the medical details are omitted, but for ten years we have a fascinating casebook, the first for any hospital in Bath.

Bellott's was also the first hospital in Bath to provide for the regular attendance of a surgeon. It was not the first in the country. The huge Savoy hospital in London, founded in 1515 from the lavish bequest of Henry VII, had a surgeon and a physician on the staff.[348] However, the Savoy was exceptional. Smaller hospitals of this period could not afford medical fees. Bellott's required only occasional medical attendance for part of the year, but even so the hospital had no physician.

Another benefactor provided the remedy. Lady Elizabeth Scudamore died in December 1651, leaving £200 to the Corporation, which it received from her husband the following year. The interest was to provide a physician for the visiting poor.[349] The first to take up the post was Tobias Venner,[350] long established as a specialist in spa medicine and author of *The Baths of Bath* and *Via Recta ad Vitam Longam* (The Right Way to a Long Life) (45). Dr Venner was his own best advertisement, since he was already 78 when he

45
Portrait of Dr Tobias Venner from the third edition of his popular work *Via Recta ad Vitam Longam* (The Right Way to a Long Life)

346   BMCA BH/1, BH/5/0, p.16; BH/6/1

347   BMCA BH/5.

348   Rawcliffe, 'The Hospitals of Later Medieval London', 9.

349   *Complete Peerage*, 11, 573; J. Wood, *Description of Bath*, 207; BaRO council minutes 24 November 1652, Furman, p.641, item 14.

350   BaRO Ms volume: Physicians appointed by the Corporation to Lady Scudamore's gift.

was appointed Scudamore physician and served until his death in 1660. Venner was a seasonal visitor to the city, coming to serve the fashionable crowd in the spring and autumn and then returning to his home in North Petherton.[351] In Bath he rented the rooms over the northern block of St John's Hospital.[352] No doubt this remarkable old man became a familiar sight in Bellott's Hospital, but any other poor visitor could also call on his services. To ensure that the poor were aware of the provision for them, a brass plaque recording Lady Scudamore's gift was put up beside the Queen's Bath.[353] A later benefactor was Lady Moyer, who donated £400 in 1722, the interest from which was for the use of the poor of Bellott's Hospital.[354]

The Corporation tightens its grip

Lady Scudamore was not the first to entrust capital to Bath Corporation for charitable purposes. Already by 17 January 1614/5, Bath's municipal charities had multiplied to the point of potential confusion and the Council decided to have a book of record made. Once a year, the mayor and justices were to take an account of all the charitable gifts to the city and do their best to see them employed according to the wishes of the givers.[355] This book is now in the Somerset Record Office.[356]

It reflects the rise of the spa. The nobility and gentry flocking to Bath were evidently moved by the poverty they found there, much of it due to the decline in cloth-making.[357] A number of gifts to the city were intended to create employment, such as the £20 from Lady Anne Sherington and the £100 from Lady Helena, Marchioness of Northampton, to be lent without interest to clothiers 'or other trades that shall employ the poor of the city'. Sir Thomas White had a more national view (46). Sir Thomas, former Lord Mayor of London and founder of St John's College, Oxford,[358] gave the Corporation of Bristol over £2,000 to be spent on purchasing lands. On 1 July 1566 he instructed that the income of £104 a year was to be paid to 23 cities and towns by rota, beginning with Bristol. Bath was included and received its first payment in 1595. The money was to be used for the free loan to four freemen of £25 each for ten years. (The odd £4 was a recompense to the administering bodies for the trouble involved.)[359] With repeated gains from Sir Thomas White's Charity and other gifts of the same type, the Corporation gradually built up a substantial capital to feed the commercial development of the city.

Other donations were intended to benefit the sick and disabled poor coming to the baths, such as another £20 from Lady Anne Sherington and £20 from Lady Elizabeth Booth. Lady Elizabeth, who lived in Bath,[360] gave a total of £260 to the city, of which £100 was to assist the local poor. Other local residents were also inclined to aid the local poor directly. Both Lady Jane Rogers [361] and Thomas Power, landlord of the Catherine Wheel in the High Street and Mayor of Bath in 1601,[362] bequeathed money for poor widows. The almsfolk were not forgotten. Nicholas Butcher of Chelwood, Somerset, gave the

351   Venner, title page; Guidott, 186-8.

352   As a sub-tenant of Susan Sherwood: BaRO 1641 survey of Bath f.174, no.2; council minutes 22 October 1638.

353   Collinson, 1, 44-45 says that it was beside the Common Pump. That was on the walkway west of the Queen's Bath: BaL plan of the baths c.1781 by Robert Dingley.

354   BaRO Furman p.670, no.18.

355   BaRO council minutes.

356   SRO DD/TB14/26.

357   Acts of the Privy Council 1582-7, 93.

358   Dictionary of National Biography.

359   BMCA TW/1/1; BaRO MS volume of accounts for Thomas White's charity; BaRO framed table of the rotation of Thomas White's charity 1570-1698.

360   BaRO 1641 survey of Bath f.50, no.3.

361   Lady Rogers had a house in Stall Street: BaRO 1641 survey of Bath f.98, no.2.

362   Bristol University Library, BaRO and BaL James, 'The Incorporation of the City of Bath', 754; Accounts of the Chamberlains, 183.

46
Sir Thomas White (1492-1567), benefactor of 23 cities and towns
including Bath, and the founder of St John's College, Oxford

Corporation a meadow called Cowlease at Ivy Bridge in the parish of Wellow,[363] the income from which was given to the poor of St John's and St Catherine's Hospitals.[364] In 1640 and 1643 the Corporation used the capital donated by Lady Booth and £175 given by Edward Stirridge to buy other lands: a pasture called Haycombe in the parish of Englishcombe and an estate at Langley Burrell, near Chippenham.[365] The income was used for a variety of charitable purposes, including clothes for poor children and fees to gain them apprenticeships.[366]

Meanwhile the Corporation had acquired direct control of St John's Hospital. John Bewshin was a sad disappointment as Master of St John's. On 22 May 1616 he was dismissed from the post, having never visited the almspeople in 20 years. The more immediate cause of corporate annoyance was that he had taken legal action over the St John's properties. As the city fathers plaintively recorded, they had a lease of these for which they should only pay £10 a year rent, while actually spending over £30 upon the almsfolk of St John's.[367] The Corporation wanted no more sudden bursts of independence from the master. Their control over the hospital would be complete if the mastership of the hospital was linked to the mayoralty, but that would mean the master changing yearly. And could the mastership be held by a lay person? The Recorder of Bath pondered the legalities and conceded that the master could be lay, but not appointed for a restricted term.[368] So on 24 September Alderman Walter Chapman was appointed as master for life.[369] For the first time in the history of St John's, its master was not a clergyman. The chapel was served by Thomas Spink, who had succeeded Thomas Hill as reader.[370]

Until shortly before his appointment, Walter Chapman had been the landlord of the White Hart Inn, opposite Stalls Church in Stall Street.[371] In the late medieval period, the most powerful burghers of Bath were its clothiers, including Thomas Chapman, great-grandfather of Walter. With the rise of the spa, the city's innkeepers became a force to be reckoned with. Generations of the Chapman family were to dominate the affairs of Bath and no less than six of them became Masters of St John's Hospital. In fact Walter was succeeded as master on 6 September 1624 by his brother Alderman William Chapman the younger.[372] The following year Eleanor, daughter of Walter, chose to be married in St John's Chapel, though this was unorthodox. The license was for Stalls Church.[373] Eleanor's sister, Judith Chivers, had a short walk to the wedding. She and her husband Robert leased the Middle House and the rooms over the southern half of the hospital.[374]

After William died in 1647, he was replaced as master by his son Walter, the mayor elect that year.[375] The post had become almost hereditary. Walter was mayor again in 1654, but he died in April. He was replaced as mayor and master by Alderman John Bigg. The Corporation had decided that the 'Mayor for the time being shall during his mayoralty be also Master of St John's'.[376] That would mean the mastership changing hands each year, though the council minutes seldom trouble to note it. Only in September 1658 was

363 BaRO Furman p.570: bundle 19; BaRO council minutes 17 January 1614/5, 26 March 1638.

364 BaRO MS volume of Haycombe and Cowleaze accounts 1646-1726.

365 BaRO Furman, p.570, bundle 19. Deed missing, so the property deduced from ensuing lease (deed no.5); council minutes 1643.

366 BaRO Haycombe and Cowleaze accounts.

367 BaRO council minutes, wrongly dated 1617 in Shickle's transcript.

368 Ibid 22 May, 1 July, 5 August 1616, wrongly dated 1617 in Shickle's transcript.

369 Ancient Deeds, 1/63.

370 BaRO account roll 62 St John's.

371 Then known simply as the Hart: BaRO 1641 survey of Bath f.96, no.1; council minutes 1 July 1616.

372 Ancient Deeds 1/ 64; BaRO Furman 528/8; BaRO MS E. Holland, Chapman genealogy.

373 SRO D/D/Ca 241, p.148.

374 Registers of the Abbey Church 1, 207; BaRO 1641 survey f.91, no.3, f.175, no.1, f.182, no.2.

375 BaRO council minutes 27 September and 4 October 1647.

376 Ibid 25 September 1654 and 30 April 1655.

The Chapman Masters of St John's Hospital
from Elizabeth Holland's genealogy of the Chapman family

Alderman **THOMAS CHAPMAN**
clothier, held the [White] Hart Inn, d.1524

WILLIAM CHAPMAN
1502-1577
sub-tenant St John's Farm

Ald RICHARD CHAPMAN
clothier, mayor, MP 1553, d.1580

PETER CHAPMAN
1506-1602
soldier, held Bear Inn

Ald JOHN CHAPMAN
of the [White] Hart, d.1603
Mayor of Bath 1584, 1600

Ald WALTER CHAPMAN=JOAN ILES
1569-1624
of the [White] Hart
mayor 1606, 1618, 1621
Master of St John's 1616-1624

Ald WILLIAM CHAPMAN=JOAN WEBB
1571-1647
mercer, mayor 1617,
1624, 1631, 1640, 1642
Master of St John's 1624-47

Ald JOHN CHAPMAN=ELIZABETH WHITE
1600-1677
of Weston
mayor 1667

ANN KNIGHT=Ald WALTER CHAPMAN
1608-1655
mercer, mayor 1648, 1655
Master of St John's 1647-55

Ald WILLIAM CHAPMAN=ANNA SPARROW
c.1642-1711
mayor 1703

Ald WILLIAM CHAPMAN
distiller, d.1729
mayor 1728

Revd JOHN CHAPMAN=MARTHA WALL
c.1676-1737
Vicar of Weston 1701-37
Master of St John's 1711-37

Ald WALTER CHAPMAN=MARY MORGAN
1670-1729
saddler
Mayor of Bath 1726

JOHN CHAPMAN
1711-1786
Rector of Newton St Loe 1755-86
Rector (1768) and Archdeacon of Bath 1769-86

MARGARET COWARD=Ald JOHN CHAPMAN
1706-1801
saddler, mayor 1744,1754
1761, 1770, 1777, 1779

SUSANNA DINGLEY=Revd WALTER CHAPMAN DD
1711-91
Master of St John's 1737-91
Prebendary of Bristol Cathedral 1746-91
Vicar of Bradford-on-Avon 1754-91

Revd JOHN CHAPMAN DD=SUSANNAH PHILLOTT
1742-1816
Vicar of Weston 1767-1808
Vicar of Bathampton and Bathford 1794-1816
Perpetual Curate of Churchill and Puxton
Master of St John's 1791-1816
Prebendary of Bristol Cathedral 1791-1816

it recorded that John Pearce had been elected mayor and would be Master of St John's for the same year.[377]

The mastership held no great advantage beyond the £2 stipend. The purpose of nominating an alderman to serve as master was that real authority should be vested in the Corporation. The council minutes are missing for 1618 to 1630, but on 1 September 1631 the Corporation ordered that no married man or woman should be chosen for St John's Hospital.[378] From then on we find notes in the minutes of placements in both St John's and St Catherine's Hospitals. With the two under the same management, almsfolk could be moved from one to the other. It seems that a certain Widow Clark did not survive the winter of 1631 in St John's, for on 2 January 1631/2 the Council decided to fill her place with the Widow Porter from the Bimbury Almshouse, while the Widow Saunders took Porter's place. Similarly in December 1646 Beatrice Gory was moved from the Black to the Blue Almshouse. Places at St John's were sought after, presumably because its almsfolk received a higher allowance. When Richard Chapman wanted to relieve himself of a decrepit old maid servant, Katherine Griffin, he proposed her for St John's. Richard was the nephew of the master, which may have given him a certain leverage.[379] More importantly the Council was heavily stocked with Chapmans and their relations. On 31 March 1645 the Council decided unanimously to admit her for life.[380] Ejections from either hospital were rare, but Sarah Dill caused so much offence by constant scolding, swearing and begging that the Council finally ordered her removal from St Catherine's.[381] Joan Sperring delivered a far more direct affront to Corporation sensibilities. She abused the mayor's wife in 'very lewd and scurrilous language'. Her punishment was to be displaced from the Black Almshouse.[382]

In 1641, the year before the country was enveloped by Civil War, Bath Corporation decided to survey its own property and that of St John's Hospital (47). Surveying in this era seldom involved mapping. The survey was simply a book of copies of leases. Nevertheless it remains a valuable source for St John's estate before the changes of the eighteenth century.[383] By this time St John's Farm had been leased to William Fry and there had been some rationalisation of the scattered medieval estate. In Gloucestershire three and a half acres remained at Cold Ashton, but the food rents at Foxcot and Gossington and the house at Cirencester had been replaced by a small farm at Bradley, near Wotton under Edge. In Somerset the distant houses at Ilchester and Wells had been retained; that at Wells was leased to the Vicars Choral. The cluster of lands east of Frome, at Berkley, Rodden and Woodman's Hill, were leased together to John Champneys of nearby Orchardleigh. However, to the north of Frome two acres at Rode and two at Beckington (probably representing the medieval lands at Standerwick) were separately leased. The looser cluster of lands around Midsomer Norton and the farms at Chilcompton, Hallatrow and Timsbury remained. However, other land at Timsbury and High Littleton was being mined for coal. The Corporation had given permission for mining in 1635,[384] and then leased the valuable works to Alderman Robert

377 *Ibid* 27 September 1658.

378 *Ibid* 1 September 1631.

379 BaRO MS Chapman genealogy by E. Holland.

380 BaRO council minutes.

381 *Ibid* 29 June and 28 December 1635.

382 *Ibid* 22 July 1666.

383 BaRO 1641 survey of Bath; M. Inskip plan of Bath in 1641.

384 BaRO council minutes 9 January 1635/6.

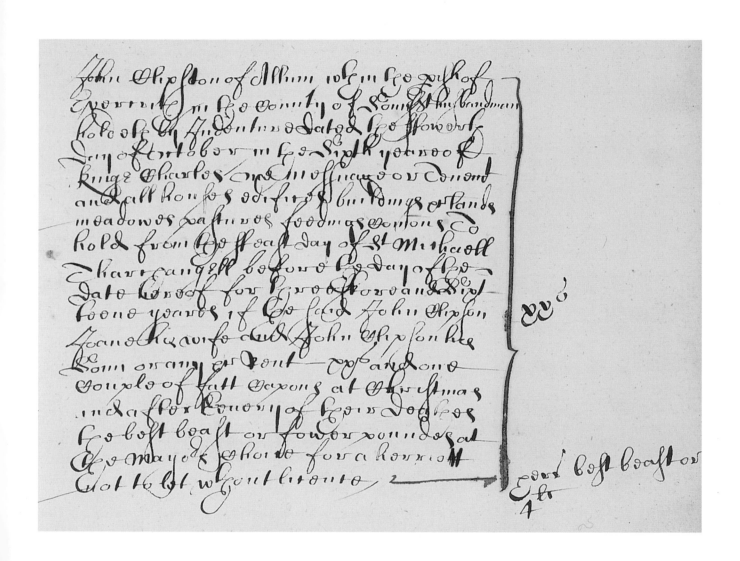

47

John Clipson held a house and lands at Alham in the parish of Evercreech at a rent of 20s a year and
a couple of fat capons at Christmas. An entry in the survey of St John's Hospital properties in 1641

Fisher in 1640. To the south, property had been acquired at Stoke St Michael and the farm at Higher Alham retained. Closer to Bath, there were lands at Keynsham, Carlingcott, Newton St Loe, Twerton, Weston and Swainswick. The rent roll for the hospital's estate outside Bath was £10 15s 8d a year,[385] while its Bath properties brought in £19 12s a year.[386]

The Corporation accounting system was bizarre by modern standards. Although on the face of it St John's Hospital had its own account, quite separate from the general Corporation account, in fact there was considerable overlap between the two. While the St John's account faithfully records the hospital income from rents, this was by no means the only income from its property. A lease would be purchased initially by a lump sum, known as a fine, and a smaller charge to cover clerical costs, known as the 'seal of the lease'. The sums involved were far higher than the rents themselves and were paid directly into the Corporation account. On the other side of the ledger, the St John's accounts could include outgoings that had nothing to do with the hospital, for example the stipend of the schoolmaster of King Edward's and repairs to the school. Before we leap to the conclusion that the Corporation was a thoroughly dishonest trustee, we should note that the outgoings on the St John's account regularly exceeded the income and that the shortfall (over £65 in 1663) was made up from the Corporation account.[387] The Corporation was guilty of little worse than muddle, but one can see how its stewardship could have come under suspicion.

Tobias Rustat

In the Civil War Bath was for Parliament. Although the city was held by Royalist forces from 1643-45, the sympathies of the majority on Bath Council remained unchanged.[388] This was to have consequences for St John's Hospital at the Restoration. In March 1661 Sir Thomas Bridges, former royalist governor of Bath, reported that the Mayor of Bath had opposed all his efforts to ensure the election of royalist MPs for the city.[389] That did not endear Bath Council to Charles II, who ordered the mayor's ejection from office. By October 1661, the Council was making efforts to placate the king, but too late.[390]

Among the king's household was Tobias (Toby) Rustat, yeoman of the robes – 'a very simple, ignorant, but honest and loyal creature'.[391] Rustat had been with Charles throughout his impoverished exile.[392] Now he seized the opportunity to enrich himself. A whisper must have reached him that Bath Corporation held a hospital estate that had greatly increased in value. The lease to John Crouch under which the Corporation held St John's had expired, so whoever held the mastership controlled the estate. Knowing that Queen Elizabeth had been the patron of the hospital at one time, Rustat boldly claimed on 29 October 1661 that the Corporation had usurped the patronage and defrauded the poor. He was willing to bear the legal costs of proving the king's right to the patronage, if Charles would appoint him master.[393] The king did so in January 1661/2,[394] but Rustat devised a variation

385 BaRO 1641 survey of Bath, f.176, no.1, ff.194-210.

386 *Ibid* 174-187.

387 BaRO account roll 106: St John's.

388 Wroughton, 189-93.

389 *Calendar of State Papers Domestic 1660-1*, 544.

390 BaRO council minutes 2 October 1661: copy of an order at Westminster 25 April.

391 *Diary of John Evelyn*, **4**, 207.

392 Renfrew and Robbins, 417. I am obliged to John Physick for this reference.

393 *Calendar of State Papers Domestic 1661-62*, 126.

394 *Ibid*, 237, 251.

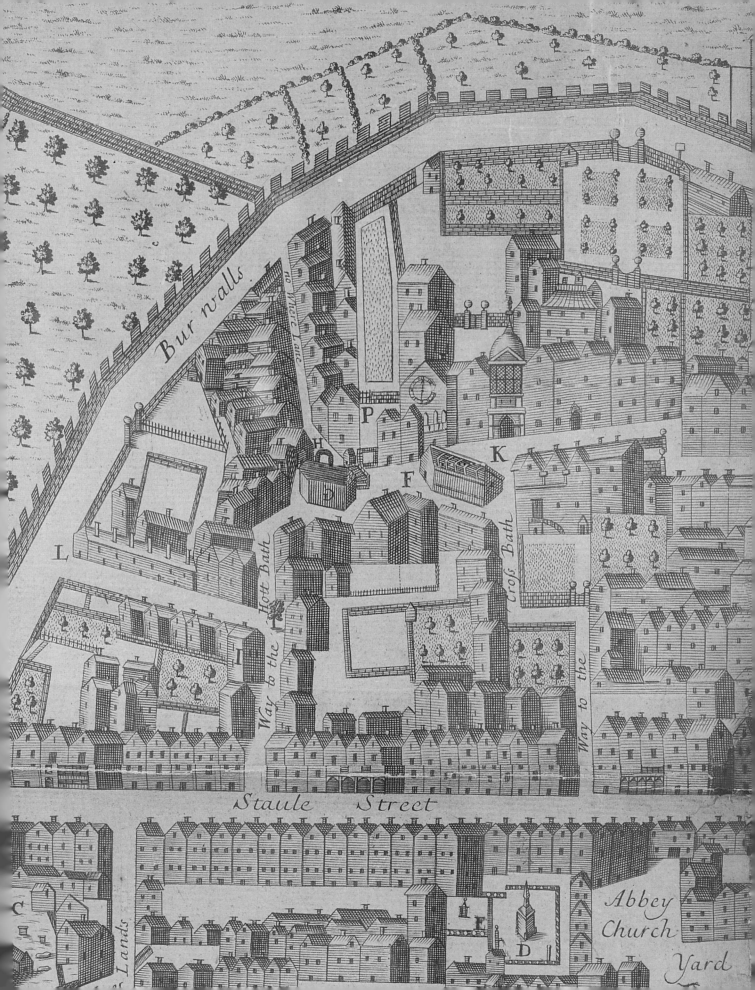

Bur walls

no Whore Lane

P

H

F

K

Cross Bath

Hott Bath

L

Way to the Hott Bath

I

Way to the

Staule Street

C

Lands

F

D

Abbey Church Yard

49
A Restoration-period chair in St John's
Hospital

395   *Ibid*, 546, 59; Renfrew and Robbins, fig.1.

396   BaRO account roll 106 is the last for St John's, dated 15 October 1663. BMCA StJH/7/1(a).

397   Venn, *Alumni Cantabrigienses part 1*, **3**, 501; Renfrew and Robbins, fig.1.

398   BMCA StJH/7/263.

399   *Report of the Commissioners for Charities* **4**, 284.

400   BMCA StJH/7/1(a).

401   Guidott, 75.

402   BaRO council minutes 13 August 1671.

403   BaRO Furman bundle 18, item 10.

404   The original is now in Lambeth Palace Library (LPL MS 931/38); an imperfect transcript made in the eighteenth century by Thomas Carew was published in 1975 (*Med Deeds*). Another transcript was made by the Revd. Shickle, Master of St John's (BMCA StJH/15/1).

on the scheme. In December the same year the mastership was transferred to Tobias's brother John, a royal chaplain.[395] Naturally Bath Council was not prepared to give up the hospital without a fight. After seeking advice from the city recorder, the formidable Puritan William Prynne, the Council resolved on 20 October 1663 to defend its title. Battle was joined. The town clerk was sent to London with the relevant deeds the following May. The case ended in a compromise. John Rustat was accepted as master for life and the estate handed over,[396] but the Corporation's right to the patronage was recognised.

That suited Toby. John Rustat was the Rector of Widmerpool and Holme Pierrepont in Nottinghamshire, where he remained until his death in 1680.[397] His appointment to St John's was simply a convenient ploy. The old leases having been cancelled, on 29 May 1665 John Rustat leased to Tobias all of the hospital's property (except the chapel and almshouses) at a rent of £130,[398] almost £100 more than the hospital rent-roll in 1641. So the allowance to the almsfolk could be raised from 1s 6d to 2s 6d per week each. Rustat's seizure of St John's was not entirely cynical.

However Rustat then raised £2,656 15s 2d by making under-leases.[399] A few survive to show how he did it. The Middle House had been leased in 1590 at a rent of £1 a year. Its value had increased and Judith Croft (formerly Chivers) was willing to pay a fine of £32 for the property and £4 a year in rent.[400] Thus Rustat recouped the £130 rent he paid to his brother and made a considerable profit. A seventeenth-century physician commented acidly on the huge increase in revenues 'to the great advantage of him that hath it…with the perpetual entailment of God's everlasting curse and blast on the treacherous head and posterity of him, that is notoriously known to have been the author of this mischief.'[401] Clearly whoever let slip the information that so profited Rustat had not made himself popular in Bath.

It will be remembered that Bellott had built his almshouse on a property of St John's Hospital in Bell Tree Lane. This arrangement posed no problems while the Corporation controlled both charities, but now there was a clash of interests. Rustat no doubt wanted an increased rent for the property. Corporation tactics included making Rustat a freeman of the city.[402] Eventually Rustat agreed to renew the lease of Bellott's Hospital at the old rent of 3s a year. His reward was to have the details of this piece of reluctant philanthropy incised in stone above the entrance to Bellott's Hospital. The deed, signed on 22 August 1672, incorporated special provision for the washerwoman of St John's Hospital. She had a room at the south-east corner of the court of Bellott's Hospital and could use the water-pipe and dry clothes in the garden.[403] That would have been more convenient than working at St John's itself, where the gardens had been leased out.

The concern of Tobias Rustat for his property preserved for us copies of all the medieval deeds of St John's Hospital. An alphabetically organised hospital cartulary was completed for him on 17 January 1678/9.[404] For the historian, this cartulary is Rustat's greatest legacy, but he wanted to be

50

The seventeenth-century silver of St John's Hospital Chapel. The communion cup was donated by Tobias
Rustat in 1675 and the paten in 1683 by Mary Joyce. Both are now displayed in the Holburne Museum, Bath

51
Memorial to Tobias Rustat in the Chapel of
Jesus College, Cambridge, probably by
Grinling Gibbons. © Crown copyright

remembered for his charity. He was a benefactor to a number of worthy causes, and particularly generous to Jesus College, Cambridge, where his father had been educated. Rustat arranged to be buried in the Chapel of Jesus College and ordered his own memorial (51), probably from Grinling Gibbons, who had done other work for him. He kept the memorial at his home in Chelsea until it was needed. The inscription was cut, leaving only the date of his death (15 March 1693/4) to be added. It tells of his faithful service to the Crown through adversity as well as prosperity, and that:

> The greater part of the estate he gathered, by God's blessing, the King's favour, and his industry, he disposed in his lifetime in works of charity, and he found the more he bestowed upon churches, hospitals, universities and colleges, and upon widows & orphans of orthodox ministers, the more he had at the year's end.[405]

John Rustat died before his brother and the Corporation resumed the selection of the Masters of St John's. However, the experiment with lay masters was over. More interestingly, the Corporation initially seems to have given more weight to merit and industry than Bath connections. It had presented Joseph Glanvill to the Rectory of Bath Abbey in 1672. Glanvill was a zealous writer of sermons with no known relatives on the Council. Selection to the mastership followed on 24 January 1675/6.[406] Since John Rustat was still alive at the time, the Council was somewhat premature. Glanvill was not installed as master by the bishop, presumably because he did not survive Rustat long enough to take up the post. He died on 4 November 1680.[407] On 1 February 1681 William Peake, Rector of Walcot, was chosen as Master of St John's.[408] Peake is a good example of industry rewarded. A Nottinghamshire man of humble background, he had gained his BA at Oxford in 1665 and was immediately appointed to the vacant position of schoolmaster at King Edward's School in Bath.[409] The young man must have made a good impression in the city for he was presented to the rectory of Walcot ten years later by William Saunders, landowner there.[410] After taking up the post at St John's, he was replaced as schoolmaster,[411] but he retained his Walcot benefice for the rest of his short life. He died on 16 November 1683 aged 40, as his memorial tells us (52). His replacement was William Clement MA, already Rector of Bath.[412]

A new use for St Mary Magdalen

We cannot tell exactly when St Mary Magdalen ceased to serve lepers, but it was after Simon Shepherd's time as master. There was a bequest in 1569 of 5s a year to the poor lazar people there.[413] The following year Shepherd died.[414] The Crown's initial response was to seize the opportunity to profit. On 31 March 1571 the hospital property was leased to John Britton, Town Clerk of Bath, for a rent of £4 15s 8d.[415] However, on 14 May the queen presented Griffin Curtis to the office of master.[416] Curtis was not a cleric, though he was a supporter of the reformed religion.[417] He was a Crown tenant and JP in Berkshire, where he remained after the appointment to St Mary

405   Renfrew and Robbins, 417-21.

406   BaRO council minutes.

407   Pleydell.

408   BaRO council minutes.

409   *Ibid* 24 April and 8 May 1665.

410   *Somerset Incumbents*, 297.

411   BaRO council minutes.

412   *Somerset Incumbents*, 235-36.

413   BaRO Furman pp.639-40, no.3; King and Watts, appendix A, no.70.

414   PRO E368/405.

415   PRO E311/13 Eliz m.104.

416   *Calendar of Patent Rolls 1569-72*, 1537.

417   *Camden Miscellany 9*, 38.

Magdalen.[418] He thus became the hospital's first absentee master and only known lay master.

Curtis was faced with an Exchequer demand for £66 19s 4d as arrears of the rent never paid to the Crown by Shepherd. Naturally he protested. On July 1576 Curtis proved in the Court of the Exchequer that the issues of St Mary Magdalen were for the maintenance of the poor inmates of the hospital, whose support he had ordered.[419] Curtis almost certainly leased the demesne farm to Thomas Clement of Englishcombe, who in 1586 left a peck of wheat to the 'poor which are in the spital house called the *Marlinge* in Holloway'. A later Clement, dying in 1651, left 12d apiece to everyone remaining in St Mary Magdalen Hospital.[420] Bath Corporation made a contribution, regularly paying 4s a year to the almsfolk.[421]

Clearly the hospital continued to function, but for whom? In 1656 Bath Corporation paid for clothes, shoes and stockings for 'Thorne's daughter placed up at the Maudlins'.[422] Why? A memorial in the chapel provides a clue (53). The marble tablet records that in 1662 Ann Nicholas chose to be buried with innocents. So it seems that the hospital was housing the mentally handicapped. If so it would need a warden. By 1665 the Corporation paid their 4s a year to the 'guide of the Magdalen'.[423]

By 1681 'the capital messuage' (chief house) at Holloway and the hospital demesne land was leased out in two parcels.[424] Probably the original hospital had been converted into the master's house by Simon Shepherd. Although the inquiry in 1560 reported that the lepers were living in 'the mansion house', Shepherd could have shifted them to poorer quarters. Later masters not being resident, it would suit them to lease the house, farm buildings, lands and sheep flock to local farmers. A 'little old decrepit' building to the east of the chapel functioned as the hospital by 1678 (54). When the antiquary Anthony à Wood visited in June that year, he described it as built for lunatics, though this may simply reflect an inability to distinguish between the mentally handicapped and the mentally ill.

> At this time there are but two, lately four, and formerly there have been six lunatics. The two lunatics that are now there (of which one is a female) are kept by an old man who is a cobbler and keeper thereof and hath paid yearly to him for their diet and lodging £13.[425]

Eighty years later John Wood's description is even more poignant:

> Saint Mary Magdalen's Hospital … is a poor cottage, situated near the east end of the chapel of that name, and was built for the reception of idiots, but there are few maintained therein; the nurse's stipend for the support of herself, and the people under her care, amounting to no more than £15 a year: This building is 47 feet in front, by about 19 feet in depth; and whoever enters it will see enough to cure his pride, and excite his gratitude for the blessings he enjoys.[426]

Oliver Cambridge was an inmate at the end of the seventeenth century. He was 'a short thick man, brown haired, a reddish beard, goeth bending forward with his knees, the forefinger of his left hand crooked.' In January 1699/1700 he disappeared from the hospital and one can imagine the concern.

52
Memorial to William Peake, Master of St John's Hospital 1681-3, in the chapel of the hospital. The Latin inscription praises his honesty, sincerity, learning and modesty

418 *Visitations of Berkshire* 2, 111; *VCH Berkshire* 4, 171; *Calendar of Patent Rolls 1569-72*, nos.1863, 1873, 1879, 3348; *op cit 1575 8*, nos. 87, 237; *op cit 1579-82*, no.1150.

419 PRO E368/405.

420 Goulstone, 27-28. Thomas Clement of Englishcombe was the lessee of half the St Mary Magdalen demesne in 1709 - see note 424 below.

421 *Accounts of the Chamberlains 1568-1602*, 89, 95, 103, 111, 117, 121, 126, 134, 141, 148, 154, 161, 167, 172, 177, 184.

422 BaRO Haycombe and Cowleaze accounts.

423 BaRO Account rolls 108-114.

424 BMCA MH uncatalogued: lease 20 July 1709 to Thomas Staples, haberdasher of London, and Thomas Clement of Englishcombe, yeoman, of half of the capital messuage of St Mary Magdalen in Holloway, now in the occupation of Thomas Staples or his under- tenant, and lands including half the garden adjoining the Chapel of St Mary Magdalen, to which chapel the said house and land had always belonged, on surrender of a lease of the same property 14 September 1681.

425 A. à Wood, 19.

426 J. Wood, *Description of Bath*, 306.

53
Memorial to Ann Nicholas, who died in
1662. Her first husband was Nathaniel
Biggs of Widcombe. The Biggs family were
tenants of the Hospital of St Mary
Magdalen, and she chose to be buried in
its chapel:

A SAVING FAITH SHE HAD, AND INNOCENCE,
AND THEREFORE HERE WITH INNOCENTS WOULD LIE,
THAT WITH THEM SHE MIGHT LIVE ETERNALLY

The hospital was on a major road. If a passing vehicle had taken him up, he could be miles away in any direction. An advertisement was placed in the *London Gazette*, offering a guinea reward for information.[427]

Times of trial

The lease to Tobias Rustat of the St John's Hospital property had been framed in the common form for the times. It was to last for the lifetimes of three named persons. The last of them died on 4 December 1711. The Revd. William Clement was still master of the hospital, though close to death. He had probably been sustained for years by the thought of the wealth he would control when the lease expired and now could not bear that it should slip from his grasp, leaving nothing for his family. On 6 December he granted the whole estate to his son Thomas, an attorney, on the same terms as in the Rustat lease. Thomas later claimed that in return he gave his father a promissory note for £1,500, from which it was intended to rebuild the chapel of the hospital and increase the maintenance of the poor,[428] but this has a hollow ring. The hospital had been defrauded.

William Clement scarcely survived this grant and a new master was installed by the bishop on 3 January 1711/2.[429] He was another of the ubiquitous Chapman clan. The Revd. John Chapman was a son of Alderman William Chapman, nephew of the last Chapman Master of St John's.[430] Local interest had once more triumphed. Alderman William had property in Weston near Bath, where the Revd. John became the vicar in 1701, while he was working for his MA at Balliol.[431] He remained Vicar of Weston for the rest of his life, regularly signing vestry minutes there,[432] so it is unlikely that he ever lived at the hospital. As soon as he was appointed master, John Chapman proceeded in Chancery against Thomas Clement and also against Bath Corporation and the Clerk of the House of Lords, who had refused to release some deeds of St John's deposited by Bath Corporation.[433]

The case was heard on 26 November 1713 by Sir William Trevor, Master of the Rolls, who deliberated and finally made an award on 13 February 1716/7. This fascinating document went much further than deciding the issue of the lease to Clement. Since this was perfectly legal in itself, it could only be set aside in the context of proper charity management. Sir William was therefore asked to rule on that as well. He reviewed the state of the hospital in detail and was highly critical. Although the true annual value of the properties had increased to about £1,200, the hospital was neglected and the six brethren and six sisters had been kept very poor. So Sir William ruled that the lease to Clement should be set aside, although Clement was to be paid £1,500 in recompense. New leases were to be made to the hospital tenants, backdated to 4 December 1711, raising a total of £3,803 5s 1½d immediately in fines, from which Clement could be paid.[434] A number of these leases survive in the archive of St John's Hospital.

Rents and fines were not to be increased without permission from Chancery.

427 *London Gazette* 15-18 January 1699/1700.

428 *Report of the Commissioners for Charities* **4**, 284-5.

429 *Somerset Incumbents*, 236.

430 BaRO MS E. Holland, Chapman genealogy.

431 Foster, *Alumni Oxoniensis 1500-1714*, 1261.

432 Hargood-Ash, 8.

433 *Report of the Commissioners for Charities* **4**, 283; BaRO council minutes 5 Feb 1711.

434 *Ibid*, 283-85, appendix C, 526-28.

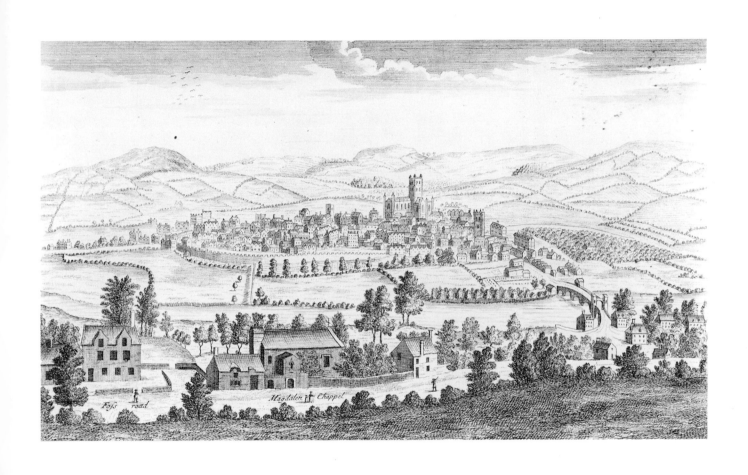

54

The Chapel of St Mary Magdalen appears on this view of Bath in 1723 by William Stukeley. To the west the Tudor hospital and its farm were by this time held by tenants. To the east of the chapel is the thatched cottage used as the hospital from at least the seventeenth century

55
A baroque stone buffet for the display of china. It was found behind panelling in 15 Westgate Street in 1906 and was moved to Fitzjocelyn House in 1956

According to John Wood, this security encouraged tenants to improve and enlarge their properties.[435] The early Georgian façade of the Bunch of Grapes and its neighbour in Westgate Street may be one of the cases Wood had in mind (56). Panelling of the period remains in the drawing room of the Grapes, while the house next door had a handsome baroque stone buffet with a shell-head and lusciously curving shelves,[436] now in St John's Hospital (56).

Sir William next considered the state of the two chapels. He was disturbed to learn that the former St Michael's had sometimes been turned into an alehouse, and once a post-office. In his view a former house of God should not become a drinking den. It should be used as the master's house or let in some more suitable way.

St John's Chapel was 'very ruinous', according to Thomas Clement. Sir William ruled that it was to be rebuilt by William Killigrew according to the model submitted to him (57-9). The details of the ruling reveal much about the building as it then stood. The chapel was not to be enlarged, so the present chapel must be the same size as the one it replaced. The house or shed adjoining the south-east end was to be taken down. No windows were to be made into the chapel out of the master's lodgings or Gibbs's house (the lodgings over the hospital.[437]) Presumably there were such windows in the Norman chapel. Finally there was to be no gallery 'on any pretence whatsoever'. Prayers were to be read in the chapel every day. The burial of the poor could continue in the chapel-yard, but no other burials and there was to be no christening or marrying. Christening would have been difficult anyway without a font, but in the late seventeenth century there had been a steady trickle of marriages.[438]

The relationship between St John's Hospital and Bath Corporation was laid down with precision. Although the right of presentation to the mastership belonged to the Corporation, this did not vest it with any right of supervision. The almspeople were not obliged to appear in the Abbey Church or attend the mayor and Corporation. The hospital was to be governed by the master. That was very clear. However, the master was not given a free hand. Sir William made detailed rulings on the hospital's management and laid down that the Lord Chancellor, the Lord Keeper, the Master of the Rolls and the Bishop of Bath and Wells could make visits of inspection. Whether they did or not, the Revd. Chapman was brought to book seventeen years later for failing to honour some of these rulings.

Sir William limited the master's freedom in handling the hospital finances by specifying the sums which were to be paid out of regular hospital income to inmates, washerwoman and nurse and for gowns. In addition (after the first batch of leases), fines should be divided, one-third being shared equally among the inmates, while the remainder went to the master, who was responsible for repairs to the chapel, hospital and clock. Sir William's rules for admittance to the hospital and the behaviour of the almspeople were equally careful. Inmates were to be selected by the master from among those who had lived in Bath for at least ten years. They must be really poor, over 50

435   J. Wood, *Description of Bath*, 227.
436   *PSANHS Bath Branch 1914-18*, 229.
437   BMCA StJH/7/117.
438   *Registers of the Abbey Church*, **2**, 481-2; BaRO CM 31 March 1651.

56
The Bunch of Grapes in Westgate Street, Bath. Nineteenth-century artist Henry
Venn Lansdown imagined how it might have looked in the eighteenth century

or disabled, unmarried, sober and civil and conform to the established Church and State. They should attend morning and evening prayers in the hospital chapel in their livery gowns. To improve their appearance, Sir William suggested that new gowns should be kept for Sundays and holy days and only given out for constant wearing after a year of use. The almsfolk should 'not be given to tippling, swearing, cursing, reviling or any other scandalous crime whatever.'[439]

439   *Report of the Commissioners for Charities* **4**, 283-8.

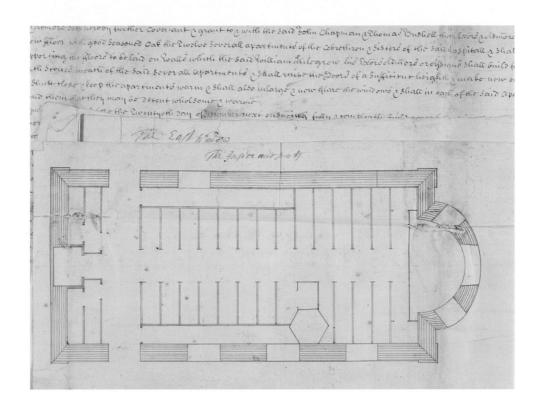

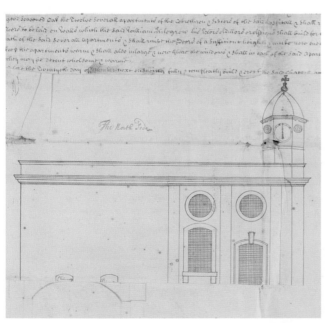

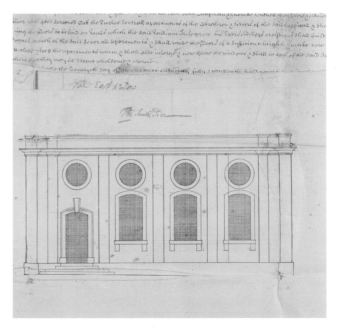

57-9

Plans for the rebuilding of St John's Chapel attached to the contract with William Killigrew 9 February 1716/7 (BMCA StJH/11/1):

TOP The stairwell to the bell-tower is shown as rectangular, but a spiral stair was actually built, which took up less space

BOTTOM LEFT Northern elevation

BOTTOM RIGHT Southern elevation

Georgian and Victorian

The Georgian rebuilding

The chapel built after the Trevor award is still in use today as a place of worship. It is an elegantly simple little building (61). Being so hemmed in by the hospital, it is somewhat dark, but the apse helps to draw in light from the east. There is little ornamentation, but the curve of the apse, the circular top windows and the cupola of the bell-tower give the chapel a flavour of restrained baroque. Killigrew's contract laid down in precise detail the specifications for the rebuilding, which was to be completed by 20 November 1717. The sash windows were to be glazed with best Bristol crown glass, the flat roof was to be of sound, firm, oak and so on.[440] Sir William's ruling that there were to be no windows from adjacent buildings was disregarded. John Chapman allowed two from the lodgings above the hospital.[441] In 1735 the Charity Commissioners ordered him to have them blocked up and plastered over to match the rest of the chapel,[442] but Chapman ignored the decree. Only after his death in 1737 were the windows closed at the insistence of his successor, the Revd. Walter Chapman.[443]

The new chapel must have astonished many. It was the first Georgian chapel in the city, a new type of ecclesiastical architecture for an age that did not bow to medieval traditions. It has little in common with its predecessor except its size. Even the clock was in a new position. Killigrew placed it on the bell-tower. However, one reminder of the past is the southern door. The main door of the Norman chapel was on that side. For over a century it had opened into the private court of the Great House. Still it would be a more convenient door for the public than the one on the hospital side. Killigrew provided a replacement. Subsequent leases of the Great House had a clause providing access to this door for the public, including those in sedan chairs.[444] The chapel was thronged daily.[445] No doubt it was particularly popular with ailing visitors lodging near the Hot and Cross Baths.

In the spring of 1726 James Brydges, Duke of Chandos, visited Bath to take the waters. His wife Cassandra was suffering from hysterical fits, while the Duke was 'wracked to death with a thousand terrible fears'. To be close to the Cross Bath, they lodged with Anne Phillips in a house on the north

440   BMCA StJH/11/1: contract 9 February 1716/7.
441   BaRO Enquiry into Somerset Charities 1734-5, **1**, 47-8, 53- 59.
442   page 95page 94PRO C93/58/16.
443   Baker and Baker, 331.
444   BMCA StJH/7/136.
445   SRO DD/TB/20/2: MS history of Bath by Thomas Carew (written 1735-50), 23-24.

60
James Brydges, First Duke of Chandos, at around the time of his visit to Bath. Portrait by Herman van der Myn

446 Baker and Baker, 298-9. Mrs Phillips had two lodging houses. Baker and Baker assume Chandos lodged in the one over the hospital. For contrary evidence see BaL microfilm of HL ST57: Brydges Correspondence, Chandos to Mrs Phillips 16 April 1728.

447 Baker and Baker, 297, n.1, 298-300; Neale, 132-34; *Registers of the Abbey Church* 1, 73, 75, 2, 419; BaL microfilm of HL ST57: Chandos to Dr Cheyne 16 May 1726, to Mr Gibson 18 October 1726; BMCA StJH/7/102, 108, 110, 113; BaRO Furman 1112, 1693; BaRO council minutes 31 March 1707, 30 September 1734.

448 BMCA StJH/7/110, 128 (a).

449 BMCA StJH/7/118.

450 BMCA StJH/7/114: lease 1717; J. Wood, *Description of Bath*, 339; Baker and Baker, 303.

451 Mowl and Earnshaw, 10-17.

452 J. Wood, *Description of Bath*, 241.

453 Baker and Baker, 300, 303; BMCA StJH/7/110 (leases 1717, 1727, 1734), StJH/7/113, StJH/7/128 (conveyance 1726), StJH/7/127.

side of Chapel Court, overlooking the chapel. The rooms pleased him not at all. Mrs Phillip's lodgings were simply a collection of bedrooms and could provide no such thing as a suite of rooms. Not only that, but none of the windows could 'keep out the least puff of wind' and in short they were 'old rotten lodgings.'[446]

Chandos was in a position to mend matters. He had a sharp nose for profit and had acquired a vast fortune through a web of financial dealings. Recognising the demand for lodgings in Bath suitable for persons of fashion, he immediately embarked upon a building venture centred on St John's. Negotiations began in May 1726. Conveniently for Chandos the properties he wanted could almost all be bought as a block, for they were in the same leasehold ownership. In October Chandos purchased from the daughters of Walter Gibbs three St John's leases and one Corporation lease (PLAN 5). These properties did have sub-tenants. One was the lodging-house keeper Ann Phillips, while a Mrs Jones kept another lodging. Such tenants would suit the duke's purpose. An old bachelor, Walter Escott, had lived in the Corporation-owned house, but he died in October.[447] Between Escott's house and the hospital was the tavern of John Billing, who sold his St John's lease to the duke.[448] Chandos also persuaded the Revd. Chapman to lease him a part of the hospital courtyard.[449] The one plot he wanted and could not get was the garden of Walter Chivers, the occupant of the Middle House. That was an irritation for years. Chandos wanted to 'run up an apartment' for himself on that ground.[450]

Chandos decided to employ a Bath-born building craftsman, John Wood. He was only 22 years old, but had been acquiring experience in London. Wood too was keenly aware of the market forces at work and the opportunities this presented. He yearned to transform his native city with noble architecture in the newly-fashionable Palladian style. Thus far it was a meeting of minds. However, the scope of Wood's ambition was quite staggering. Whole landscapes had already formed in his mind. The limitations of the Chandos development were to frustrate him, while his youthful idealism and impracticality irritated Chandos.[451]

On 23 January 1726/7, John Wood contracted with Chandos for the rebuilding of the two lodgings of Mrs Phillips.[452] One was a large house on the north side of the hospital courtyard, leased together with the Elizabethan formal garden. Chandos planned an even larger house, taking in part of the site of Billing's tavern. In the end he decided to divide the new house in two: one part (later known as Chapel Court House) opened into the hospital courtyard, while the other part fronted the lane.[453]

Mrs Phillips's other lodging was over the hospital. The rooms of the almsfolk on the ground floor were no concern of the duke's. Wood had the awkward task of modernising just the top storeys of an Elizabethan building. One can imagine how that must have chafed a budding architect of his ambition. Mongrel façades could do him no credit. However, John Wood was a young man dealing with an important patron. Rather than try to dictate from the start that Chandos should rebuild the alms-rooms at his own expense, Wood

61
St John's Chapel (now St Michael's), looking east. The windows were plain originally. The present tracery and stained glass was inserted in 1879. The reredos was donated in 1890

62
John Wood House (the former hospital range) from the west. Wood intended a grander façade to the court, with a regular arcade, but was frustrated by his client. The arches are of varied widths. A staircase led to a first-floor door where there is now a window wider than the rest (second from the right)

put forward suggestions piecemeal. Over May and June 1727, he proposed to pull down and rebuild the wall against the Cross Bath to gain an extra foot, to rebuild the west wall in ashlar for a better appearance, to widen the passage through the building and to rebuild the partition walls, since they would not support the weight of what was intended above. Not all of his proposals were accepted. Chandos paid him £100 for pulling down the front and back walls of the hospital, but Wood was not permitted to totally demolish and start afresh from the foundations.[454] His frustration had still not cooled when he came to write his recollections twenty years later. Geometry and symmetry were the essence of architecture for Wood, but he had to build on a Tudor plan that was more of a parallelogram than a rectangle. 'There is scarce a right angle in the whole building,' he raged. The passage through the hospital range is at a slant today as a result.

Wood treated the court side as the front of the building (62). Not only is it faced in ashlar, while the east is rubble-built (63), but Wood originally intended a grander façade on the west. To replace the 'ancient colonnade', there was to have been a regular arcade of nine arches, he recorded wistfully, with the centre three projecting to support a pedimented frontispiece:

> In the tympan of it I proposed to place the figure of the head of Saint John the
> Baptist, together with several other ornaments that embellished the old frontispiece,
> or rather tower, in the centre of the east side of the building.

In short, the decorative emphasis was to be switched from east to west. He did not entirely get his way in this. Although the western wall was rebuilt in ashlar, Wood was not permitted his decorated pediment or a new arcade. It looks as though he re-used at least the arches of the old colonnade. Wood also had to contend with alterations to his plan at the request of the tenant, which he felt destroyed the beauty of this façade.[455] Mrs Phillips was a thorn in Wood's flesh throughout, making continual complaints to Chandos. Water-closets were then a relatively new invention and Wood's struggles with an unfamiliar technology led to some particularly embarrassing problems.[456] Despite the ensuing delays, both new buildings were ready for assessment in November. The almspeople were able to return to their chambers by Christmas. They had been lodged elsewhere at the duke's expense.[457] In total Chandos paid Wood £3,139 2s 9d for just this first stage of rebuilding.[458]

Then in 1728 he employed Wood on the second stage. Some 'good, large, handsome rooms' (64) were built on the Elizabethan formal garden, capitalising on fine views over the city wall to the green hills beyond. Chandos was intent on rapidly recouping his investment. More rooms meant more paying guests, so the new building was a deep, five-storey block. It had nearly 70 rooms, not counting cellars and pantries. For the first two years Chandos ran it through a housekeeper, Jane Degge, who was distantly connected to the Duchess Cassandra. Among the first guests were closer relatives of Cassandra – Lord Castlemaine's family.[459] Chandos was aiming at quality as much as quantity in his lodgers. Designed to be easily divided, Mrs Degge's lodging became two houses, later nos. 1 and 2 Chandos Buildings (65). In the eighteenth

454 BaL microfilm of HL ST57: Chandos to Wood 24 May 1727, to Mrs Phillips 6 June 1727, to Revd. Chapman 14 June 1727, to Wood 3 November 1727; Neale; fig. 8.

455 J. Wood, *Description of Bath*, 303-5.

456 Baker and Baker, 307-8; Mowl and Earnshaw, 33-35.

457 BaL microfilm of HL ST57 Chandos to Mr Cope 9 November 1727, to Revd. Chapman 21 December 1727; Baker and Baker, 306.

458 Neale, fig.8.

459 BaL microfilm of HL ST57: Chandos to Wood 12 January and 29 February 1728; Baker and Baker, 317-23, 331-3; BMCA StJH/7/108: lease to Chandos 28 February 1735.

63
John Wood House from the east. Wood treated this
as the back of the building, so it was merely rubble-faced

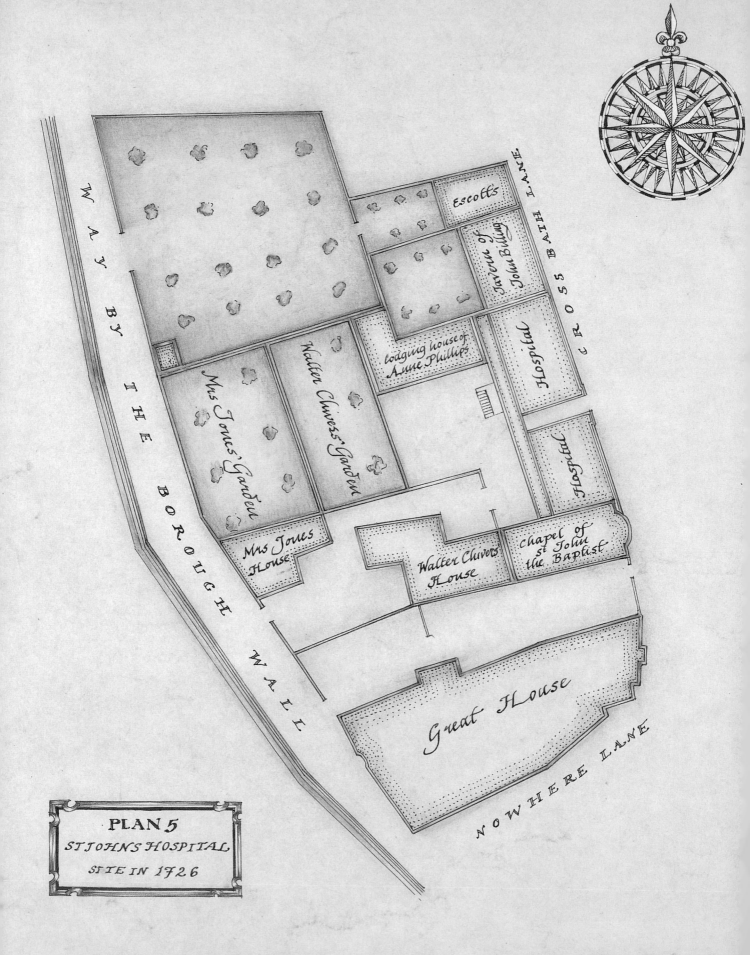

WAY BY THE BOROUGH WALL

Escotts

Tavern of John Billing

CROSS BATH LANE

Hospital

Hospital

lodging house of Annie Phillips

Walter Chivers' Garden

Mrs Jones' Garden

Mrs Jones House

Walter Chivers House

chapel of st John the Baptist

Great House

NOWHERE LANE

PLAN 5
ST JOHNS HOSPITAL
SITE IN 1726

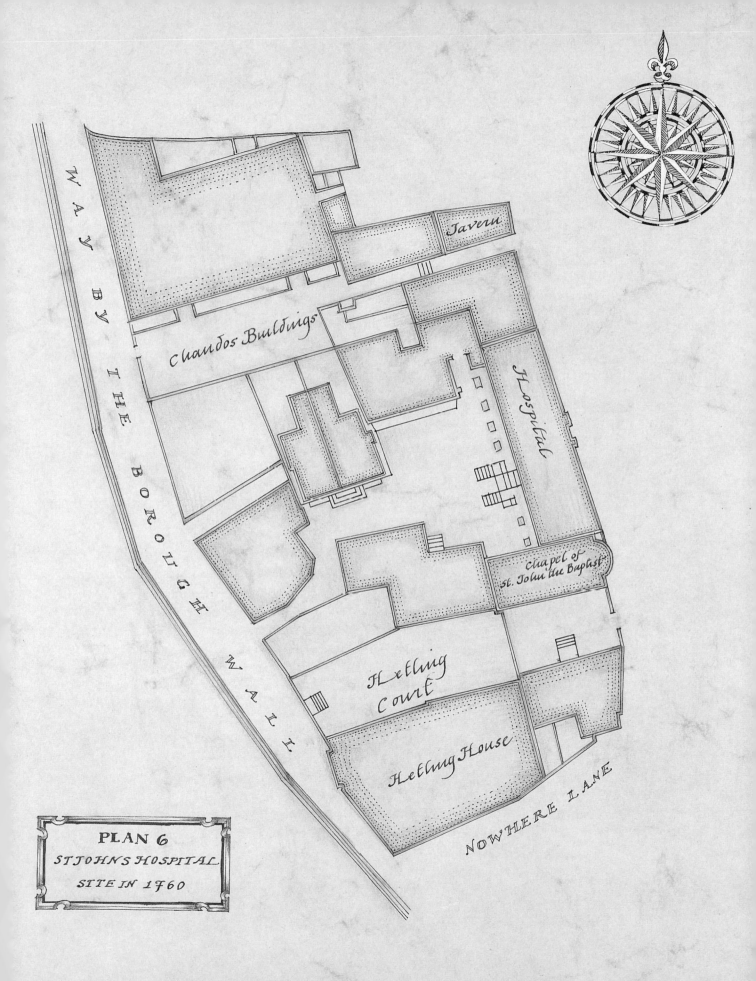

WAY BY THE BOROUGH WALL

Chandos Buildings

Tavern

Hospital

Chapel of St. John the Baptist

Hetling Court

Hetling House

NOWHERE LANE

PLAN 6
ST JOHNS HOSPITAL
SITE IN 1760

64
Chandos Buildings was fitted up in expectation of noble lodgers. Sketches by A.M.Tylee in 1886 for the *Bath and County Graphic*

460 BMCA StJH/7/126; *The Post Office Bath Directory* (1866), 438.

461 Neale, fig. 8; BaL microfilm of HL ST57: Chandos to Wood 23, 29 December 1727, 5 July 1728, 11 February, 22, 30 March, 2 December 1729, 9, 19 March 1730; BMCA StJH/7/108; BaRO Bath public houses licensed 1 Nov 1776; *A Directory for ... Bath* (1854), 227; *The Post Office Bath Directory* (1913), 658; Chandos's coat of arms is still painted on glass over the door.

462 J. Wood, *Description of Bath*, 339.

463 *Ibid*, pl. opposite p. 344.

464 Baker and Baker, 311-13; BaL microfilm of HL ST57.

century the whole Chandos development was known as Chandos Buildings. Now the name is given only to the passage Chandos created to Mrs Degge's grand lodging house.

On the north side of the passage lay the narrow Corporation plot that Chandos had acquired. When he bought it, it had a house facing St Michael's Lane, with a back gate into the formal garden. Chandos initially demolished the house just to enlarge the passage, but later gave way to the temptation to maximise his investment. A narrow house (later 3 Chandos Buildings) went up mainly on Corporation ground, with only a sliver on the land of St John's. The complications this caused were eventually resolved by an exchange. A wine merchant, Mr Carey, was its first tenant. Despite the protests of Ann Phillips, he was permitted to have a single-storey, two-room tavern beside his house. In 1784 the house was leased by a tea-dealer, who probably used the former tavern as a shop, but in the early nineteenth century it reverted to tavern use as the Chequers, one of several pubs in Bath to use that name. This Chequers remained in business until 1866.[460] Where once the tavern stood people now make their way into the Little Theatre. The house façade is all that survives of John Wood's work on Chandos Buildings.

Chandos House has been more fortunate (67). A sensitive conversion in recent years has preserved more original features than in any of Wood's other buildings for Chandos (66). It was built in 1729-30 as a new lodging-house for Mrs Jones. Beneath the house wine vaults were made for Mr Carey, so they had their own entrance from the lane by the city walls. Still the house and its vaults were soon in the hands of the same family. Mr Carey's brother Robert bought the house from Chandos in 1736 for his sister. The next development was almost inevitable. By 1776 wine merchant Francis Chalie was running a pub in Chandos House. Naturally it became the Chandos Arms, which thrived until the outbreak of the First World War.[461]

All these houses were built as closely as possible to a uniform design, but one can understand why the result failed to satisfy Wood.[462] Bath's old heart was a tangle of buildings and boundaries that gave no scope for the grand geometry of squares and circuses. His own contemporary development of Queen Square was on virgin ground outside the city wall. While his design for one of the façades is similar to his work for Chandos,[463] the impact is very different. Chapel Court, despite its Georgian façades, retains an intimacy and irregularity that recall an earlier age. For the modern eye, that may add to its charms, but not for Wood.

However, it was not the lack of perfect symmetry that disturbed the occupants. Chandos passed on a endless drizzle of complaints from his tenants about thin partitions, loose tiles and smelly drains.[464] By the end of the development, the duke's patience was exhausted. His irritation overflowed on 29 August 1730 and he wrote to Wood about Chandos Buildings and Chandos House:

> It is the opinion of almost every one who has seen them & especially who have
> lodged in them that no two houses have been worse finished and in a less

65
Chandos Buildings (now demolished) photographed *c.*1900 by Mowbray Green.
The regularity of Wood's façade had been destroyed by lengthening windows

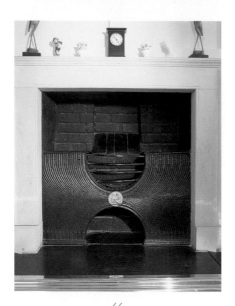

66
An elegant mid-Georgian fireplace in a
ground floor room of Chandos House

465   BaL microfilm of HL ST57 Chandos to
Wood 29 August 1730.

466   J. Wood, *Description of Bath*, 303.

467   BaRO Enquiry into Somerset charities 1734-
5 1, 53-59.

468   BaRO Enquiry into Somerset charities 1734-
5 1, 68b-c.

469   Baker and Baker, 329; BMCA StJH7/113.

470   J. Wood, *Description of Bath*, 265; BaRO
Enquiry into Somerset charities 1734-5, 1, 80;
Manco, 'History of Binbury', plot 15.

471   BMCA StJH/7/114.

472   *Registers of the Abbey Church* 1, 101.

473   *Ibid* 2, 423.

474   Neale, 139.

475   BMCA StJH/7/113-4. Lease of 3 Chapel
Court 14 October 1760 has a plan showing Mr
Sainsbury's house adjoining.

workmanlike manner by anyone who pretended to be an Architect & had any
regard for his own Reputation or the Interest of the Person who was his Benefactor
& Employed him.[465]

The hospital residents were equally aggrieved. Although Wood claimed
to have made their rooms 'much more capacious and convenient',[466] their
comfort was scarcely the prime consideration. Their light was blocked by
the new lodgings to the north and the staircase in the courtyard. The staircase
jutted a foot or two further into the court than the previous one. A pipe from
the duke's water closets passed through Abigail Collibee's room, causing a
great nuisance. Worst of all, the demolition of the old staircase had removed
their water-trough beneath the stair, supplied by a pipe under the hospital
passage. Such of the poor as could not fetch it were forced to buy water.[467]
All this emerged in the enquiry into Somerset charities in 1734.

When Chandos heard that his development was coming under fire, he
lost no time in sending his agent to protect his good name. The duke protested
that any encroachments on land of St John's were made 'entirely without
his knowledge or direction' and that he wished to take nothing from the poor.
The Commissioners were soothing. They assured his grace 'that his name
or character had not been mentioned before them but with the utmost respect
and without the least calumny'.[468] In fact the Georgian development had
squeezed to a minimum the area the almsfolk could call their own, but Chandos
had by then distanced himself. With the enquiry on the horizon he sold his
lease of the lodgings once run by Mrs Phillips to an old servant of his, John
Leaves. A new lease to Leaves in September 1734 excluded that part of the
courtyard that Chandos had taken, which was returned to the use of the
brethren and sisters.[469]

John Wood's work for Chandos did bring him one joy. While he laboured
on the site, he lodged in the Crown beside the Hot Bath.[470] He was ideally
placed to woo Jane, the daughter of Walter Chivers, who lived in the Middle
House.[471] It must have been a whirlwind courtship, for their son John was
christened on 25 February 1727/8.[472] Walter Chivers lived until 1731,[473] but
perhaps in poor health, for Chandos negotiated with Mrs Chivers in his fruitless
attempts to gain their garden. In November 1729 Wood offered to approach
his mother-in-law with an offer of £200. Chandos replied dryly 'By what I
have seen … she has not such regard for you as gives me room to hope she
would be persuaded by you.'[474] So it proved.

The garden was not built on until after November 1753, when the lease
was acquired by a carpenter, William Sainsbury. It was common in this period
for either a carpenter or mason to act as a developer, leasing a suitable site
and then gathering a team of craftsmen who could build to his designs, perhaps
taken from a pattern book. Sainsbury probably started work soon after he
gained the lease, for he had built at least one house on the garden by October
1760 and two by July 1765, when he was given a new lease of both.[475] These
are now nos. 4 and 5 Chapel Court (69). Although built so much later than
the Chandos development, they still have an early Georgian look. Provincial

67
Chandos House today from the north

68
The sinuous stair-rail of no.5, Chapel Court,
a show-piece of fine carpentry by William
Sainsbury, who built the house

476 Following Tobias Rustat's acquisition of St John's property, the Corporation paid him the 3s ground rent for Bellott's Hospital and 2s for Butthays, although Butthays is only specifically mentioned in the initial payment of arrears. From 1680 the 5s was paid to the Master of St John's unitl 1718. After 1707 it was for Bellott's and the town mixon (BaRO account rolls 117-158).

477 Keevil, fig.2: plan of Walcot marked to show the lands of St John's.

478 BaRO 1641 survey of Bath f.84, no.1, f.178, no.2.

479 *Registers of the Abbey Church* **2**, 481; BMCA StJH/7/262.

480 *Bath Journal* 23 February 1747, 4.

481 J. Wood, *Description of Bath*, 231, 338; BMCA StJH/7/226- 229.

482 BMCA StJH/7/308.

483 J. Wood, *Description of Bath*, 232, 242, 246, 341-2.

484 The façade has the date and the rebus of a rose and well. *Bath Journal* 22 October 1744, p.4, col. 2 advertised for sale the corner house in Kingsmead Square, built by Thomas Rosewell; *Registers of the Abbey Church* **1**, 67, **2**, 481.

485 Colvin, 529-30; BMCA StJH/7/154: Ireson had taken a plot of land from Joseph Jones, lessee of St John's Farm after the death of Hobbs. For Jones see BMCA StJH/7/308.

486 BMCA MH uncatalogued deeds.

builders tended to lag behind the changing tastes of the capital. This conservatism has left some delightful touches of baroque, such as cupboards which echo in timber the stone buffet from 15 Westgate Street. Perhaps the most charming feature is the sinuous stair rail in no.5 (68), en exhibition of Sainsbury's skill in carpentry.

Wood's Queen Square was not the only development beyond the city walls. As the booming spa began to throw its tentacles out into the green fields around, St John's Mead, by then known as Little Kingsmead, acquired a new value. Also the hospital in 1719 retrieved Butthays, which had been leased to the city since 1438 and had become the town's rubbish dump.[476] All this made a tempting area for development, although as one descended towards the Avon, the ground became progressively more liable to flooding.[477] North of the Bristol Road, St John's had better land. It is not surprising that the first area to be built up was the former garden of Westgate House, just outside and north of the West Gate.[478] By 1695 the Londonderry Inn occupied this prime position. The fives court shown there on Gilmore's map of Bath must have been in its yard. The inn thrived for over two centuries, becoming the Globe and later the Seven Dials.[479] Plays were performed at the 'great room' in the Globe.[480] To the north of the Londonderry Thomas Greenway built St John's Court in 1720 (70).[481]

John Hobbs, a sail-maker and timber merchant of Bristol, leased St John's Farm in 1717[482] and employed John Strahan to lay out Beaufort Square, Kingsmead Square and Avon Street. All are shown on John Wood's plan of Bath in 1735. Wood was seldom generous to his rivals. However, his criticism here fell less upon Strahan than the jobbing builders under him, who were castigated as too undisciplined to follow Strahan's designs. Although Beaufort Square achieved a decent regularity, he could find nothing to praise in Kingsmead Square.[483]

Rosewell House would naturally not appeal to Wood (71). This is the ornate baroque that followers of Palladio disdained. It was built in 1736 for Thomas Rosewell, son of the first landlord of the Londonderry.[484] The design has been attributed to Strahan, but is much more in the style of Nathaniel Ireson. Ireson was a mason and architect who had settled in Wincanton, Somerset, and who favoured just this type of provincial baroque. In the mid 1730s he developed the north side of Kingsmead Square.[485] He was therefore in the right place at the right time to build the house for Rosewell. John Wood's was the prevailing vision that shaped the Georgian city, but to modern eyes Bath is the richer for this intriguing dissident.

Meanwhile, work was going on at St Mary Magdalen (72). The 'capital messuage' had been divided in two, but Alderman Milo Smith reunited it. He was leasing both halves by 1717.[486] The two parts were probably the former master's house and the farm house. Smith was a man of substance, who owned a quarry in the parish, and so could improve the property. Holloway House, set in a farmyard west of the chapel, looks as though it had become more of a mansion than a simple tenant farm. It was demolished in 1904 to make

69
Nos. 4 and 5 Chapel Court today

70
The ornate house of Beau Nash, part of the development of St John's Court in 1720, drawn by S.H.Grimm in 1790 (BL Add Ms 15546 f.127). The parade of statuary around the roof is long gone

way for Magdalen Road and Park Avenue.[487] The Tudor house against the chapel (54) was pulled down by the Smith family. A Judas tree now flowers magnificently each spring on the site. Magdalen House still stands at right-angles to the chapel (73). There was a house there in 1757 (72), which was described as ancient in 1806.[488] If so the present house must be a Regency rebuilding.

The simple cottage east of the chapel which served as the hospital needed regular re-thatching and repair.[489] It was to be completely rebuilt. Revd. Duel Taylor was appointed Master of St Mary Magdalen in 1760.[490] He was the Rector of Bath, which also made him the Vicar of Widcombe and Lyncombe, the parish in which the hospital stood.[491] He saw the need for a chapel of ease in Holloway, so that his parishioners there did not have to walk over to Widcombe every Sunday. The once isolated Chapel of St Mary Magdalen now had new buildings springing up around it. So in 1760 the Revd. Taylor repaired the chapel and fitted it up for divine service, with the aid of the residents of Holloway.[492] John Smith, son of Milo, helped the work by building his own pew.[493] The following year Revd. Taylor rebuilt the hospital (74), as an inscription records. It remained small. On the ground floor was a kitchen (10ft by 11ft) which doubled as a living room, with two smaller rooms off it, each 5ft by 6ft. Above were two bedrooms.[494]

The Charity Commission of 1734

The first major enquiry into Bath charities under the Elizabethan Charitable Uses Act took place in 1734. On 5 August George II authorised an enquiry into charities throughout Somerset, Ilchester only excepted. The Commissioners were mainly county gentry, chaired by Thomas Carew of Crowcombe (75), who took a close interest in St John's.[495] Another Commissioner was that leader of Bath fashion, Richard 'Beau' Nash, the city's master of ceremonies (76). They requested the sheriff of Somerset to empanel a local jury to meet on 20 September in King Edward's School in Bath, at that time housed in the disused Church of St Mary Northgate. The Commission sat there and at the Guildhall for months, diligently probing into Bath charities. Statements were taken. Those responsible for the charities were compelled to appear. Very little was achieved by all this activity, but the evidence provides fascinating glimpses of life in the Bath hospitals. The enquiry had been triggered by complaints that the endowments for the maintenance of the Rector of Bath, the school and the hospitals of Bellott, St John the Baptist, St Catherine and St Mary Magdalen had been misgoverned, misemployed and misconverted.[496]

The jury sympathised with the brethren and sisters of the Hospital of St John the Baptist. John Chapman had blithely disregarded the Trevor award. He had not only permitted the Chandos development, with all its drawbacks for the hospital residents, but eroded their standard of living. Their income had been reduced from 5s to 4s 2d a week each and the quality of the gowns

487   BMCA MH/8/28(b).

488   *Report of the Commissioners for Charities* 6, 740; BMCA MH uncatalogued lease to William Redman 20 October 1806. The house was Paradise Cottage in the nineteenth century, but was changed to Magdalen House in 1903 (BMCA MH/7/8, MH/8/29).

489   BaRO Enquiry into Somerset charities 1734-5, 1, 80-85.

490   *Report of the Commissioners for Charities* 6, 556; BaRO Acc 59, bundle 2, nos 49/50, p.24.

491   In the medieval period the Church of St Thomas à Becket in Widcombe was a chapel belonging to the Church of St Mary of Stalls in Bath. After the consolidation of city parishes in 1583, it was linked to the Abbey Church.

492   *Report of the Commissioners for Charities* 6, 556; Inscription in the chapel; *Bath Chronicle and Weekly Gazette* 6 November 1760.

493   BMCA MH uncatalogued lease 8 May 1767 to John Smith of half the capital messuage and the seat in the chapel built and used by John Smith.

494   BaRO Acc 59, 2/53. I am indebted to Dr Carpenter for this reference.

495   An early eighteenth-century transcript of St John's cartulary among the papers of Thomas Carew (SRO DD/TB/20/2), was published in *Med Deeds*.

496   BaRO Enquiry into Somerset charities 1734-5, 1, 1-6, 10-12.

71
Rosewell House in 1851. It was built in 1736 for Thomas
Rosewell, probably by the mason and architect Nathaniel Ireson

72
The Chapel of St Mary Magdalen appears
on this engraving after Thomas Robins of
Bath in 1757. Behind it are the roofs and
chimneys of a house where Magdalen
House stands today. To the left is Holloway
House. To the right of the chapel is the
hospital before its rebuilding. Across the
river Avon Street runs up from a small quay
to the Westgate. Inside the city wall the
Chandos development stands out among
the older, gabled houses

73
Magdalen House today

74
The eighteenth-century hospital of St Mary
Magdalen, now Magdalen Cottage, the
home of the caretaker of the chapeL

497 Baker and Baker, 328.

498 BaRO Enquiry into Somerset charities 1734-5, 1, 26, 28-29, 35, 44, 47-51, 53-5; PRO C93/58/16.

499 Appointed at some time between 16 June 1724, when George Bradford issued a lease as Master and 9 June 1729, when Revd. Thomas did so: BMCA MH uncatalogued deeds.

500 Collinson, 1, 172.

501 BaRO Enquiry into Somerset charities 1734-5, 1, 7, 21, 80- 85; BMCA MH uncatalogued deeds.

502 BaRO Enquiry into Somerset charities 1734-5, 1, 33-4.

issued to them had declined. Chapman had failed in his obligation to pay for a nurse for them and for heating and repairs. In addition he retained the first three weeks pay for each new hospital entrant, to pay for the burial of his or her predecessor. It was a catalogue of meanness. More surprisingly for a member of the clergy, Chapman stood accused of permitting alcohol to be sold and billiards played in the former chapel of St Michael. In fact Chapman had leased it with a clause forbidding the sale of alcohol, but the lease had been bought by Chandos in 1729.[497] Had Chandos noticed that clause? The absentee Chapman was unlikely to check up. The Commission ordered him to fulfil his obligations under the Trevor award and fined him £20 for not having supplied a nurse. Hospital vacancies were to be filled promptly and no more than 5s deducted from the newcomer's pay for the shroud and funeral bell of the deceased.[498]

The Master of St Mary Magdalen faced a similar inquisition. The patronage of this hospital had remained with the Crown, which bestowed the appointment upon a series of clerics with other benefices. The current incumbent was the Revd. David Thomas of Erlestoke, Wiltshire.[499] Richard Jefferies opened the action with a petition on behalf the poor persons of St Mary Magdalen's Hospital. (He was related by marriage to Milo Smith, who held the hospital's demesne farm.[500]) He claimed that it had been endowed with large possessions, but that 'of late years many of the lands have been secreted, rents withheld and money embezzled which should have been applied to the relief and maintenance of said poor persons.' These were strong words, but David Thomas promptly disarmed his critic by agreeing with him. He had spent considerable money and effort in trying to discover exactly what the endowment had been, but in vain. He was under the impression (no doubt from the chapel inscription) that the hospital had been founded and endowed by Prior Cantlow, but could find nothing in writing. This led him to suspect some embezzlement. The master was open with the Commissioners, producing a rental of the hospital properties and details of other income. One startling fact to emerge was that the master was paid a premium of about £20 and the nurse a guinea for each person admitted to the hospital, presumably by their relatives. In 1734 there were only three inmates. According to Revd. Thomas:

> There is a nurse that makes it her whole business to attend the poor persons at the hospital; they have constantly their bellies full of wholesome diet; they are not troublesome to any of the town and they have things befitting persons in their circumstances ... I am frequently myself at Bath, and I never come there without giving the nurse cheese, meat, bread or money of my pocket to encourage her to be kind to the paupers. I do also furnish them with necessary clothes.[501]

However, the main target of the enquiry was Bath Corporation. On 23 September the Commissioners ordered the Corporation to produce charters and any other proof of the endowment of St Catherine's and Bellott's Hospitals.[502] That of Bellott's presented no problem. Bellott's deed of gift had been retained and separate rentals kept for the estate at Ludwell in Donhead St Mary, Wiltshire, which supported the hospital.[503] A survey of

75
A portrait of Thomas Carew MP by Thomas Hudson. Carew chaired the Charity Commission for Somerset in 1734.
Fascinated by local history, he delved deep into the past of St John's Hospital. His own copy of its cartulary is still among
his papers. He became the first president of the Bath Hospital (now the Royal National Hospital for Rheumatic Diseases)

these lands in 1652 and a map in 1749 both estimated the total as around 60 acres.[504]

St Catherine's Hospital was a different matter. There the Corporation could not comply because of the 'perplexity and confusion of the several grants deeds and writings' and asked for an adjournment until 7 November. The Corporation then produced the grants and deeds of Corporation-held property 'but the same being above seven hundred in number and most of them so very old and wrote in so obsolete hands and the writing so decayed by length of time' that the Corporation was 'not capable of reading or scheduling the same' and so was 'obliged to send them to London to be transcribed, scheduled and methodized,' which would take at least four months. The Corporation was allowed more time, but even then failed to produce the required evidence.[505] What did emerge was damning. King Edward had provided for the creation of a school and the support of 10 poor people and yet the local jurors could not see that the Corporation had ever made any provision for any poor persons whatsoever out of his endowment. Of course the city chamberlain's accounts prove that the Corporation had continuously maintained St Catherine's Hospital, but with whose money? Was this the hospital of the Edwardian endowment? The jurors clearly thought not.

There had never been separate accounts kept. The payments to King Edward's School and St Catherine's came out of the general city account, which was fed by the rents of ex-priory properties, among others, but by now there was no way of telling which were which. The Commission struggled with the problem. Edward's charter did not specify the properties individually, so the Commission consulted the rental made when they were in Crown hands. It was singularly unhelpful. The local jury, faced with a list of around 100 tenants from two centuries earlier holding 'one cottage' or 'one shop', could scarcely be expected to identify the properties concerned. Only in five cases was there something more solid to seize upon: St Werburg's Church[yard], the Bell and the Hart were all named, and there was also a mill and 'a tenement in Westgate' [Street] which they took to be the house over the West Gate.[506] The jury declared those five properties to be of the Edwardian endowment.

By June 1735 the Charity Commissioners had lost patience. They issued a decree condemning Bath Corporation for misapplication of revenue. The Corporation was to be displaced by Trustees including the Bishop of Bath and Wells and Rector of Bath, to whom the five properties were to be given. In addition the Corporation was to pay the trust £500 and identify all the other ex-priory properties. Although the decree was never implemented, some of the details are revealing. The trust was to provide for 10 poor men, who 'shall always behave themselves orderly, piously and soberly and constantly attend divine service in the Abbey Church,' taking communion once a month. Anyone neglecting these religious duties was to be expelled from the charity. The poor men were to receive 3s 6d each weekly and 'new gowns on Christmas day of grey cloth, value 20s, whereon shall be marked in white cloth E 6 R'

503   Ibid, 2, 38; BMCA BH/5/0, 3, 16.

504   BaRO Furman bundle 18, no.11; *Report of the Commissioners for* Charities 4, 294.

505   BaRO, Enquiry into Somerset charities 1734-5 1, 74-6, 79; BaRO Furman, 678/2, 6, 8-11, 14.

506   In fact the 'tenement' was a garden and the Bell Inn that had belonged to Bath Priory was not the one they knew. *Report of the Commissioners for Charities* 4, 511-20; SRO T/PH/VCH6 microfilm of PRO SC6 3144; SRO DD/X/HY 1 (Bath Priory Rental 1503).

76
Richard 'Beau' Nash, Master of Ceremonies for Bath
society 1705-61. Miniature portrait by Nathaniel Hone

(for Edward VI Rex).[507] The concept of what was fitting in the recipients of charity was only one step away from the medieval. Prayers for the founder's soul might have been abolished, but his name should be ever before them.

Bath Corporation had resolved back in September 1734 to fight the case,[508] but it was unnecessary. Presumably those nominated as Trustees were not inclined to engage in a costly legal battle to gain possession. Public censure had one result, though. From then on the Corporation was anxious to present King Edward as the founder of St Catherine's. This was not difficult. Bathonians had lost sight of the origins of this 300-year-old charity. A seventeenth-century Bath physician thought that the hospital was founded by seven sisters named Bimbury.[509] John Wood was easily convinced that St Catherine's was built after the grant by Edward VI. He loved a romantic story. He supposed that it was finished in the reign of Mary, which for him neatly explained both the black gowns of the residents (mourning for their youthful founder) and the name St Catherine (in compliment to Catherine of Aragon, mother of Mary).[510] This ingenious nonsense would have pleased the Corporation.

New vistas

The records of the Charity Commission show a great deal of worthy endeavour, but little actually changed as a result. However, some of the Commissioners who had been most diligent in probing into the old institutions were active in creating a new one. By time of the enquiry, plans were afoot for a new hospital for poor visitors. Once again the inadequacy of provision had been recognised. The population was rising, which would inevitably mean more cases coming to Bath. Between Prior Holloway's rebuilding of St John's and the Commission of 1734 the population of England had more than doubled.[511] Also the upsurge in scientific curiosity was changing expectations of medical care.

The new hospital differed from its predecessors in significant ways. It was not the creation of a single will, but many. It drew on the energies and goodwill of local worthies and the deep pockets of aristocratic visitors. Beau Nash was notably successful in cajoling money from those he ruled as master of ceremonies. Thomas Carew of Crowcombe steered through the necessary private Act of Parliament and became the first president of its governors. A site was found on Upper Borough Walls, part of which was leased from St John's Hospital.[512] The new Bath Hospital opened in 1742 was an imposing institution, designed by John Wood. It was recognisably closer to the modern concept of a hospital. From the beginning it had both surgeons and physicians, among them Jeremiah Peirce and Edward Harington, who had been respectively surgeon and physician at Bellott's from 1733, and a resident apothecary with a dispensary. The seeds of the future were there. Over the centuries it evolved with changes of name into the specialist centre for research and treatment that we know today – the Royal National Hospital for Rheumatic Diseases.[513] Bellott's and the Leper's Hospital were thrown into the shade. Ultimately

507 *Report of the Commissioners for Charities* **4**, 511-20

508 BaRO council minutes 30 September 1734.

509 Guidott, 76.

510 J. Wood, *Description of Bath*, 199, 306.

511 Smith, 10, 165-6.

512 BMCA StJH/7/239.

513 Rolls, 9, 12, 23, 39, 167; BaRO MS vols. appointments to the gift of Lady Scudamore.

77
Jeremiah Peirce, Surgeon to Bellott's Hospital 1733-55.
Detail from a painting by William Hoare

they were to become redundant, but in the case of Bellott's, it took a surprisingly long time.

Even the tiny Leper's Hospital survived until the radical changes to the smaller baths in the last quarter of the century.[514] The Lazars' Bath and its hospital were demolished when the Hot Bath was rebuilt on a more convenient site. The elegant new building, designed by John Wood the younger, was ready for the spring season of 1778.[515] It did not include a pump room, so the Corporation needed another building for those who simply wished to drink the waters. One was ready to hand - the Great House, by this time known as Hetling House, after the family who lived there. For centuries it had had its own supply from the Hot Bath spring. Conveniently for the Corporation, the eastern part of the house, housing the private pump, had been rebuilt earlier in the century.[516] The Corporation bought up the lease of that part in 1778.[517] It was known as the Hetling Pump Room or Hot Bath Pump Room. Next in line for renovation was the Cross Bath, which was rebuilt in 1783-4.[518] However, these fine Georgian baths were still approached down narrow medieval lanes and packed around with property.

Private occupiers digging foundations, cellars or wells might damage the hot springs. Equally important was the desire for broad and elegant approaches to all the baths and between the newly expanding Upper Town and the old city centre. In 1788 the Corporation planned several new streets and the widening of old ones. A private Act of Parliament the following year gave the authority for the Corporation's Improvement Commission to purchase property that lay in the way. The proposals were dramatic (78). To clear the area around the Cross Bath, it was intended to remove St John's Hospital and sweep away a mass of property to the east for a new, colonnaded Bath Street. Bell Tree Lane and St Michael's Lane were to be straightened, widened and re-named Beau Street and Nash Street, in honour of Beau Nash. Hetling Court was to be opened at the west end to become Hetling Street. The narrow Nowhere Lane was at the wrong angle to form part of this new scheme. Evidently the aim was to get as close as possible to a regular grid, with long vistas down to a remodelled Cross Bath at the centre. So the plan included demolishing the George Inn to create a new Hot Bath Street.[519]

Although these plans were not fully carried out, the area around the baths was certainly opened up and valuable properties of St John's, including the George, vanished in the process.[520] St Mary Magdalen lost two houses: the former Crown, immediately south of the new Hot Bath, was pulled down in 1804 and a property on Bell Tree Lane was demolished to complete Beau Street in 1824.[521] In some cases, the Corporation and St John's arranged an exchange, so that the charity gained property of equivalent value elsewhere. In other cases the charities were paid the market price and should have invested this in other property. St John's generally did so.[522] The Master of St Mary Magdalen supposedly instructed his agent to use the £200 from the sale of the former Crown to make a desirable purchase. Instead it was used to fund a mortgage to the artist Thomas Barker on his house on Sion Hill.[523]

514 Carpenter, 'The Leper's Hospital at Bath'.

515 BaRO Council Minutes 30 October 1775, 1 July 1776, 16 May, 29 June 1778; BaRO Chamberlain's Accounts 25 April, 19 July 1777; Bath Chronicle 4 January 1776; J. Wood, Description of the Hot-Bath.

516 J. Wood, Description of Bath, 227; Bath Journal 8 July 1745; observations of the fabric.

517 The Corporation later gave St John's another property in exchange. BaRO CM 30 March and 6 April 1778; BMCA StJH/7/137(b); BaRO Furman bundle 21; Report of the Commission for Charities 4, 527.

518 Manco, 'The Cross Bath', 68.

519 Neale, 250-58.

520 BMCA StJH/7/101.

521 Manco, 'The History of Binbury', plots 15, 20.

522 Report of the Commissioners for Charities 4, 529.

523 Report of the Commissioners for Charities 6, 557; Barkers of Bath, 15.

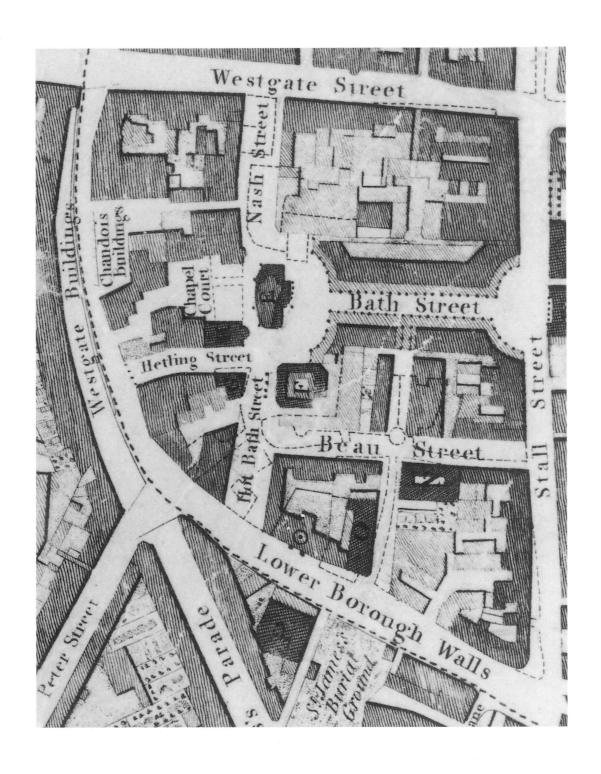

78
The planned new city centre, with St John's Hospital removed. The dotted lines show frontages as they actually stood.
Only part of the plan was carried out. Detail from a map of Bath in 1793 by Harcourt Masters

Nepotism, pluralism and absentee masters

For St John's Hospital the Georgian period was the Age of the Chapmans. The Revd. John Chapman, master 1711-37, was succeeded in turn by the Revd. Dr Walter Chapman and his nephew the Revd. Dr John Chapman. Between them the three Chapmans held the mastership for over a century, almost coinciding with the reigns of the first three Georges. Bath Corporation had returned to nepotism. Dr Walter's father Alderman Walter was from a rising branch of the Chapman family, who were predominantly leather-workers (sse page 81). They came to dominate the Council in the eighteenth century, just as their innkeeper and mercer cousins had done in the seventeenth.[524]

Walter was appointed master on 8 October 1737 at the age of only 26.[525] He was studious enough to have gained an MA from Pembroke College, Oxford.[526] (His Doctorate in Divinity came later.) The years at Oxford seem to have been the most exciting of his life. Among his fellow students was Samuel Johnson. Johnson was the gifted son of a bookseller, painfully conscious of his poverty among the gilded elite at Oxford.[527] One can see why Walter Chapman, the intelligent son of a saddler, might be among his favoured companions. In later life, as Johnson grew into a literary giant of his generation, Dr Walter evidently came to take pride in this youthful association above all else. Beyond the bare facts of his life, it was the only thing mentioned in his obituary.[528]

Like his predecessor, Dr Walter was a pluralist. On 11 February 1745/6 he became one of the six Prebendaries of Bristol Cathedral.[529] Then in 1754 he was appointed Vicar of Bradford-on-Avon.[530] There he was involved in a curious episode. In 1764 Hester Bishop, aged 24, and John Vennell, a weaver of Bradford-on-Avon, asked the vicar to put up the banns for them, but John's mother forbade the marriage. Now comes the interesting part. The Revd. Chapman was not rash enough to act himself in a clandestine marriage, but his servant, Thomas Dick guided the disappointed couple to a chapel 'near the Hot Bath in Bath' and fetched the clergyman, who duly married them.[531] In short Chapman induced his chaplain at St John's to break the rule barring marriages in the chapel. Dr Walter either smiled upon young love or perceived a certain urgency in the matter. The chaplain was a Cornishman named Grigg, educated at Launceston. He clearly did not see it as any part of his duty to keep the chapel clean. It was festooned with cobwebs in his day.[532] By 1783 Dr Walter had retired and the church of Bradford-on-Avon was served by a curate.[533] He died in April 1791 at his house at Shirehampton near Bristol, at the grand age of 80.[534] He had been Master of St John's for 54 years, the longest-serving master in the hospital's history.

He was replaced by his nephew the Revd. Dr John Chapman, aged 48, who had just gained his doctorate in divinity at Oxford.[535] 'His style of preaching', we are told 'was marked by luminous arrangement, strong argument and classical simplicity.'[536] Dr John was already well-supplied with clerical livings. Like his namesake he was Vicar of Weston. He also held the perpetual

524 BaRO MS E. Holland, Genealogy of the Chapmans.

525 *Somerset Incumbents*, 236.

526 Foster, *Alumni Oxoniensis 1715-1886*, 240.

527 *Dictionary of National Biography*

528 *Gentleman's Magazine* **61**, 489 (May 1791).

529 BrRO EP/A/42/2.

530 W. Jones, 121.

531 *Calendar of Bradford-on-Avon Examinations*, 26-27 (no. 93).

532 *Letters from Bath*, 87.

533 *Wiltshire Returns...1783*, 41-2 (no.23).

534 *Gentleman's Magazine* **61**, i, 489 (May 1791).

535 Foster, *Alumni Oxoniesis 1715-1886*, 239.

536 *Bath Chronicle* 24 April 1816.

79
Revd. Dr Walter Chapman, Master of St John's Hospital 1737-91. This portrait
was presented to St John's Hospital in 1924 by his descendant Ruth Young

curacies of Churchill and Puxton, Somerset, which were in the gift of the Dean and Chapter of Bristol.[537] It must have helped to have an uncle in the Chapter. On 18 May 1791 he took over his uncle's prebend in Bristol Cathedral,[538] then on 4 June he became Master of St John's Hospital. The Dean and Chapter were also patrons of the united living of Bathford and Bathampton, given to him in 1794. Until then he had been signing vestry minutes at Weston. He may have moved to the vicarage at Bathford for a few years, but by 1812 he was living at the Paragon in Bath.[539] When he died there on 21 April 1816, aged 74,[540] he was replaced by his wife's nephew, the Revd. James Phillott the younger.

Phillott broke the Chapman reign, but not the pattern. His family had risen to prominence in Bath in the eighteenth century. Joseph Phillott, grandson of a French immigrant, was the lessee of the Three Tuns in the middle of the century and later of the Bear Inn.[541] He was also a founder partner in the Old Bath Bank.[542] His sons Joseph and Charles served on Bath Council.[543] Their influence can be seen in the appointment of their brother, the Revd. James the elder, to the Rectory of Bath. He was also Vicar of Stanton Drew and Rector of Stanton Prior. In 1815 Revd. James the younger succeeded his father in Stanton Drew and Stanton Prior, which became his home.[544] On 6 May 1816 Bath Council elected him Master of St John's Hospital.[545] This amassing of benefices was nothing remarkable in this age and attracted no particular comment at the time. It was left to stern Victorians to censure the nepotism and pluralism of their forefathers.

At least the Georgian Masters of St John's did not stray too far from Bath. All could visit quite easily. The same could not be said for the Revd. Dr Richard Roberts, the absentee Master of St Mary Magdalen. Roberts came from a Bristol family who could not afford to support him through university, but with the aid of a scholarship he left Oxford with an MA in 1759. He had become the curate to Revd. Taylor by the time newly-repaired Chapel of St Mary Magdalen opened in November 1760. On the death of Revd. Taylor in 1767, Roberts replaced him as Master. However, such a post could not satisfy an ambitious man. In 1769 he was appointed High Master of St Paul's School in London. From then on Roberts cared little for the hospital and nothing at all for the residents of Holloway. During his marathon 55 years as master, he supported no services in the chapel. Roberts did permit the chapel to be used, as long as he was not expected to do more than keep the roof in repair. Services were held from time to time by various local clergy, either out of goodwill or paid for by local residents, but there were periods when the chapel was closed.[546] For example in 1816 the Revd. Charles Crook, Rector of Bath and Vicar of Widcombe, joined several of his Holloway parishioners in sending a petition to Dr Roberts for services to be held there.[547]

A greater cause for concern was that the charity, never large, had dwindled to the minimum. When Roberts took over as master, there were two or three 'idiots' in the hospital, then called Maudlin House (now Magdalen Cottage). By the time that Nathan Strange was appointed as housekeeper about 1803,

537 Collinson, **1**, 112, 118, 160, **3**, 581, 599.

538 Le Neve and Hardy, **1**, 227; *Diocese of Bristol*, 182.

539 Hargood-Ash, 10. I am obliged to Godfrey Laurence for this reference.

540 *Bath Chronicle* 24 April 1816.

541 BrL MSS 4528: Bath Single Sheets, 9: cutting; BaRO Furman 2520, 2519, 2520.

542 BaRO PP275; Clews, 122.

543 Collinson, **1**, 27; BaRO PP275.

544 *Bath Journal* December 1865.

545 BaRO council minutes.

546 Foster, *Alumni Oxoniensis 1715-1886*, 1208; *Bath Chronicle and Weekly Gazette* 6 November 1760; BaRO Acc 59/2/49-50, p.67; *Report of the Commissioners for Charities* **6**, 556, 558, 738; Warner, 240.

547 BaRO Acc. 59/2/49-50, pp.49, 52-3, 107.

there was only one. Clearly as inmates died, the vacancies had not been filled. The lone survivor was an old man, who came originally from Norton St Philip and had been placed in the hospital some 75 years earlier. On 28 July 1806, the *Bath Journal* reported:

> The poor inoffensive idiot whom the passenger may have seen for nearly half a century past sitting at the door of the Magdalen Hospital in Holloway died last week aged 92. He has been for some years the only patient supported in that institution and we doubt not that the intention of the benevolent founder will be fulfilled by the speedy appointment of some other proper object to fill the vacancy.

Would Roberts have actually left the hospital empty without this polite reminder of public interest? We shall never know. As it was Nathan Strange was sent a replacement, Thomas Howse of Bath. When he died around 1814, he too was replaced.[548] However, towards the end of his long term as master Roberts was to encounter a great deal more public interest - in fact a thorough inquisition.

The Brougham Commission

By this time the unwieldy process of appointing local gentry to act as charity commissioners had lost its appeal. There had not been a commission under the Elizabethan statute since 1787. The Court of Chancery had always had the power to redress abuses, but it involved such interminable delays and crushing expense that few cases were brought to its attention. Sir Samuel Romilly MP was determined to rectify matters. His Act of 1812 provided that petitions presented to the Lord Chancellor or the Master of the Rolls on a breach of charitable trust had to be heard in a summary way and acted upon. He envisaged justice swift and sure, but it was not to be. The Act was hastily and loosely drafted and was interpreted by the courts in a restrictive way. More radical change was required. That cause was now ardently pursued by reformer Henry Brougham MP. He campaigned for a parliamentary commission to investigate charities. He drafted a statute which was so heavily amended by the House of Lords that the final Act of 1818 was a mere shadow of the original. However, public feeling was with Brougham. A year later the Government brought in its own Charitable Foundations Act, which adopted many of the provisions of Brougham's original bill.[549] Like modern parliamentary commissions of enquiry, the Brougham Commission's role was to investigate and report. The many volumes of its reports became a directory of charities, with a mass of detail on their history and funding. The weakness of the commission lay in its limited power to redress abuses. It could, however, draw the attention of the Attorney-General to matters of concern.

The commissioners set to work with commendable speed. In February 1820 they began investigating the charities of Bath and surrounding parishes, hearing witnesses and taking evidence. Their report was published in September the same year. This included all the charities within the city limits. The report

548 *Report of the Commissioners for Charities* 6, 735-7.
549 G. Jones, 160-67.

on St Mary Magdalen was not published until 1822, probably because of the need to clarify its origins. Experts were required to transcribe ancient scripts in medieval Latin. However, since that only revealed that the hospital had originally been used for lepers, it did not help the commission at all in deciding how the foundation should properly be used in their own age. Faced with evidence that on the appointment of Revd. Roberts, 'it was considered to be the duty of the master of this hospital to maintain two or more idiots in the hospital, and to perform, or procure to be performed, divine service regularly in the chapel on Sundays', they could only conclude that he had failed.

The care of the handicapped resident was not criticised. He lived and ate with Nathan Strange and his wife, who had the hospital rent free. It was the absent master's use of the revenues which caused concern. The facts were certainly disturbing. Over the period of his mastership the Roberts had collected £3,575 8s in fines for new leases, £30 each for the two people he had admitted to the hospital and £21 18s a year interest from the mortgage on the Sion Hill house. All went into his own pocket, giving him an average income of around £85 a year for doing little more than sign a few documents. All that Nathan Strange received to maintain the man in his care was the annual income from rents of less than £15. Roberts did pay for his clothing and bedding. He must also have paid a fee to his local agent. However, it is clear enough that the mastership had become a lucrative sinecure.[550]

Roberts did not long survive the publication of the report. Seizing the opportunity, the father of the Rector of Bath approached a local M.P., assuring him that if Revd. Crook were master, he would keep the Chapel of St Mary Magdalen open.[551] It was a rash promise. George IV appointed Revd. Crook as successor to Roberts on 12 August 1823.[552] Crook rapidly set about repairing the chapel at a cost of £600, which encouraged three residents of Holloway to pay for its enlargement at the same time. We see the results in a drawing by Thomas Shepherd (80). The old bell-tower scarcely higher than the chapel roof had been replaced by a substantial tower. A new crenellated east end extended the length of the chapel. Ironically the expensively rebuilt chapel was closed in 1832, since the new Church of St Mark in Lyncombe rendered it redundant, in the rector's view.[553] The closure triggered off a case in Chancery against Crook.

Five Bathonians provided the Rolls Court with a catalogue of abuses. They followed the Brougham Commission in arguing that the Master of St Mary Magdalen had a duty to provide divine service for the inhabitants of Holloway and also to accommodate more than one handicapped person in the hospital. In fact for several years Crook had not even admitted one. The last inmate died before Crook's appointment and from Christmas 1824 he let the hospital to Mrs Sarah Chunn and her husband at £12 a year. Two applicants for admission to the hospital were turned down, on the grounds that they were not from the Bath district. Early in 1827 Crook did admit a handicapped child named Sarah Radford, making a new arrangement with Mrs Chunn that she could live in the hospital rent free, in return for taking care of Sarah.

550 *Report of the Commissioners for Charities*, **6**, 555-558, 735- 745.

551 BaRO Acc 59, bundle 2, nos 49/50, p.53.

552 SRO DD/BR/bb 9.

553 BaRO Acc 59, bundle 2, 49/50, pp.19, 21-2, 38-9.

80
St Mary Magdalen drawn in 1829 by Thomas H. Shepherd. The tower and battlemented east
end were new additions. The Judas tree was well-grown, so it was probably planted by c.1800

He charged Sarah Radford's sponsors £31 10s and then refused to refund any part of it when she died within the year. Another idiot, Mary Phillips, was admitted shortly afterwards on payment of another £31 10s. When the case was heard in 1836, the judge ruled that an admission fee was illegal. However, the court recognised that the charity was not bound to provide divine service for the people of Holloway.[554] Even so after Crook died a new master, the Revd. John Allen, was appointed in 1838 on a promise to the Lord Chancellor to keep the chapel open.[555]

At St John's Hospital, Phillott could give the Brougham Commission a rather better account of himself. At his expense a Bath clergyman held regular services in the chapel, with the women sitting on one side and the men on the other. The residents complained of nothing except the annoyance of noise from the rooms above theirs early in the morning and late at night. It was shameful that under Dr. John Chapman the hospital residents had been made to pay for their own repairs, just as under his namesake a century earlier. Only since Phillott's arrival had that changed. Although Dr. Chapman had raised the pay of the combined nurse and washerwoman to £12 in 1813, the residents were still only receiving 4s 2d a week. The supply of gowns and coals had been replaced by a payment of £2 a year. Phillott had improved matters. Finding that there was a surplus from rent income, he divided this between the residents. The Commission pressed him into raising their pay instead to the 5s a week laid down by the Trevor award.[556] The income from fines was shared between the master and brethren and sisters as Trevor had stipulated. These payments were irregular, but could dramatically overshadow rent income.

The value of the property of St John's Hospital had increased enormously. Before the report was published, rumour had clearly been at work and an unpublished county survey was highly critical. The author estimated the annual rent roll at nearly £10,000. 'What abuse of common sense to suffer thirteen infirm persons to enjoy such a princely income.' He suggested an Act of Parliament to permit this wealth to be spread more widely among the poor of Bath.[557] This was a glimpse into the distant future of St John's, but at the time the author was misinformed. The annual value of the estate was calculated at over £11,000 in 1818, a huge rise from just over £600 in 1711, but this was the value to the tenants. The income to St John's from rents was only £129 5s 4½d, an actual fall from £150 15s 2d in 1711. The hospital was not yet feeling the full benefit of the Georgian development of some of its property, particularly St John's Mead. The value of what had been St John's Farm had increased from £60 in 1711 to £6000 in 1818, but this was not reflected in raised rents to St John's. This was not seen as unfair at the time. It was generally accepted that where lessees bore the costs of developing property, they and their heirs should reap the benefits of the investment for anything up to a century. Ultimately the lease would expire and the landlord would acquire an improved property at no cost to himself.

The estimated value to tenants was used to calculate the size of fines for

554   BaRO Acc 59, bundle 2, nos.49/50.
555   *Bath Journal* 12 August 1854.
556   *Report of the Commission for Charities*, **4**, 291-92, 522-25.
557   Collinson, **1**, 43, supp. 37-8.

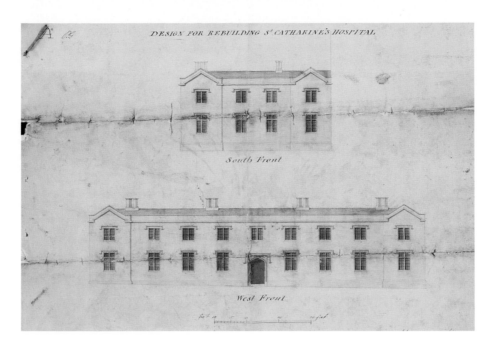

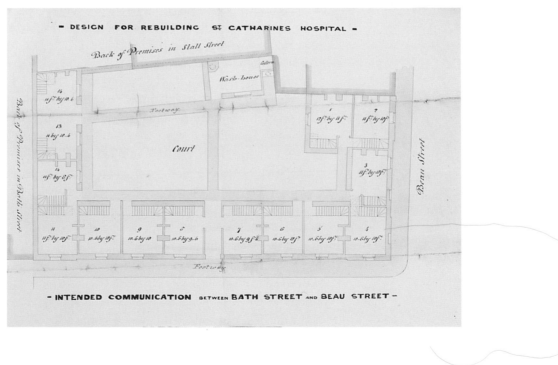

81-82
Designs by George Manners for rebuilding the Hospital of St Catherine 1826:
TOP elevations
BOTTOM plan

new leases. So when the lease of the developed part of St John's Farm expired in 1813, new leases had been granted, the fines for which totalled £5,000. One-third had been promptly divided between the residents of St John's as laid down by the Trevor award. This would have given each resident a lump sum of about £139, while the master received about £3,333. Some properties in Avon, Monmouth and Princes Streets and Beaufort Square had been leased by Dr. Chapman to his own steward, the Bath solicitor John Physick, without the payment of any fine. However, this was explained. Physick had simply held the properties in trust for St John's until new lessees could be found.[558] The Commission was satisfied. It was not until later in the century that the fundamental inequity of this division of the fines was challenged.

With the Corporation charities, the situation was much as the eighteenth-century commission had found it. All was in order at Bellott's Hospital. It was now kept open from Lady Day (25 March) to Michaelmas (29 September) each year. The patients were cared for by a resident nurse, supplied with medicines and attended regularly by an apothecary and the physician appointed from Lady Scudamore's gift, at this time Dr John Ford Davis. The physician was no longer expected to treat all the poor coming to Bath, but only those in Bellott's, which was accepted by the Commission as a reasonable return for £8 a year. The Corporation produced impeccable accounts. The only fault that could be found was that the smaller parts of the Ludwell estate had been leased for three lives, rather than 21 years, as laid down in the foundation deed. The Corporation promised amendment as soon as possible.[559]

It was King Edward's School and St Catherine's Hospital that presented problems. The Brougham Commission accepted St Catherine's without question as part of King Edward's foundation. Nor did they have any complaint about the running of it. The 14 rooms housed 10 poor women who were paid 3s 6d a week each and a black gown every two years, along with another four women who received no pay or gown. St Catherine's had become a single-sex charity. Vacancies in the paid places were generally filled from among the four who only had a free room.

However, the decree of 1735 had been completely ignored. Bath Corporation had made no attempt to disentangle the Edwardian endowment. With the documents before them, the Commissioners could appreciate the difficulties. They managed to identify the five properties listed by the jurors in 1735. These had yielded an average annual income of £86 13s in recent years, while the Corporation was paying out about £100 a year for the Black Alms charity alone. The schoolmaster's salary was £84 a year. Then there was the cost of school repairs. Building a new school in Broad Street had cost the Corporation £3,933 13s 9d between 1752 and 1755. It looked as though the Corporation's charitable outgoings far exceeded the income from the Edwardian endowment. In fact Edward had given the city around 100 properties, but which were they? The Corporation acted swiftly to forestall further investigation. On 24 April 1820, it resolved that Fountain Buildings (on the site of St Werburg's), the White Hart, the Bell Inn and Monk's Mill

558 *Report of the Commission for Charities*, **4**, 288-89, 523-24.
559 *Ibid*, 292-95, 297, 530-33.

St Catherine's Hospital in Black Alms

April-1851.

83
St Catherine's Hospital in 1851

should be set apart as the estate of the charity. (Westgate House had been demolished.) After surveying the properties and seeking the approval of the Bishop of Bath and Wells, the Corporation passed a formal resolution on 25 May 1822 to keep separate accounts for the Grammar School and Black Alms.[560]

Two years later the new United Hospital was begun on the site of the old rectory house of St James, north of St Catherine's Hospital. If St Catherine's was moved elsewhere, then the old site could be vacated for the use of the new hospital. The Corporation had a free plot south of Bath Street and plans were drawn up for the new building in September 1826.[561] The cost was estimated at £1800. However, after the censures of the Brougham Commission, the Corporation acted with care. Under an Act of 1821, this exchange of property required a trustee to act for the charity. In October 1828 the mayor wrote to the bishop asking him to nominate a trustee. The mayor stressed the benefits to the charity. The present building was so ancient and ruinous as to be positively dangerous. To make it safe would cost far more than the charity revenues permitted. The Corporation therefore proposed to build a new, more commodious hospital at its own expense, with comfortable and healthy apartments. At the end of the year the City Surveyor, George Manners, was instructed to start building.[562] An inscription on the present hospital tells us that it was completed in 1829.

The Manners design is in keeping with the times (81-3). The passion for nostalgic architecture had taken root in the previous century and now was sending up awkward, uncertain shoots everywhere. A mock-Tudor style, with gables, mullions and hood-moulds no doubt seemed appropriate for a charity that now claimed to be founded by Edward VI. The neat ashlar and perfect geometry give the game away. This is a Georgian building playing charades. Still the desire to express the antiquity of Bath's first municipal charity is strangely touching. More importantly the residents now had modern accommodation. When Sophia Dillon died there in 1870, after 12 years in the hospital, her relations expressed their gratitude for the comfortable home she had been given.[563]

The age of reform

In the 1830s pressure for electoral reform swept the country. It was to bring in its wake a major change for the Bath charities. Initially the aim was to broaden the electorate for members of parliament. Bath MPs were selected by just thirty people - the mayor, aldermen and councillors, so thousands of Bathonians joined the campaign for change. The Reform Act of July 1832 extended the vote to over 28,000 Bath citizens – those who had property worth £10. There was great excitement in the city when an election was called in December 1832. After a vitriolic 'poster war', Bath elected the popular local liberal General Charles Palmer and fiery radical newcomer John Roebuck. Roebuck aimed to destroy closed corporations like Bath's, in which power

560   Ibid 269-83; 5, 453-55; 6, 567-73.

561   BaRO Philip George Papers, King Edward's, Chancery 13.

562   BaRO plans, Philip George Papers bundle 84.

563   BMCA BMC/3 1866-73, 256 and undated cutting.

84
Residents in St Catherine's Hospital courtyard around 1900

85
William Hunt (1800-1885) as Mayor of Bath in 1869. He was a Trustee of Bath Municipal Charities for nearly half a century. Of the original trustees appointed he was the only one who survived to see the Municipal Charities take over the management of St John's Hospital. Portrait by Edwin L. Long

had been wielded by a tiny elite. He found many like minds in the new parliament, which in 1835 passed the Municipal Corporations Act. It was the end of the old oligarchies. Now the Corporation of Bath had to be elected by its citizens.[564]

Under the new Act corporation charities were to be managed by a separate body,[565] so the Bath Municipal Charities Trust was born. The Master of the Rolls was presented with a list of substantial and upright citizens of Bath. They included two of Bath's leading Radicals, James Crisp and William Hunt. Hunt had chaired Roebuck's election committee.[566] On 17 October 1836 the Master of the Rolls appointed seventeen of them (appendix 4) as Trustees of the Free Grammar School, the Black Alms (St Catherine's Hospital), Bellott's Hospital and various gifts to the Corporation including Lady Moyer's, Lady Scudamore's, Lady Booth's and Sir Thomas White's.[567] The status of St John's was as yet unclear. The Corporation held the patronage, so was it a municipal charity? The point was settled by Lord Chancellor Cottenham in 1837, who ruled that St John's was an ecclesiastical and not a municipal trust. The master therefore retained control, though this was not to last.

The Trustees instigated a Chancery suit against Bath Corporation to reclaim more of the Edwardian endowment. James Crisp was the force behind it. His determination and stamina pressed the case on for 15 wearying years.[568] A solicitor's clerk working on it used a friend of his, Thomas Fisher, to elucidate the sixteenth-century Crown rental of ex-priory properties. Fisher was more enthusiastic than expert. Still one further property was finally wrung from the Corporation in 1851.[569]

A new scheme for King Edward's School and St Catherine's Hospital was issued by Chancery on 9 June 1849. This established rules of procedure for the Trustees and gave them the power to appoint a salaried clerk or secretary. It was only fitting that Thomas Fisher should become the secretary. The apparatus of the present trust was now in place. The Trustees had to act within a framework of provisions for the running of the charity, although some flexibility was permitted to meet changing circumstances. It laid down that St Catherine's was to house 14 poor women of Bath aged 55 or over. They were to be paid 3s 6d each Saturday morning (5s if the income permitted) and given a black cloth cloak worth 30s every alternate year. All must attend some place of public worship at least twice every Sunday, unless prevented by illness or incapacity.[570] The wording here is significant. No longer were the 'city almsfolk' tied to the Abbey Church. Freedom of worship was accepted. However, two very different charities remained yoked together by their history. It was not until 1872 that the logical step was taken of separating King Edward's. The management of the school and endowment then passed to a new board of governors, who were required to pay £280 a year out of the endowment towards support of St Catherine's Hospital, which remained with the Bath Municipal Charity Trustees.[571]

Meanwhile Bath Corporation petitioned Chancery in 1849 for permission to sell the patronage of St John's.[572] The hospital residents by this time were

564 Neale, 337-9, 343-50, 364; Brooks.

565 *Statutes of the United Kingdom* **13**, 1013-1065: 5 & 6 William IV cap. 76, especially clause 71.

566 Neale, 347.

567 BaRO Philip George Papers, King Edward's 6.

568 BMCA BMC/3 1852-55: tribute to James Crisp after his death 24 August 1852.

569 The former Warborough (St Werburg's) Mead, on which Bladud's Buildings had been erected. BMCA BMC/8 Fisher to Bath Municipal Trustees 25 November 1862; BMC/3 1858-60 St John's, 39- 42; BMC/3 1861-5, 82.

570 *The Scheme for the Future Government...of the Free Grammar School and Saint Catherine's Hospital* (1849).

571 BMCA BMC/3 1866-73, 370; StCH/1.

572 BaRO Council Book 1843-54, 397.

The humble Petition of Six Poor Men and Women
Living in Darkness and Dampness
in the Rich St. John's Hospital of Bath.

——————

"Enlighten our dismal Darkness"
"we beseech the Oh! DUNCAN."

IMPROVEMENTS OF BATH.

——————

I wish to bring into public notice the neglected and decaying part of the City about Hetling court, Chandos house, and St. John's Chapel court and premises, for as a Local Act is likely to be obtained—now, if ever, seems to be the time to improve that Neighbourhood.

As regards the office of Master to St. John's Hospital—it is a sinecure in the gift of the Corporation—since he has no parish duty, and the preaching, and the reading of prayers in the Chapel, have been assiduously performed for him.

An admission of more Trustees being about to take place, some alteration for the benefit of *many more* Inmates might be made; and I therefore intreat some of the Corporation, or any other benevolent persons, to view and examine the *dark and confined* Rooms, in which the aged Poor have to finish their lives, and probably some Subscribers might be admitted to assist its extent and improvement.

AN OBSERVER.

Bath, 24th February, 1851.

86
Two pleas for the reformation of St John's Hospital

becoming desperate. They were surrounded by damp and decay, misery and neglect, while the mastership was a rich sinecure. In the past they and their sympathisers might have grumbled quietly, but the old order had been overturned. They shouted. In February 1851 a flyer was printed pleading for the Corporation 'or any other benevolent persons' to view the 'dark and confined rooms, in which the aged poor have to finish their lives'. Another flyer besought Bath's Radical MP Viscount Duncan to 'enlighten our dismal darkness' (86). The language was powerful, the sense of injustice strong. Whether or not Duncan used his influence, Lord Chancellor Truro decided in 1851 that St John's was not an ecclesiastical, but a municipal charity (reversing the decision of his predecessor.) Deprived of the power to sell, the Corporation wanted to appoint members of its own body as Trustees, but this too was frustrated. Thomas Fisher claimed that the Mastership of St John's was part of the Crown property granted by Edward VI for charitable purposes.[573] This was nonsense, but it served its purpose. In 1853 the future patronage of St John's Hospital was vested in the Bath Municipal Charity Trustees by order in Chancery.[574]

The Trustees immediately started to prepare a new scheme for the hospital, which would bring it under their management. Ten new Trustees had been appointed to fill vacancies in 1852, including Thomas Jolly of the Milsom Street business (appendix 4). This was the team that now considered the future of St John's.[575] They included strong churchmen of several denominations, but opinion on the religious question did not divide along predictable lines. Jolly, a member of the Church of England, even suggested that the chapel should be closed altogether. While he was overruled, the majority favoured a clause proposed by another firm supporter of the C of E, Augustus Barretté, which did not restrict residents to worship in the chapel. He 'did not want to deprive his dissenting fellow citizens of participation in charities which should be open to the whole community',[576] a wise approach to an issue upon which feelings were easily inflamed.

Nonconformity was strong in Bath. There were sects to suit every taste, who met in each other's houses until sufficient chapels could be built. Daniel Harrison, who described himself in the 1830s as 'the inventor of the new system of mental calculation' lived in 1 Chandos Buildings and registered a room next door in no. 2 as a Dissenter's Meeting House. It had become a Baptist chapel by 1849.[577] Meanwhile a room in Hetling House was used for a few years by a splinter group from the Somerset Street Baptist Chapel.[578]

These were years of ferment for England's charities. Since print was cheap and literacy growing, the swirling currents of opinion were splashed liberally upon the pages of a growing press. Public debates were published verbatim including noises off. Reports of speeches would be interspersed with (cheers) or (cries of 'shame'), to convey the atmosphere. Nor did the press stop at merely reporting. Journals would thunder out denunciations as they saw fit. The power of the press is one of the themes of Anthony Trollope's *The Warden* (1855), the first of his popular Barsetshire novels. Set in the cathedral town

573   *Ibid*, pp.528, 612, 627; *Bath Journal* 9 June 1860; BMCA BMC/3 1858-60 St John's, 41-5: letters Thomas Fisher to Chancery 11 November 1851, 29 June 1852.

574   *Law Reports Chancery Division 1875-6*, **2** (1876), 559; BMCA BMC/3 1858-60 St John's, 51-2.

575   BMCA BMC/3 1858-1860 St John's.

576   *St John's Hospital…Meeting held at the Guildhall*.

577   SRO D/D/RM 11; *Bath Directory* (1837), (1849), 100.

578   SRO D/D/RM 11; BaL TS K. J. Birch, 'The Baptists of Bath', 27 and appendix 5.

87
The old Bellott's Hospital by Henry Venn Lansdown

of Barchester, it tells the tale of an ancient hospital which becomes the focus of a national scandal. While the value of its endowment was rising, the income of the inmates had been fixed long before. The ever-increasing remainder went into the pocket of its Warden, a clerical post held by the Cathedral Precentor. Some have supposed *The Warden* to be based on St John's Hospital,[579] but Trollope privately admitted that his model was the Hospital of St Cross at Winchester. Trollope went to school at Winchester, so naturally he was gripped by the Chancery case involving the Hospital of St Cross in 1853. Many of its details are mirrored in the novel.[580] *The Warden* beautifully illustrates the spreading unease over cases such as these.

In Bath the able pen of Walter Savage Landor was recruited to expose conditions in St John's. He wrote to *The Examiner* in September 1855:

> Sir, I was desired, a few days ago, to visit a hospital here called the Blue Alms. The surgeon conducted me through a dark passage into a darker chamber, apparently very low, but I could not see clearly the ceiling. The humane surgeon had removed its old inmate, who was suffering by the close and noxious air. Only the lower rooms are allowed to the poor and sick, the upper are let out for lodgings. The beneficiary chaplain receives several hundreds a year, six or seven. His name is Phillott. The hospital is such a dungeon as no criminal would be confined in, even after condemnation...Before the Reformation the poor were fed by the clergy; since the Reformation the clergy have been fed by the poor.

Help was on its way. A series of parliamentary commissions had worked diligently through into the 1830s. Now the time was ripe to create a permanent regulatory body. The Charity Commission of England and Wales was formed by the Charitable Trusts Act of 1853.[581] It had powers not only of enquiry, but of advice, arbitration and authorisation. It could permit charities to sell, buy or develop real estate. Legal proceedings on behalf of charitable trusts could not be taken without its permission. Even so new schemes to establish or vary the purpose of a trust could still only be legalised by Chancery or Act of Parliament. It was a logical development for the Charitable Trusts Act of 1860 to give this power to the Charity Commission. These Acts remained in force for the next century.[582]

The Act of 1853 had immediate repercussions in Bath. As it chanced the Master of St Mary Magdalen, the Revd. John Allen, died in the same year and the Government received a flood of applications for the post. Thomas Fisher leapt into action. He urged the Lord Chancellor, the Prime Minister and the Solicitor General that St Mary Magdalen ought to be a charitable institution and its funds ought not to line the pockets of a non-resident master. The Lord Chancellor therefore declined to fill the vacancy.[583] Instead the Charity Commission approved a new scheme for St Mary Magdalen, which was authorised by Act of Parliament on 14 July 1856. This placed what was now to be called the Magdalen Charity under the control of the Municipal Charities of Bath. It was the appropriate authority. Holloway by this time was in effect a suburb of Bath; in 1900 the parish of Lyncombe and Widcombe was legally incorporated into the city.

579 Young, 16.

580 Trollope, *The Warden*, with introduction by O. Chadwick (London 1995), xii-xv.

581 Amended in 1855. *Statutes of the United Kingdom* **21**, 912-24 (16 & 17 Vict. c.137); **22**, 919-24 (18 & 19 Vict. c.124).

582 Nathan, 5-6.

583 BMCA BMC/8 Letter Fisher 25 November 1862; BMC/3 1861-5, 83.

88
Bellott's Hospital today

The new scheme provided for a chaplain, whose services would be paid for out of pew rents. The remainder of the income was to be invested and accumulated until the sum of £5000 was raised, with which to buy or build a new home for 'poor idiot children' from Bath or thirty miles around. The Commission was enlightened in its approach. It envisaged this institution not only caring for such children, but training and improving them 'to the utmost attainable extent'.[584] On taking over, the Trustees found that Mrs Sarah Chunn was still occupying the hospital rent-free although the last idiot in her charge had died. However, she was also the sextoness of the chapel, keeping it clean and opening pews, so the Trustees decided to leave her in possession.[585] Magdalen Cottage has remained the home of the Magdalen Chapel caretaker ever since.

Meanwhile the future of Bellott's Hospital was under review. Was there still a need for it? It had been long overshadowed by Bath General Hospital (now the RNHRD). Applications were falling. When the Bath Municipal Charity Trustees took over Bellott's they did their best to advertise its existence by printing leaflets, which they circulated to every parish for twenty miles round, but to no great effect.[586] Another problem was the seventeenth-century building. It was now so dilapidated that on 23 April 1853 the Trustees decided to close it as unsafe. Should it be rebuilt? If so, how were the funds to be raised? Also the lease by Tobias Rustat had long since expired and had never been renewed. The Charity Trustees felt that a new lease was imperative if they were to rebuild and deferred the whole matter until St John's Hospital should come into their hands.[587] One suspects a lack of enthusiasm for the struggle to maintain a charity of no benefit to Bathonians. While Bellott's remained restricted to visitors, the General Hospital had opened itself to Bathonians in 1835.[588]

When Bath General Hospital announced plans for a new wing in 1856, it seemed as though the perfect solution had presented itself. Why not use Bellott's gift to endow a ward there which would carry his name? Even the Charity Commission initially advised that Bellott's should be absorbed by the larger hospital. The General Hospital approved the offer in 1857. By now, though, a chorus of disapproval was ringing out. At a public meeting at the Guildhall on 1 September 1857, Dr. Randle Falconer, physician at the General Hospital, spoke in favour of the absorption of Bellott's, but he was in the minority. The meeting was in favour of rebuilding. Meanwhile the Revd. Phillott helpfully agreed to grant a new lease of Bellott's Hospital at a nominal rent. In a complete about-face, the Trustees then decided in 1858 to rebuild Bellott's. The Charity Commission devised a new scheme which would permit enough to be borrowed from the charity estate to make this possible.[589]

Rebuilding began in 1859. In a touch typical of the age, a bottle containing a list of the Trustees and a copy of the scheme was placed below the foundation stone on 7 June. The architects were the partners Cotterell and Spackman, Surveyors to the Municipal Charities.[590] In December there was a timely

584   *An Act for…Saint Mary Magdalen Hospital near Bath* (1856).

585   BMCA BMC/3 1855-58, 165-6.

586   Falconer, 4-5.

587   BMCA BMC/3 1852-5, 83.

588   Rolls, *Hospital of the Nation*, 59.

589   BMCA BMC/3 1855-8; Falconer; *Bellott's Hospital, Bath. Scheme for the Management* (London 1858).

590   BMCA BH/9/2.

windfall. General Joseph Smith of the East India Company Service had died in Bath in 1790, leaving a legacy of £500 to the Bath hospitals, which had been lying forgotten in Chancery ever since, where it had grown to about £3,500. The Court of Chancery awarded £1,055 8s 4d of this to Bellott's Hospital. Plans were at once made for two extensions to the new building, one containing day rooms, the other a bathroom, dressing room and coal store.[591] The new hospital was opened on 1 August 1860.

Although 30 years later than St Catherine's, Bellott's is a clumsier exercise in nostalgia. The old coat of arms was placed over the door and mock-medieval relieving arches over the windows, like raised eyebrows (88). The half-hearted gesture fails to captivate. The old Bellott's was a charming, if crumbling, anachronism in a Georgian city. The new Bellott's simply looks perpetually startled by its surroundings. But visitors using the bright new building were delighted. In March 1875 a man slowly recovering from a six-month attack of rheumatic gout and fever was recommended by his doctor to try the Bath waters. He took lodgings at first, but finding Bellott's very different from what he had expected, he moved there and preferred it. He found that the matron made inmates comfortable and was surprised that the wards were not generally full.[592] The Trustees did their best to advertise; new leaflets were printed extolling the amenities.[593]

89
Dr Randle Wilbraham Falconer, physician at the General Hospital 1856-81. In 1859 he became a Trustee of St John's Hospital. He was mayor of Bath in 1857 and president of the British Medical Association in 1878

The battle for St John's

Dr Randle Falconer was among a new group of Trustees appointed to the Municipal Charities in 1859,[594] who revised the proposed new scheme for St John's Hospital. Falconer successfully pressed for the removal of the clause giving freedom of worship. There was a wave of outrage in Bath. In a packed and heated public meeting, Falconer again found himself fighting the tide of opinion.[595] But this was just a skirmish before the real war. The Trustees were agreed on the need for radical change in the way the estate of St John's was managed, but they faced heavy opposition from its tenants, as well as the master. All the ingredients were there for lengthy legal action.

The Charity Commission reported in 1860 that the hospital owned between 300 and 400 houses in Bath and its neighbourhood, but these were let on such low rents that the total rental was only around £250 p.a. The problem was the tradition of letting on leases for three lives. Periodic fines for new leases boosted the average yearly income to around £1,260, but the annual value of hospital estates if in hand would be about £12,000. At the instigation of the Bath Municipal Charity Trustees, the Attorney-General filed an information in Chancery on 16 August 1864 with two aims: an immediate order banning the master from letting any more property on fines or long leases or lower than the best obtainable rents, and the settlement of a new scheme. The Bath newspapers, fed full details by the Charity Trustees, gave pages of dense print to the story. They indignantly pointed out that the master, a non-resident clergyman, took two-thirds of the income, leaving only around

591 BMCA BMC/3 1858-61, 123, 126, 129, 139-40; BH/9/1: plans by Cotterell and Spackman.

592 *Somerset and Wiltshire Journal* 29 May 1875, letter to the editor.

593 BMCA BH/10/3: leaflets printed c.1875.

594 BMCA BMC/3 1858-61, 89, 104.

595 *St John's Hospital ... Meeting held at the Guildhall.*

£420 p.a. for the real purposes of the charity. It was a matter of urgency to have a new scheme in place, since James Phillott was now very aged. Were he to die the vacancy would have to be filled within six months.[596] No sooner was the Chancery case filed than Phillott granted new leases, though whether for his own benefit or that of anxious lessees is unclear.[597] On 22 December Chancery judged that the Trevor award was not binding and could be superseded. All the St John's properties had been erected for 95 years and some for 125 years, so some tenants had enjoyed properties much longer than the 99 years considered reasonable for a building lease. They had no right to renewals of their leases at fixed rents.[598] Naturally the lessees took a different view and their case was presented at Lincoln's Inn on 15 November 1865.[599]

In the midst of this legal wrangling, James Phillott died at the rectory house of Stanton Prior on 30 December 1865. *Keenes' Bath Journal* printed a wry obituary:

> In the absence of any recorded distinction, academic or otherwise, gained by Mr Phillott himself, we may, without disparaging whatever abilities he possessed, fairly conclude that he was mainly indebted for his rich and multifarious livings to the circumstance that he was a member of an ancient and influential Bath family, who had the dispensing of the rich morsels pertaining to what some people persist in designating 'the good old times'.[600]

His death brought matters to a climax. The Bath Charity Trustees quickly convened a special meeting. They hoped to appoint a chaplain, not a new master, and use the money saved to extend the benefits of the charity to a larger number. With Bath's population now around 60,000, the need for care for the poor elderly had increased. They were also in favour of commuting life-hold to 75-year leases.[601] The lessees of St John's responded by holding their own meeting to consider how best to protect their interests. About two dozen attended, with Jerom Murch, a leading light of Bath Corporation, in the chair. As a result the Charity Trustees met again on 25 January 1866 to confer with a deputation from the lessees.[602]

The momentum of events was preserved by the Attorney-General, who sent a representative to Bath on 3 February to receive suggestions for a new scheme for St John's. His visit was advertised in advance and the meeting was packed. Alderman William Hunt spoke for the Bath Charity Trustees, while Murch spoke for the lessees. Murch's own interest was in keeping St John's land near his own house as open country, preserving his view. He had purchased the leases for that purpose and feared that under the Charity Trustees, the land would be let for building. Naturally he urged a clause in the scheme giving lessees the right to purchase. Three charitable institutions also put in pleas to purchase the site of their buildings, or that part of it which stood on St John's land: Bellott's Hospital, the Mineral Water Hospital and the Bath Penitentiary for Fallen Women at Ladymead House in Walcot Street. There was even a deputation from the Bath Anti-Pew Association, objecting to a proposal to let those pews in the hospital chapel which were not required by inmates. Pew-rents would exclude the local poor.[603]

596 *Bath Chronicle* 18 August 1864; *Keenes' Bath Journal, Bath Express* 20 August 1864.

597 BMCA StJH/1/1 1857-1865.

598 Peach, 44-5; *In Chancery. Cause between … attorney general and … the hospital of St. John … in Bath* (privately printed 1864).

599 *Keenes' Bath Journal* 2 December 1865; and see *Bath Chronicle* 20 December 1865.

600 *Keenes' Bath Journal* 6 January 1866 and see the *Express* 6 January 1866.

601 *Bath Journal* 6 January 1866; *Keenes' Bath Journal* 6 January 1866.

602 *Bath Express* 20 January 1866; *Keenes' Bath Journal* 27 January 1866.

603 *Bath Journal* 27 January 1866; *Bath Chronicle* 8 February 1866; *Bath Express* 10 February 1866.

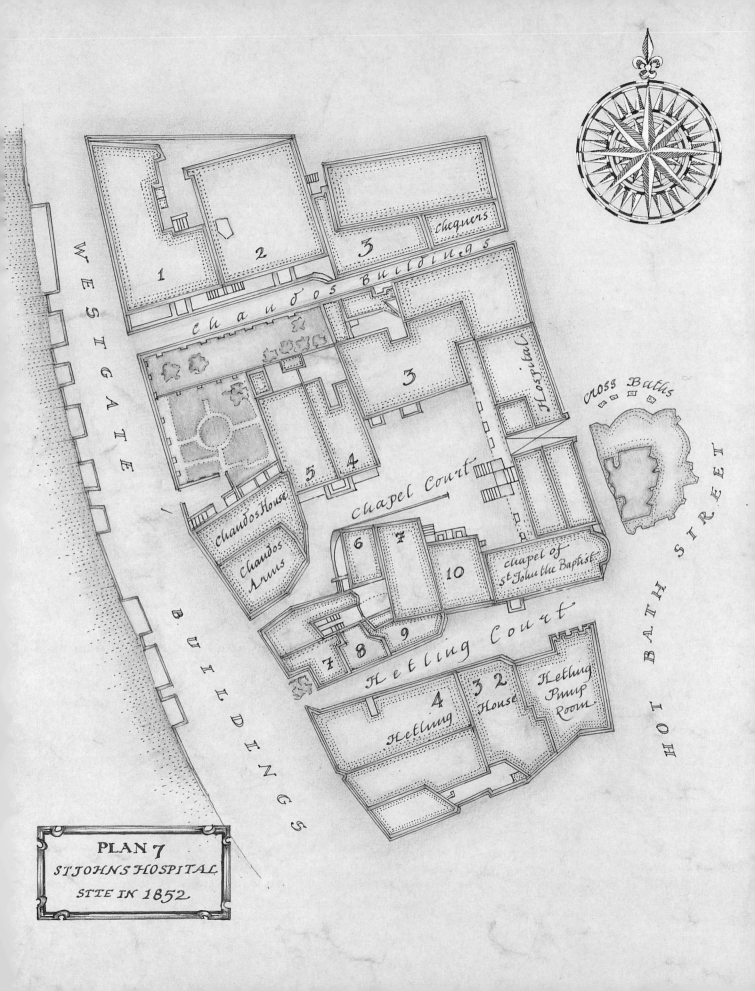

WESTGATE

Chandos Buildings

1

2

3   Chequers

Chandos Buildings

3

Hospital

CROSS Baths

5   4

Chandos House

Chandos Arms

Chapel Court

6   7

10   chapel of St John the Baptist

7   8   9

Hetling Court

7

4   3 2   Hetling
Hetling   House   Pump
Room

BUILDINGS

HOT BATH STREET

PLAN 7
ST JOHNS HOSPITAL
STTE IN 1852

After this promising start, Chancery then took eight years to mull the matter over. In the meantime the Attorney-General would not permit the appointment of a new master either by the Charity Trustees or the Bishop of Bath and Wells. So the Revd. William Luckman, who had been appointed chaplain of St John's by Phillott in 1863, continued to serve the chapel unpaid. Provision for the three remaining residents of St John's was made by the lawyer of the late master, who held the funds of St John's.[604]

However, no-one could complain of lack of consultation. When the Attorney-General had devised a scheme for St John's, his solicitor appeared at Bath Guildhall on 23 January 1874 to receive comments on it. The Attorney-General considered that, as a church charity, Trusteeship should be restricted to members of the Church of England, which roused strong protest from the Bath Charity Trustees. Thomas Jolly revived his idea of letting out the chapel, as there were other places of worship nearby, but failed to win the audience. One clergyman felt that it was important to have a chapel close at hand for the sick and aged who could not walk far to worship; to destroy the chapel would be 'sweeping away one of the living witnesses of the purposes of the foundation.'[605] The Attorney-General then grafted some of these suggestions, including the cancellation of the religious restriction, into the prepared scheme. On 8 June 1877 Chancery finally issued a new constitution for the hospital, placing it under the Bath Municipal Charity Trustees.[606]

Rebuilding by Bath Municipal Charities

At last the Charity Trustees could act and they lost no time. Firstly, appointments were made. William Luckman was selected as master.[607] The paid officers of the Municipal Charities – Edward Turner Payne (Clerk and Receiver) and Henry Spackman (Surveyor) – gained the same posts with St John's. The latter post, by an oversight in the scheme, was actually illegal. No provision was made for a Surveyor to St John's until 1911, but one was certainly needed.

The new scheme provided for the immediate repair and enlargement of the hospital to accommodate 12 almspeople (and their husbands and wives) in greater comfort. On 29 August Spackman reported on the state of the old hospital rooms and the floors above. He had prepared plans to convert the whole building (90). Of the original three passages through the building, one was to be blocked on the street side, while another became a private entrance to the porter's lodging, leaving only the centre passage open. Off this two internal stairs led up to segregated accommodation for men (on the south) and women (on the north). Each apartment had a bedroom and sitting room and there were communal wash-houses on the ground floor, fed with mains water. John Wood's external stair was redundant and it was removed. It was a major remodelling. Spackman considered the walls, main timbers and roof to be sound, but windows, doors, floors, ceilings and internal fittings should be ripped out. This provided the opportunity to replace all the small-

604 *Keenes' Bath Journal* 6 January 1866; Peach, 33.
605 *Bath Chronicle* 29 January 1874.
606 BMCA BMC/1.
607 BMCA StJH/13/1.

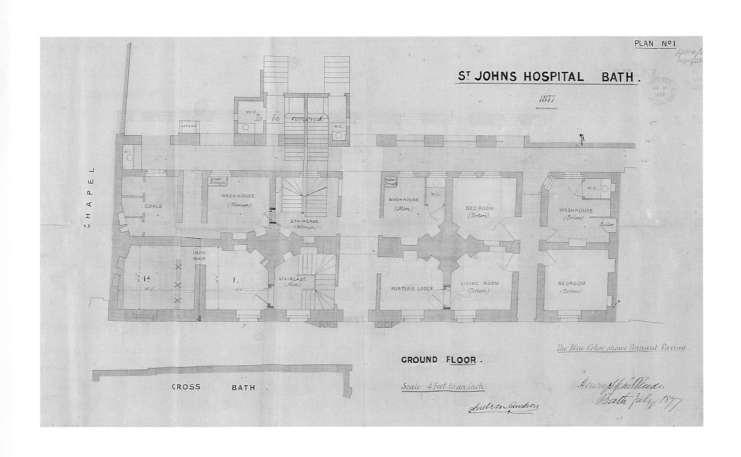

90
Henry Spackman's plan for alterations to St John's Hospital (BMCA StJH/11/2)

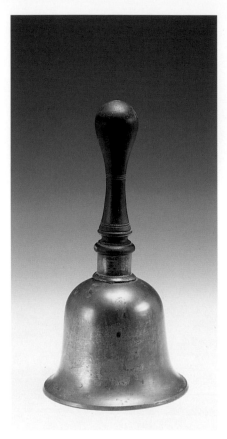

91

The porter's bell, rung to warn visitors that St John's was about to be locked up for the night

paned Georgian windows with sheet glass, and raise the ceilings and enlarge the windows of the top floor to let in more light. To give the façade towards the Cross Bath more dignity, cornices were added above the windows. The contract for the work was signed on 25 October with a finishing date of 25 February 1878. In March gas fittings were supplied to light the building.[608] Dark and dismal rooms were to be a thing of the past.

Meanwhile a married couple were selected as porter and matron and Dr Fox appointed as Medical Officer. It was not until 1 July that all was ready. The Mayor of Bath was asked to speak at the official opening. As irony would have it that year's mayor was Jerom Murch. His approving comment that the estate of St John's 'had already greatly increased in value and was likely to yield a still larger income' reads oddly from the man who did not want development spoiling his view. However, his pleasure that religious restrictions had been removed was genuine. Murch had been an Unitarian minister.[609]

New rules for the inmates were posted up in the hospital. The outer doors were to be unlocked at 7 a.m. and closed by the porter at 10 a.m., after he had rung a bell warning visitors to depart. The inmates were to 'conduct themselves with becoming respect towards the Trustees and the Master and all their officers'. The porter and matron were to check all gas taps every day and inspect the rooms at least once a week for 'disorder or want of proper cleanliness'. It was a strict regime. The hospital scheme permitted the expulsion of almspeople 'given to insobriety, or immoral, insubordinate, or unbecoming conduct'.[610] However, the Trustees took it in turns to visit the almsfolk regularly, to check on their welfare. The first visitors found the inmates most grateful and contented with their new home, apart from the lack of cupboards. That essential item had been forgotten.[611]

The Trustees then turned their minds to the chapel. In the spring of 1879 Spackman surveyed it and condemned the floor. It was old and decayed and unpleasant smells built up when it was closed overnight. The roof needed re-covering and the old windows replacing. Once again Spackman's instinct was to gut and refit. The box pews were now old-fashioned, and plain sash windows were no longer considered appropriate for churches. Gothic had become almost compulsory in ecclesiastical architecture. However, after the expensive refitting of the hospital, St John's could barely fund necessities. Frills like window tracery were out of the question. So the Municipal Charities dipped into one of their other pockets and lent St John's £325 from Sir Thomas White's Charity to pay for most of the alterations, on the understanding that Luckman and his congregation would raise funds for the new windows. An agreement was signed with the builder George Cross in July.[612]

While excavating under the floor to lay concrete, the workmen found fragments of Norman, Gothic and Jacobean work, reminders of the antiquity of St John's. Once a new floor was in place the apse was laid with tiles, marble and Draycot stone steps. New pine benches were fitted and the pulpit replaced by a reading desk. As an afterthought, a new entrance was made to the vestry direct from the chapel, with a niche to display the mementoes of the original

608 BMCA StJH/11/2; BaRO Chapman calotypes: a photograph of the eastern façade before the remodelling by Spackman shows it without the present window cornices. It also shows the door to the northern passage, retained as the porter's private entrance.

609 *Bath and Cheltenham Gazette* 3 July 1878; Kolaczkowski, 157.

610 BMCA StJH/1/2 1882-88, rules pasted into the front of the volume. Also see StJH/13/9: porter's journal 1878-1884.

611 BMCA StJH/2/1: visitor's book.

612 BMCA StJH/11/2. The sum agreed initially was £295, but costs rose.

St. JOHN'S HOSPITAL, BATH.

DUTIES OF PORTER.

Issued by the Trustees of this Hospital under the powers conferred upon them by the Scheme under which the Hospital is administered.

The Porter with his Wife shall reside in the Apartments provided for them by the Trustees, and except with the consent of the Trustees shall not permit any person to reside with them and shall not receive any Visitors who shall stay for more than a week without the consent of the Master.

The Porter shall be responsible for closing the outer doors of the Hospital at 10 p.m. precisely, after which hour except in cases of urgency, no person not actually resident in the Hospital will be allowed to enter or remain in the Building.

The Porter shall be responsible for the cleanliness of the passages and staircases in the Building, also for the condition of the wash-houses, and will do all necessary dusting, washing, and cleaning in the Clerk's Office and Strong Room as directed by him.

The Porter shall light the gas in the passages and on the staircases and shall extinguish such lights every night before retiring for the night and shall exercise a general supervision over the gas arrangements in the Hospital.

The Porter shall keep the pavement adjoining the Hospital building clean and properly swept, pursuant to the directions of the Urban Sanitary Authority.

The Porter by himself or his Wife shall give any needful assistance directed by the Master, Trustees, or Medical Officer to invalid or decrepit Co-Brethern and Sisters.

The Porter shall give all needful assistance in the Chapel and Vestry as desired by the Master, and shall ring the Bell for the period of a quarter of an hour before each service and act as Sacristan.

The Porter by himself or his Wife shall keep the Chapel and Vestry clean and properly dusted and shall assist each week at the payment of the Co-Brethren and Sisters and the Out-pensioners.

The Porter shall keep a general watch over the persons who may seek or apply for entrance into the Hospital, so as to prevent the intrusion of improper persons.

The Porter shall record in a Journal the name of any Co-Brethren and Sister absent throughout the night without the leave of the Master or the Visitors.

The Porter by himself or his Wife shall visit the rooms of the Co-Brethren and Sisters at least once in each week and report in any case of disorder or want of proper cleanliness which may be observed.

Any infraction of the Regulations affecting the Co-brethren and Sisters shall be reported to the Master by the Porter who shall make an entry thereof in the Journal.

92
Duties of the porter at the renovated St John's Hospital

93
Harvest festival in St Michael's Chapel before the Second World War. All the stained glass was intact and the walls were decorated

chapel. Luckman raised funds not only for window tracery 'to a Florentine design' but for expensive stained glass from Ward and Hughes (93-4). It took several years and Revd. Luckman clearly drew heavily on his friends in the Church. Those commemorated by the windows included three clergymen, among them the Revd. John Skinner of Camerton, now best known for his Journal of a Somerset Rector. Luckman donated another window himself as a memorial to his own three children. The total cost of the windows was around £1,200,[613] which represented a tremendous effort for a small chapel.

Out into the community

The Trustees had been anxious to spread the income of St John's to benefit more of the needy, not just those in the hospital. The new scheme had the flexibility to permit this. The Trustees could give 10s a week to non-residents living in Bath or within three miles of the city limits.[614] Ten out-pensions were made available when the hospital re-opened.[615] By 1918 the number had grown to 139.[616]

The Trustees were also concerned with their social responsibilities elsewhere. It must have been an embarrassment to these upright citizens to find themselves collectively owning some of the worst slums in Bath (95). The development of St John's Mead had aimed at the middle rather than the upper end of the property market. When John Wood built North and South Parade by the river he had gone to the trouble of raising the ground above flood level. By contrast flooding was an annual problem in Avon Street. Effluent from its sewers, pigsties and a slaughter house would wash back into the house basements. No wonder that in the cholera outbreak of 1831, 27 out of 49 deaths in the city were in this street alone, while a number of the remaining deaths were in adjacent streets. By the time St John's came under the control of the Charity Trustees, Avon Street was notorious for poverty and vice.[617]

In July 1880 the city's medical officer of health, Dr. Brabazon, reported on the insanitary conditions of houses in Avon Street, concluding 'that the structural condition of many of these houses is quite enough to account for the lamentable attacks of disease which occur.' The immediate reaction of the Trustees was to pass this damning report on to the Charity Commission with a strong recommendation that the land be sold. However, subsequent discussions with the Commission and Bath Corporation produced acceptable proposals for change. St John's commissioned its own estate survey from Spackman, who agreed entirely with Dr. Brabazon. He reported that many of St John's properties were 'of very inferior character and in a bad state of repair' of which Avon Street was the worst.[618]

The Artizans' Dwellings Act of 1882 sought to encourage the provision of cheap but healthy accommodation for the industrious poor.[619] In 1883 Spackman viewed a range of such buildings in Ebury Street, London, which inspired plans for a similar block on Avon Street. Dilapidated buildings in

613   Peach, 48; StJH/11/2; three of the window's were not put in until 1883 (BMCA BMC/3).

614   Scheme for the Management ... of the Hospital of St John the Baptist ... in ... Bath (1877), clause 38.

615   BMCA StJH/14/1: register 1878-94, 81.

616   PSANHS Bath Branch 1914-18, 257-6; BMCA StJH/14/2: pensioner's receipt book 1915-9.

617   Neale, 211-17.

618   St John's Hospital: Abstract of Surveyor's Report (1882).

619   My thanks to Robin Lambert for useful discussion of this point.

94
The east window of St Michael's Chapel. The stained glass
by Ward and Hughes shows Christ among the lilies

New Court and Avon Street were pulled down to clear a site. In November 1885 St John's Buildings (96) was opened by the deputy mayor to a chorus of approval. It had five floors of bed-sitting rooms and flats to let, with accommodation on the ground floor for the caretaker and a shared laundry and drying room. The interior walls were glazed brick for cleanliness.[620] A set of rules posted on the walls (97) showed the concern of the Trustees with health and safety. All tenants had to be vaccinated and no infectious diseases were permitted. Children were not allowed to play on the stairs.

Perhaps it was also with the sensation of aiding a worthy cause that the Trustees in 1889 sold to the Rector and Churchwardens of Bath Abbey the virtual freehold of Hetling House. Canon Richard Brooke was granted a 200-year lease at an annual rent of £25.[621] So Hetling House became known as the Abbey Church House.

Meanwhile there had been slow progress with the Magdalen Charity. Soon after the Trustees took it over, they had made contact with another charity in Bath with the same aims, the School for Imbecile Children in Belvedere, founded in 1846.[622] By 1884 Edward Turner Payne, Clerk to the Charity Trustees, happened to be the sole surviving trustee of this institution. He suggested that the two charities should merge, and the Trustees urged this course upon the Charity Commissioners. The pace of discussion was forced in 1887 when the Lunacy Commissioners ordered the closure of the Belvedere home because it had too little space for exercise. Thirteen children needed to be rapidly rehoused. For years the search had been going on for a suitable site for the new Magdalen School.[623] Now the Trustees in desperation advertised for a house within 10 miles of Bath with three or four acres of land. Rockhall House on Combe Down with two acres of garden seemed ideal.[624] The Trustees were happily beating the owner down to an acceptable figure when the Charity Commissioners and Lunacy Commissioners wrote to say that Rockhall was far too small. However, extra land was available, so the purchase went ahead and an architect was appointed to design the necessary additions. Preparations were in train for the opening when the Lunacy Commissioners once more intervened. Unless a public footpath could be diverted, they could not give their approval. The Trustees could do nothing about the footpath and so began the search again for a suitable site, although the Rockhall school opened anyway in 1889. The amalgamation was agreed in principle and the Charity Commissioners began to prepare a new scheme for the combined charity.[625]

In the same year a 20-acre site on Claverton Down was bought with official approval and the Trustees could plan a purpose-built school. But they found that the cost would be well beyond the £5,000 envisaged by the Charity Commission. It was estimated at between £14,000 and £15,000. Even if the funds could be found, there would be nothing left to run the school. The plan therefore came to nothing and the Magdalen School remained at Rockhall.[626] The new scheme for the amalgamated charity was finally made legal on 29 January 1894.[627]

The move to Rockhall had divorced the charity from its chapel. The

620   BMCA StJH/1/2 1882-88, nos. 287, 351, 368, StJH/1/3 1882-90: Spackman report 16 June 1883, BMC F: plans and elevations; *Bath Herald* October 1885; *Bath Chronicle* 5 November 1885.

621   Including parts of the building which had been converted into separate dwellings (2-5 Hetling Court): BMCA StJH/7/137 (a).

622   BMCA BMC/3 1855-58, 116; Carpenter, 'The Bath Idiot and Imbecile Institution'.

623   BMCA BMA/3 1858-61, 10.

624   BMCA BMC/3 1881-7, nos. 862, 869; MH 11/1.

625   BMCA BMC/3 1881-7, nos. 349, 374, 393, 405, 412, 436, 438, 495, 531, MH/1/2.

626   BMCAe MH 1/4, MH/3 1888-89, MH/11/2. See Carpenter, 'The Bath Idiot and Imbecile Institution' for a more detailed account of the Rockhall school.

627   BMCA MH/3 1888-9: scheme for amalgamation 3 February 1891; *Scheme for the Management ... of the Magdalen Hospital School Approved ... on the 29th of January, 1894* (1917). Amended in 1904 (BMCA MH/1/6).

95-96
TOP A wood-engraving of Avon Street c.1870. By this time it was a notorious slum
BOTTOM St John's Buildings, Avon Street photographed in January 1974, just before demolition

children and those caring for them could scarcely walk the two and a half miles from Combe Down to services at Holloway. The Trustees had been happy to keep the chapel open while they had no other responsibilities under the charity, but faced with a choice between needy children and the chaplain's stipend, they voted on 11 June 1890 to discontinue services. However the Lord Chancellor did not agree and the chapel remained open.[628]

628   BMCA MH/2/2.

St. John's Hospital, Bath.
ARTIZANS' DWELLINGS.
RULES.

1.—The Rooms consist of 15 Sitting and Bedrooms, to be let, 7 in sets of 3, and 8 in pairs, and 6 single Living rooms, with the joint use in each case of a Laundry and Drying-room, and W.C. They will be let by the week, from Tuesday to Tuesday, seven days' notice on either side to terminate the tenancy. No application for rooms will be entertained unless every member of the Applicant's family has been Vaccinated. The Applicant must also agree to remove any person suffering from Infectious Disease from his rooms to the proper Hospital.

2.—The rents to be paid weekly, in advance, at the Porter's Office, on Mondays, between the hours of 8 and 10 a.m., or 5 to 8 p.m.

3.—No Arrears of Rent will be allowed, and immediate notice to quit will be served if the Rent be not paid in conformity with Regulation No. 2.

4.—The Passages, Stairs, and Water-Closets must be washed every Friday, and swept every morning before 10 o'clock. This must be done by the Tenants on each floor, in turn, but the Tenants may make arrangements with other persons to do such washing and sweeping for them, provided that such arrangements are approved by the Porter, and are made through him.

5.—Washing must be done only in the Laundries. Tenants will not be permitted to use the Laundries for the washing of any clothes but their own. No clothes shall be hung out of the Windows or on the Landings The Laundries and Drying-rooms will be placed at the disposal of the Tenants in rotation The Tenant of this set of rooms will have the use of the   Laundry for   hours on the   day in each week, and of the Drying-room for   hours on the following day. Each Tenant shall wash and cleanse the Laundries and Drying-room effectually after using the same.

6.—No Carpets, Mats. etc., can be permitted to be beaten or shaken after 8 o'clock in the morning. Refuse must not be thrown from the doors or windows. Each Tenant shall, before the hour of 9 a.m. on each day, remove from his room all Ashes, Refuse, or other Offensive Matter, and deposit the same in the proper receptacles provided for the purpose. Liquids, or anything likely to cause an obstruction, must not be thrown down the Dust Shafts; no Refuse may be thrown into the yard. The Tenants will be required to keep the Windows of their rooms cleaned and in proper order, and to cause their Chimneys to be swept at least once in every six months Coals will only be allowed to be brought into the building before 12 at Noon, and not later on any day.

7.—The Porter or Matron will inspect the Rooms of the Tenants at least once in each month, and report in the Porter's Journal any want of proper cleanliness which may be observed.

8.—Tenants must pay all costs for the repairs, etc., of Windows, Keys, and Grates, lost, broken, or damaged in their rooms.

9.—Children will not be allowed to play on the Stairs, in the Passages, or in the Laundries or Drying-rooms.

10.—Dogs must not be kept on the premises.

11.—Tenants cannot be allowed to Paper or Paint the walls of their rooms.

12.—No Tenant will be permitted to underlet, or take in Lodgers, or to keep a Shop of any kind.

13.—Disorderly or Intemperate Tenants will receive immediate notice to quit.

14.—At 11 p.m. the outer doors will be closed for the night, but each Tenant will, on payment of One Shilling, be provided with a key, to admit him at all hours. The key must be given up on the Tenant quitting his rooms, and the Shilling will then be returned to him.

15.—Tenants are required to report to the Porter any Births, Deaths, or Infectious Diseases occurring in their rooms.

16.—Any Tenant not complying with these Rules will receive notice to quit.

F. GOODALL, PRINTER, 18, WESTGATE BUILDINGS, BATH.   11244.

97
The rules posted at St John's Buildings

The Twentieth Century

Awareness of the past

Struggle and setback

The expanding hospital

Renovation

The changing face of St John's

Moving into the next century

Awareness of the past

The turn of the century saw a mood in St John's of reflection on the past. In 1875 woollen merchant Frederick Shum joined the Trustees and served as chairman from 1899 to 1912. He was fascinated by Bath's history and had a scholarly turn of mind, reflected in his election as a Fellow of the Society of Antiquaries of London in 1867.[629] In 1899 he published *Early Bath Books*, following this in 1913 with *A Catalogue of Bath Books ... on the Hot Mineral Springs*, which he described as the fruit of 75 years of enquiry and research.[630] He was a stalwart of the Somerset Archaeology and Natural History Society, particularly the Bath and District Branch.[631]

In March 1899 the Revd. Charles Shickle became Master of St John's. He had served the community in Bath in a variety of ways for more than 30 years. A native of Norwich, he fell in love with Bath when he came to it as a young curate and never left. From curacies in Twerton and Woolley he progressed to teaching at Bath College and then became Rector of Langridge in 1885.[632] Shickle developed a deep interest in the city's past. He was elected a Fellow of the Society of Antiquaries in 1902.[633] Although Shum had catalogued many printed works on Bath, they could only reveal a part of the city's history. So Shickle began reading original manuscripts. It was no easy task. Those before 1700 are written in unfamiliar scripts and sometimes in Latin. Shickle set himself the immense task of laboriously transcribing such records, so that they could be read by all. Local historians owe him a great debt. Although some Bath records had been published by the Somerset Record Society, Shickle felt that the city would benefit from its own series. His translation of Bath Corporation's medieval deeds became the first volume of the Bath Records Society.[634] Alas it was also the last volume. The enterprise died with him.

Naturally Shickle was particularly interested in the Bath Municipal Charities and made a mass of notes for a projected new history.[635] It was he who rediscovered the true origins of St Catherine's Hospital.[636] He loved to recapture the past. A Restoration-period chair in St John's intrigued him and he had a replica made for the boardroom.[637] He also presented the Trustees

629 *Bath Post Office Directory* 1875; BMCA BMC/3 1893-1902, 323; BMC/3 1903-13, 455-6; Library of the Society of Antiquaries of London.

630 Shum, vii.

631 *PSANHS* **41**, 117; **46**, 223, **53**, 216; *PSANHS Bath and District Branch* 1904-1908, 5, 39, 99, 145, 191.

632 BMCA StJH/1/2 1894-1900, no.1036; *Bath Chronicle and Herald* 31 December 1927: obituary.

633 Library of the Society of Antiquaries of London.

634 *Ancient Deeds*; *Bath Herald* 20 April 1922.

635 BMCA StJH/15/1.

636 BMCA BMC/3 1903-13, 233; *Ancient Deeds*, 4/104.

637 BMCA StJH/1/2 1906-11, 26-7.

98
Frederick Shum FSA, Chairman of the Trustees
of Bath Municipal Charities 1899-1912

99
Revd. C. W. Shickle FSA, Master of St John's
Hospital 1899-1927

638 Photographs of Tobias Rustat's portrait, the earliest deeds of St John and the papal decree regarding the cemetery, sketches of Bellott's and St Catherine's and old print of St Catherine's (BMCA StJH/1/2 1900-6, 106, 292; BMC/3 1903-13, 239; BMC/3 1913-24, 370).

639 *Bath Herald* 27 June 1904.

640 McLaughlin.

641 BMCA StJH/15/1, bundle 6. Rosewell House was known at the time as Bishop Butler's House. Also see the Trustees' obituary of Shickle, praising his constant concern for the residents and pensioners in his care: BMCA StJH/1/2 1927-32, no. 63.

642 BMCA StJH/1/2 1888-93, 197 (no.427).

643 BMCA StJH/1/2 1906-11, 490 (no.771), StJH/1/3 1908-18, 68 (no.472).

with pictures of historical interest.[638] Under the influence of Shum and Shickle the long association between St John's and Bath Corporation was gracefully acknowledged. In 1904 the Mayor of Bath and other members and officers of the Corporation were invited to a service in the chapel on the festival of St John the Baptist.[639] Representatives of the local authority have attended the annual event ever since.

Shum and Shickle were part of a rising tide of awareness of Bath's past, in particular the city's glorious architectural heritage. In 1909 this gave birth to the Old Bath Preservation Society.[640] Soon the Trustees of St John's found themselves under pressure. In 1910 the Society urged the removal of disfigurements from Rosewell House. Shickle was sympathetic, but helpless. As he pointed out, the charity had been founded to serve those in need and was struggling to meet the demand. Whatever Shickle's interest in the past, his feeling for present suffering was greater. He could only suggest that the Society might raise a subscription for the work.[641]

It was an omen of things to come. Bathonians were awakening to the riches around them. At first attention focused on the more eye-catching buildings, but as the twentieth century progressed the feeling grew among conservationists that Bath should be seen as a whole. It would be short-sighted to preserve only its architectural gems, when Georgian middle-class and artisan housing creates so much of the city's character. St John's owned swathes of Georgian buildings, most of which were not regarded as anything out of the ordinary when they were built. Some had become slums. At the start of the century it would have seemed senseless to the Trustees to put conservation of such buildings before their responsibilities to their pensioners and their tenants. By the end of the century, conservation had been accepted as another responsibility of Bath Municipal Charities.

Struggle and setback

However, the most dramatic change for St John's in the twentieth century was the turn of the tide in its finances. This was a slow and difficult business. As long leases expired, the charity could find its property returned in ruins. Investment in repairs or development was needed before it could be re-let on better terms.

By 1900 Chapel Court had become shabby and disreputable (100-101). The heyday of the spa had long passed. The Chandos development intended for fashionable visitors was now in a city centre that had been abandoned by the affluent in favour of the leafy suburbs. In 1890 prostitutes had to be cleared out of Chapel Court.[642] Chandos House was used by a firm of brewers and wine and spirit merchants, who ran the Chandos Arms (102-3). A clutter of workshops and similar buildings crowded between the former Middle House and Westgate Buildings (PLAN 7). The site was cramped; the buildings crumbling. So the Trustees razed the workshops in 1911 to make a garden for the inmates (104), later named after Revd. Shickle.[643]

100-101
Photographs c.1900 by Mowbray Green
LEFT Chapel Court
RIGHT No.6 Chapel Court

102-104

TOP Sketches from the *Bath and County Graphic* of Chandos House used by T. A. Pearce & Co, brewers and wine and spirit merchants. They sold their own brand of whisky called Chandos. The artist was told that the cellar had once been a debtors' prison. The truth is quite the reverse. From 1837 to 1846 there was a charity at Chandos House with funds for the release of those imprisoned for debt. With barrels of wine stored there, the iron grille on the cellar door was to prevent people breaking in, not breaking out

BOTTOM The Shickle garden with its original decorative ironwork

105
The boardroom in 4 Chapel Court and its furnishings and fittings

106
The Chapel of St Michael before the
Second World War. Charles Matthews,
Porter of St John's Hospital and Verger
from 1925, stands before the railings

When the lease expired on 4 and 5 Chapel Court in 1907, the Trustees seized the opportunity to allocate some space to their own use. Two rooms on the first floor of no. 4 were thrown into one to create a panelled boardroom (105). The front room below became an office with a telephone, while other rooms were allocated to a newly-appointed caretaker and handyman. The front room on the ground floor of no. 5 became the pension room, where the residents were paid each week.[644] The charity was still far from wealthy; St John's account was periodically in overdraft.[645] It was not yet the time to expand. So, apart from those three rooms, 4 and 5 remained leased to tenants and subsequently to staff.

St John's was to live through fire and blitz before the real expansion could begin. The fire destroyed some of the best of Wood's work for Chandos, but it was not without a certain grim humour. Between the wars, when society threw off its corsets, Bath had a colony of colourful artists and actors. The flamboyant actress Consuelo de Reyes lived at 2 Chandos Buildings, renamed 'Citizen House'. Her lease included the upper floors of 1 Chandos Buildings, while the Labour Exchange occupied the ground floor. De Reyes converted Citizen House into an 'Educational, Dramatic and Art Centre', but her ambitions grew. She aimed to build a small theatre, which could also be used as a cinema. Bath Corporation granted her 7 St Michael's Place and building permission for the Little Theatre in 1934. In the same year the Corporation served a demolition notice on 3 Chandos Buildings, so the Trustees of St John's were happy to lease it to de Reyes for incorporation into the Little Theatre.[646] Alas Citizen House was destroyed by fire on the night of 23 February 1936. The two children of Consuelo de Reyes were rescued by ladder from her flat on an upper floor, but this did not entirely console her for the loss of her theatrical costumes. She raged that she could always have more children, but her costumes were irreplaceable – or so the story goes.[647] Perhaps it was a stab at Wildean wit. Fortunately a strong south wind preserved St John's from the flames.[648] After war was declared in 1939, a large air-raid shelter was built on the site.

The railings around the chapel (106) were taken for the war effort, while the stained glass in the lower side windows was removed to safety. Unfortunately it was stolen during the war. However the symbols of the evangelists are still in the round windows, and the east window survives, since it was covered with a grille and left in situ.[649] Several charity properties were among those bombed in the 'Baedeker raids' in April 1942. Perhaps the saddest loss was a large part of the Abbey Church House. The whole west front of the Elizabethan house was turned into rubble overnight (109-110). Meanwhile the Chapel of St Mary Magdalen had its stained glass shattered and its roof burned (107-108).

In 1946 a country drained by years of war began to think of rebuilding. The Magdalen Chapel was re-roofed in 1947,[650] though it had to wait a few years for new stained glass. The opportunity was taken to create a window that celebrated the interwoven history of Bath's three medieval hospitals

644 BMCA St JH/1/3 1890-1908 nos. 1098, 1129, 1140, 1147, StJH/1/2 1906-19, nos. 195, 215, 228, 274, 275-7.

645 BMCA StJH1/2 1894-1900, 410, StJH/1/2 1906-11, 349.

646 BMCA StJH/1/2 1931-34, 153-4, 158, StJH/7/111, 112; *Bath Directory* 1933; recollection of Mrs Joan Fear.

647 Recollection of Mrs Joan Fear.

648 BMCA StJH/1/3 1935-41, 62-3, StJH/1/2 1931-34, 457, StJH/15/1, wallet marked 'Old Papers', Master's report 14 July 1936.

649 Recollections of Mrs Joan Fear.

650 BMCA MH/2/4.

107-110
top Two views of The Chapel of St Mary Magdalen after the bombing on April 1942. © Crown copyright
bottom Two views of Abbey Church House after the bombing on April 1942. © Crown copyright

111
The east window of the Chapel of St Mary Magdalen. It was designed by Michael Farrer Bell to symbolise the three medieval foundations now linked under Bath Municipal Charities. On the left is St Catherine, with a medallion below of St Catherine's Hospital. In the centre is Christ with St John the Baptist. On the right is St Mary Magdalen, above her chapel

651 *The Critic* 2 October 1952; *The Builder* 8 October 1954; F. Beresford-Smith; personal communication David Beresford-Smith.

652 BMCA BMC/3 1947-57, 21; MH/3 1940-49, 308.

653 BMCA MH/3 1940-49, 324, 327-8; BMC/3 1947-57, 71.

654 BMCA BMC/3 1934-46, 430, 437, 463, BMC/3 1947-57, 21-2, 30, BH/1 1947.

655 Under a scheme approved by the Charity Commission in July 1951. BMCA BMC/3 1947-57, 42, 130.

656 BMCA BMC/3 1947-57, 49-50, 53.

657 Recollections Mrs Joan Fear.

658 BMCA BMC 9 B4; Wedlake, 84-5.

659 BMCA StJH/7/114, 115.

(111). The Abbey Church House was restored by the Abbey authorities from 1950 to 1952 (113). Ironically, from the ruins arose a new façade more appealing than the old one. The building had been brutally altered over the centuries, as one can still see on the northern side. Instead of simply rebuilding the west front as it had stood before the raid, architect Frederick Beresford-Smith chose to recapture its Elizabethan appearance.[651]

Under the National Health Service Act of 1946, the Ministry of Health in October 1947 laid claim to Bellott's Hospital and the Magdalen Hospital School.[652] The management of the school was transferred to the Ministry in 1948, although the Chapel of St Mary Magdalen was retained by Bath Municipal Charities, along with the endowment, which became the Magdalen Educational Foundation.[653] Bellott's had been closed since November 1944, while the Trustees debated its future in a desultory way. The threat of imminent take-over by the State gave an urgency to their thinking. The building belonged to St John's Hospital, so the Trustees could simply declare that the lease to Bellott's was at an end. In that way they could retain the property and put it to a new use as an extension to St John's.[654] Thomas Bellott's endowment was converted into a fund to assist patients in Bath hospitals.[655]

The expanding hospital

So it was in the midst of post-war austerity that St John's Hospital began its growth spurt. The Surveyor to St John's at this time was Alan Crozier-Cole. He recommended converting Bellott's Hospital into six units, each containing a bedroom and a living room with a sink. There would be communal bathrooms and lavatories. In addition there was to be a flat on the ground floor for the warden.[656] The new almshouse opened on 1 April 1950 with Mrs Joan Fear as warden. As the daughter of the porter of St John's, she was thoroughly familiar with the work of the hospital.[657]

In the same year Crozier-Cole prepared plans for rebuilding Chapel Court House and the building backing onto it (which had been a warehouse for some years) as an extension to the hospital. Although Wood's façade to Chapel Court was substantially retained, behind it he designed a new building, to be named Fitzjocelyn House (114-5). Today the demolition of a building by John Wood might seem almost inconceivable, but at the time Crozier-Cole's approach was seen both practical and architecturally sensitive. At least demolition of the old building provided the opportunity for excavation. One of the Norman fragments found beneath the hospital so attracted Crozier-Cole that his final designs in 1956 incorporated it in the wall facing St Michael's Place.[658]

In the 1960s the Trustees turned their attention to the south side of Chapel Court. The former Middle House had long been divided into 6 and 7 Chapel Court and 10 Hetling Court (116).[659] When the Trustees wanted to convert the block into a second extension to the hospital, Crozier-Cole initially hoped to retain part of the façade, but after a good many changes of plan the whole

112-113
TOP The Chapel of St Mary Magdalen with the Judas tree in bloom
BOTTOM Abbey Church House today

114-115

TOP No 3 Chapel Court photographed in 1945. It was apparently divided into two houses. Lettering over the left-hand door once read CHAPEL COURT HOUSE. To the right it seems was LORA HOUSE though only a few letters remain. In 1956 Crozier-Cole replaced the left-hand door by a window, while the door and window in the corner made way for a larger entrance

BOTTOM Reginald Fitzjocelyn House from Chapel Court today

116-117

TOP The block west of the chapel photographed in 1963 before its demolition. The house
next to the chapel was 10 Hetling Court; the gabled houses were 6 and 7 Chapel Court

BOTTOM Chapel House today. It is linked with John Wood House by a bridge above the door of the chapel

118

The Lamb and Flag of St John the Baptist
over the door of Chapel House. St John
said of Christ: 'Behold the Lamb of God'.
So the Holy Lamb is one of the symbols of
St John. Another is a long-stemmed cross.
Heraldry combined the two and decorated
the cross with St George's flag

building was finally demolished in April 1967. In 1969 the new Chapel House was complete (117), containing 15 flats, the Master's Lodge, the vestry and a strong room for the archive. It is connected to John Wood House by a bridge over the chapel door. Crozier-Cole aimed at a modern interior encased in a shell that echoed the building he replaced, so retaining the Georgian atmosphere of Chapel Court.[660] Over the entrance he placed the symbols of St John the Baptist as they appear in heraldry: the Lamb of God holding St George's flag (118).

It was only when the hospital had expanded this far that the porter finally stopped following the rule laid down in 1878 that he should make the rounds with a hand-bell before locking up at 10 p.m.

All this rebuilding was naturally a drain upon the charity funds, but in 1967 William Rosenberg left a legacy to St John's Hospital, which encouraged new plans. Rosenberg had been a wholesale fruit and potato merchant in Bath, who moved to Jersey before the war.[661] He remembered St John's in his will in gratitude for the hospital's care of his mother. The site of Citizen House had been standing vacant since the war and now the Trustees hoped to build another extension there. When they found that the legacy would not entirely cover costs, they decided in 1974 that St John's should become a housing association, in order to borrow the remainder from the Housing Corporation.[662] In the same year Norman Bence took over from Alan Crozier-Cole as Surveyor to St John's, so it was under his supervision that Rosenberg House was completed in 1975 (119). The building incorporates John Wood's façade for 3 Chandos Buildings.

However, simply retaining or replicating façades did not satisfy the conservationists of this era. Under Norman Bence and his successor Derek Jones, St John's adopted a policy of greater respect for historic fabric. This bore fruit in the treatment of Chandos House. For decades the former wine merchant's and public house had been leased to the Salvation Army. The Trustees commissioned architects William Bertram and Fell to renovate and convert it into residents' flats, retaining such period features as the staircase. This extension was opened on 19 June 1984 by HRH Princess Anne. St John's Hospital had finally reclaimed to its original use the bulk of its medieval site.

Inevitably the expansion of St John's meant some loss of family atmosphere. In the 1970s the 'pension room' in 5 Chapel Court was the scene of musical evenings for residents, but it had been outgrown by the end of the decade. Its successor is the Princess Anne Room in Chandos House, which houses a variety of social gatherings.

Renovation [663]

Meanwhile the properties generating St John's income had become dilapidated once more. The condition of St John's Buildings became a public scandal. When it was built, this block filled a crying need, but it had not been renovated

660   BMCA BMC/9D3, 9D8, 9E.

661   BMCA StJH/5/4, StJH/1/2: 1961-8: meetings 18 May and 18 September 1967; *Post Office Directory of Bath* 1911, 1921.

662   Personal communication from Christopher Couchman.

663   Otherwise unattributed information for this section was kindly supplied by Derek Jones.

119-120
TOP Rosenberg House, opened in 1975
BOTTOM The court of St Catherine's Hospital in 1997. The wrought iron pergola is an Italian
well-head, presented to St Catherine's in 1945 by Arthur Ingrim, Clerk to the Trustees

since. It still had gas lighting. In the winter of 1973 *The Bath Chronicle* reported that seven old people were living in 'a grim Victorian building' with no electricity, hot water or fixed heating. One 75-year-old tenant declared, as he shivered over his paraffin stove, that he would rather be in prison – 'At least I'd get some warmth and three square meals a day'. The *Chronicle* noted with relish that his landlord was none other than St John's Hospital – a charity caring for the aged. Furthermore Alderman Sydney Smith, as the Chairman of both the Trustees of St John's and the Bath City Council Health Committee, had been in the awkward position of lecturing himself on the necessity to improve tenants' living conditions. However, the *Chronicle*'s diatribe fell on the retreating back of Alderman Smith. The Trustees had already sold 'Heartbreak House' to the Corporation for £30,000.[664] It was demolished in 1974.

In the following decade the Trustees received regular reminders from Bath City Council's Housing Department about the run-down condition of its residential estate. Other property, for example in Lower Swainswick, was demolished because of the shortage of funds for renovation. Improvements were also needed to the hospital complex. Conditions in John Wood House and Fitzjocelyn House were seen as primitive in an age of rising expectations. Although gaslight had given way to electricity, heating was still by coal fires. These were not ideal for the elderly, as Dorothy Clease, Matron of St John's (1962-79) recognised. Even when operating single-handed, she took care to bring in the coal and light fires for those not able to manage for themselves. Residents had to share public bathrooms on each floor and wash clothes in white porcelain sinks on the landings.[665]

It was against this background that Derek Jones was appointed as the first full-time Surveyor in 1982. The Council supported the twin aims of renovation and conservation. Conservation and housing improvement grants helped to fund major refurbishments to both the hospital and the residential estate. All the hospital's flats were made self-contained by installing bathrooms where required, while kitchens were modernised. Meanwhile, with the aid of an English Heritage grant, the eastern façade of John Wood House was repaired and cleaned, giving the hospital a more welcoming face.

Grants from the local authority and English Heritage also aided the renovation of St Catherine's Hospital, which was converted into ten flats by architect Richard Le Fevre (120). The converted building was re-opened on 7 October 1986 by John Wroughton, then Headmaster of King Edward's School, in recognition of the long historical association between the school and the almshouse. In the 1920s the wife of the headmaster felt that it was 'regrettable that more interest is not taken by Edwardians in the ten old women in their black cloaks who live in the pleasant little court of St Catherine's'.[666] In more recent years the pupils of King Edward's Junior School have been encouraged to visit St Catherine's, particularly at Christmas.

Once residents had been made comfortable, the Trustees and their Surveyor could turn their minds to the appearance of Chapel Court. In 1991 façades

664 *Bath and Wilts Evening Chronicle* 12 December 1973.
665 Recollections of Irene Lewis.
666 Symons, 64.

were cleaned and the windows of John Wood House carefully replaced in their original style, with the aid of grants from Bath Preservation Trust and the City Council. Only then did the Trustees and staff consider their own comfort. The offices at 4 and 5 Chapel Court were no longer adequate for the growing charity. By returning the houses closer to their original state, the offices could be expanded and a committee room created.[667] This provided an opportunity to renovate the buildings and restore their Georgian character.

The changing face of St Johns [668]

In the last twenty-five years the pace of change has accelerated. St John's has not only grown, but altered its way of operating. The Board of Trustees, for so long a male preserve, began to accept women in 1972. As trustee Sir Gerald Beadle pointed out, there was nothing in the schemes to prevent this.[669] Today there are five women on the Board of Trustees (appendix 5). However there was a more profound shift. The loan from the Housing Corporation had long-term consequences. It has been paid back, but St John's remains a housing association. Once an organisation is registered as such it is not permitted under current legislation to de-register. Under Housing Corporation rules St John's therefore has to ask all residents to pay maintenance charges, although not at commercial rates. Previously residents had been receiving £1 a week. Since St John's and St Catherine's have been serving the same purpose for centuries, their amalgamation was a logical step. Under a new scheme approved in 1984 the charity is now officially The Hospital of St John the Baptist with the Chapel of St Michael annexed with St Catherine's Hospital.

The growth of St John's has caused other changes. The leap in the number of residents required an increase in nursing staff. Today the Matron and her deputy are aided by trained nurses and assistants. This permits a high standard of care. Residents are seen every day and can contact staff at all times, day and night. Also the work of the Surveyor's office has increased sufficiently to warrant the appointment of two Assistant Surveyors, one in 1984 and the second in 1997. A part-time Clerk of Works was appointed in 1984 and the post became full-time in 1998.

The post-war Welfare State diminished the need for out-pensions. However, in the 1980s Government determination to cut Social Security spending left very limited help available to those with special financial needs. The number of cases referred to St John's grew. The volume of work was more than existing officers could reasonably handle, so an almoner was appointed in 1989. The cases are mainly of financial hardship under the St John's Hospital Relief in Need scheme. A smaller number of grants are made from the Bath Dispensary Charity (now also under the control of Bath Municipal Charities), which gives relief in sickness where the State does not provide, and the Magdalen Educational Foundation for children who by reason of disability of mind are in need of special educational treatment.

121
The residents enjoying coffee in Chapel Court on a summer's day

667 The committee room has been named the Albert Lansdown Room, in memory of the former porter, verger and foreman employed by St John's for 57 years.

668 This section is an amalgamation of information kindly supplied by Mrs Charlotte Bayntun-Coward, Christopher Couchman, Quentin Elston, Joan Fear, Irene Lewis and Richard Millar.

669 The first woman Trustees was Mrs Gulielma Maw: BMCA StJH/1/2 1969-74: 21 September and 19 October 1972.

The increased volume of work has born hard upon the Trustees, who have a heavy schedule of board and committee meetings. In addition they have maintained the visiting rota instituted in the last century. All residents are visited at least once a month by at least one Trustee. As the number of residents has increased, so has the length of the visiting round. However the Trustees are in no doubt of the value of these personal contacts, without which management can so easily become divorced from the realities of daily life in the hospital.

The profound social changes in post-war society are reflected among the residents. Before the Second World War, many more people were in service. If they lived in their employer's house during their working lives, they could be in desperate need of a home in old age. St John's was still providing for pre-war servants up to the 1970s, for example Mrs Dorothy Genge, who was old enough to recall Queen Victoria's funeral in 1901. In her youth she lived at Windsor Castle as a royal dressmaker, but was paid a pittance in royal service. She sought to improve her position by becoming the lady's maid to an American millionairess, but servants could seldom save a great deal. St John's could provide a pleasant haven in old age for those who had worked hard and long for little reward. However, the post-war years of rising wages changed the lives of a large section of the working class. Now an applicant to St John's might be the widow of a working man who had been able to buy his own home, but whose income has fallen to the poverty line as a pensioner.

The most recent operational change has been technological. Quentin Elston, Clerk to the Trustees since 1993, encouraged a rapid conversion to the new computer technology and staff are now equipped and trained for the electronic age.

Moving into the next century by Quentin Elston

Although St John's provides a degree of care beyond the normal for sheltered accommodation, it is not currently registered either as a residential home or nursing home, so when residents reach a certain degree of frailty they have to leave the community that has become their home. Dissatisfied with this, in 1991 the Trustees began to consider converting Bellott's Hospital into an 'extra-care unit' for its own community. There have been obstacles in the path. Converting an old building on a tight city centre site is more difficult than designing a new purpose- built one for a clear green field. Since Bellott's could only accommodate 10-12 persons, which in the commercial world is not considered economic, St John's would have to subsidise the care to a very great extent. However the Trustees pressed on with the plan, and after close scrutiny by the Charity Commissioners, an amendment to the charity's scheme was agreed, enabling the development to take place. It is expected that the new Bellott's will open in 1999.

It had also become clear to the Trustees that whilst the accommodation provided by St John's was comfortable and well-serviced, the expectations of those applying to the Hospital were rising. The Surveyor and his staff were constantly employed in refurbishing and improving the almshouses. The Trustees concluded that only so much could be done within the confines of their listed buildings, and whilst the existing almshouses would continue to be occupied for the foreseeable future, a new development was required.

The Trustees attempted to identify possible sites for a new, modern almshouse. This was itself not an easy task; land is in short supply in the 'bowl' of Bath and is expensive. A number of sites were considered, including the hospital's land in Walcot. A site in Kingsmead, which is within a few hundred yards of the heart of the Hospital in Chapel Court, was eventually found. Negotiations with the owner took place and plans were drawn up. This seemed the perfect site: it was large enough to provide a substantial almshouse and an additional extra-care unit, so doubling the accommodation provided by St John's. Unfortunately, after many months of work, the purchase fell through. But shortly thereafter a new site unexpectedly became available.

In the autumn of 1996 agents contacted the Trustees on behalf of their client who owned land and buildings adjacent to the Royal United Hospital in Combe Park. The site was outside the city's conservation area and did not have on it any listed buildings which might hamper development. With the site would be sold office accommodation, which could be leased to the existing 'blue-chip' occupier, providing a good covenant and income, which in itself represented a good investment for the charity. The site was ideal.

This time the negotiations, whilst lengthy and complex, proved fruitful. The purchase of the site was completed shortly after St. John's day 1997. The terms of the purchase meant, however, that the Trustees would not be able to fully develop the site until 2002, but within two years the charity would be able to commence work on part of it to create a new almshouse

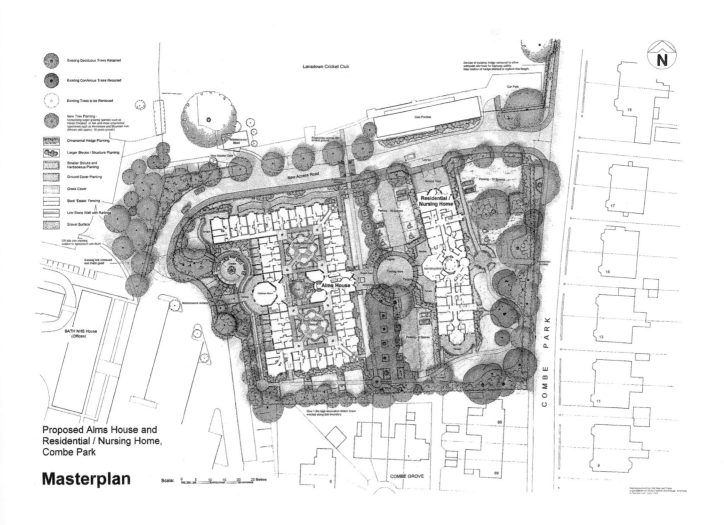

Proposed Alms House and
Residential / Nursing Home,
Combe Park

Masterplan

Scale: 0   5   10   15   20   25 Metres

122
A proposal for the new almshouse and residential/nursing
at Combe Park by architects Hutton Nichols Goodenough

containing a minimum of 50 self-contained flats. An extra-care unit providing 30 or more beds of nursing home accommodation would follow shortly thereafter (122). The next hurdle for the Trustees was how all of this was to be funded.

In the 1980s and 1990s a number of long leases in the Hospital's estate expired and long standing rent reviews were settled. As a result, the Hospital's rental income from its properties in and around Bath began to rise significantly. It was this rising sum of surplus income that enabled the Trustees to first consider expanding the almshouse. Much credit for this improvement in the charity's finances must be given to Christopher Couchman who was the Clerk to the Trustees from 1971 to 1993. His prudent, insightful and judicious management of the charity was of the utmost importance to its fortunes. By 1997 the Trustees were able to complete the purchase of the Combe Park site solely from the accumulated funds of the charity, with the expectation that the new development could be funded from the Hospital's own resources without the need to approach a lender – a very different situation to that which faced the Trustees in 1974 when Rosenberg House was built.

During the weeks leading up to the publication of this book, two events linked the present with the past. For some years the Bath spa waters have been flowing away unused. What were once busy, bustling streets around St John's were quiet. In the autumn of 1998, plans were completed for a new spa, which will draw visitors to the area once again. The baths, beside which Bishop Fitzjocelyn founded his hospital have again prompted a development to benefit the city. Outside Bath, the Trustees improved on an ancient holding at Michaelmas 1998 by purchasing an additional 50 acres of land for the farm at Alham which was granted to St John's c.1200.

As the Trustees and their officers and staff look forward to the new millennium, they do so with a degree of confidence and optimism, but they are by no means complacent. Very high standards both in the administration of the charity and the care of the almspeople have been achieved, and the Trustees wish to maintain and improve those standards. All aspects of the running of the Hospital both charitable and 'commercial' become more complicated as every day passes, a symptom of late twentieth-century life. With this there is always the danger of taking a short-term view. The Trustees are, however, very much aware of the history of the Hospital and the work of their predecessors. They always work diligently, with both commitment and care, to ensure that they govern the charity with the long-term good health of the Hospital in mind, hoping that in the future when an historian looks back, it will be written that St John's Hospital successfully met the challenge of a new century.

Appendix 1

Masters of St John's Hospital

c.1193	Nicholas
By 1256	Adam
By 1266/7	Robert
By 1280 Jan	Henry
By 1286	William
	John Hasting
1305 2 May	Nicholas Brent
1317	Adam of Corston
By 1332	John Ballington
By 1338	William of Chelwood
1343 7 Sep	Thomas Gosmale
by 1349	Walter Harding
1349-59	Adam Hatfield
By 1377	John Ashwick
1399	John Shaftesbury
1428 28 Sep	Peter Buryman
[1459	John Philips acting]
1460/1 9 Jan	John Vobe
1470?	Edmund Gyll
1483 24 Jul	Robert Alday
1520 8 Nov	James Horton BCL
[1527-c.1532	Prior of Bath]
c.1532	John Simons
1561 19 Apr	Thomas Greenway STB
1580	Richard Bewshin
1586/7 20 Feb	John Bewshin
1617	Walter Chapman
1624 6 Sep	William Chapman
1647 4 Oct	Walter Chapman
[1655-1662	Mayor of Bath]
1662/3 12 Feb	John Rustat
1680 1 Feb	William Peake BA
1683 5 Dec	William Clement MA
1711 3 Jan	John Chapman
1737 8 Oct	Walter Chapman MA
1791 4 June	John Chapman DD
1816 12 Jun	James Phillott
[1866-77	William James Grant
	Luckman acting]
1877 21 Nov	W.J.G. Luckman
1892	Robert E. Whittington
1899	Charles W. Shickle
1928	Frank Elam Wheatcroft
1930	George Alexander Bunbury
1937	Charles L. Malaher
1941	Guy Lauder FitzMaurice
1946	Frederick Richard Bishop
1953	Norman Howe Parcell
1956	Oswald Lunn Martin
1958	William Luxmore Jameson
1970	Reginald Jackson
1975	Gilbert Jessop
1988	Thomas Gilbert Horwood
1990	Frederick George Harte

Appendix 2

Masters of St Mary Magdalen

By 1263	Nicholas
By 1377	Edward
By 1411	William Heyford
[1486-1539	Prior of Bath]
1539	Simon Shepherd
1571	Griffin Curtis
By 1693	George Bradford
By 1729	David Thomas
1739	James Thomas
1760	Duel Taylor
1767	Richard Roberts
1823	Charles Crook
1838	John Allen

Appendix 3

Physicians appointed to Bellott's Hospital by Bath Corporation

1653-59	Dr Tobias Venner
1660-62	Dr Robert Peirce
1663-65	Dr Thomas Brewer
1666-1705	Dr Robert Peirce
1706-16	Dr Henry Parker
1717-31	Dr Charles Bave
1732-33	Dr Richard Ford
1733-49	Dr Edward Harington
1750-85	Dr Rice Charlton
1786-1815	Dr Henry Harington
1816-1835	Dr John Ford Davis

Appendix 4

Trustees of the Bath Municipal Charities

1836-51

Augustus George Barretté, solicitor
Henry Alexander Barry, esq (d.1852)
William Thomas Blair, esq
James Bryant, carrier
James Crisp, hat manufacturer (d.1852)
Charles Davis, gent (d.1849)
John Edridge, esq
Benjamin Higman, printer (d.1848)
William Hunt, esq
Edward Jay, solicitor (left Bath by 1852)
Michael Theobald Langton, esq (d.1844)
Joseph Pearson, gent (d.1844)
James Sexton, esq (d.1846)
James Grant Smith, brewer
John Stone, esq
Arthur West, esq (left Bath by 1852)
George Horwood White, music teacher (d.1848)

1852-58

Edmund Lloyd Bagshawe
Augustus George Barretté
William Thomas Blair (resigned 1858)
Hon Revd William John Brodrick (resigned
    1858)
Richard Willson Brown
James Bryant (resigned 1859)
Frederick Dowding
John Edridge (d.1856)
Edward Fletcher (resigned 1859)
Richard Francis George
William Hunt
Thomas Jolly
William Long (resigned 1858)
George Moger, junior
James Grant Smith (d.1856)
John Stone (d.1858)
William Titley

1859-72

Edmund Lloyd Bagshawe (d.1885)
Augustus George Barretté (d.1868)
Benjamin Bartrum (d.1876)
Richard Willson Brown (d.1860)
Robert Dyer Commans
Frederick Dowding (d.1861)
George Edwards (retired 1873)
Dr Randle Wilbraham Falconer
Richard Francis George (retired 1873)
William Hunt
Thomas Jolly
George Arthur Jones (d.1872)
Richard King
Charles Frederick Marshall
George Moger
Revd Edward Douglas Tinling (retired 1873)
William Titley

1873-74

Edmund Lloyd Bagshawe (d.1885)
Benjamin Bartrum (d.1876)
[Sir] Robert Stickney Blaine (d.1897)
Robert Dyer Commans (retired 1903)
Charles Ekin (resigned 1881)
Dr Randle W.Falconer (d.1881)
William Hunt, esq (d.1885)
Thomas Jolly (d.1889)
William Crucknell Jolly (d.1904)
Revd Charles Kemble (resigned 1874)
Richard King (d.1890)
Charles Frederick Marshall (d.1897)
George Moger (d.1880)
William Titley (d.1882)

Appendix 5

Trustees of the Bath Municipal Charities

1998

Susan Fuge SRN
Alan Gerrard Meecham MA
William Bosley MSc PhD
Edward Peter Craig Kelly RN CEng M.I.Mar.E
Marianna Clark MB ChB
Robert Jeremy Barber
Richard James Millar MC FCIS
Barbara Kathleen Dewey B Ed
Anthony John Rhymes
Arthur William Henry Hind Dip.Arch RIBA
Brian James Langdon MA D.Phil
Gillian Dallas
David Beswick Lloyd MB BS DRCOG
Avis Joan Langdon Cert Ed

Appendix 6

Chairmen of the Trustees of the Bath Municipal Charities

1867-99	Robert Dyer Commans
1899-1912	Frederick Shum
1912-20	John Eddan Commans
1920-35	John Mannett Ealand
1935-56	Roy Carmichael Leedham Fuller
1956-63	Henry Mallory
1963-69	Edward Rhodes Cook
1969-72	Commander Arthur Henry Bullen Day
1972-78	Sydney Arthur Smith
1978-80	Bernard Selwyn Padfield
1980-82	Robert Preston Jones
1983-85	Rear-Admiral Thomas Heron Maxwell
1985-88	Very Revd Dean Fenton Morley
1988-93	Alan Gerrard Meecham
1993-96	Dr William Bosley
1996-	Richard James Millar

Appendix 7

Clerks and Receivers to Bath Municipal Charities

1852-59	Thomas Fisher
1859-86	Edward Turner Payne
1886-1933	Edward Newton Fuller
1934-48	Arthur Irvine Ingram
1948-71	Basil Henry Sheldon
1971-93	Christopher Hugh Couchman
1993-	Quentin Timothy Starr Elston

Appendix 8

Surveyors to Bath Municipal Charities

1853-68	Jacob Henry Cotterell
1868-1904	Henry Spackman
1904-08	Charles Chantry Spackman
1908-47	William Benjamin Rolfe
1947-74	Alan Crozier-Cole
1974-82	William Norman Bence
1982-	Derek Morgan Jones

Appendix 9

St John's Hospital Accounts c. 1530

Annual income:

Rents of assize	£22 8s 5d
Pension from the bishop of Bath and Wells	£5
Tithes of St Michael's	£1 6s 8d
TOTAL	**£28 15s 1d**

Annual outgoings:

Stipend of 2 priests (hospital and St Michael)
£14 6s 8d

Alms to poor people:

To Thomas Walsheman and his wife weekly 4d each	(yearly £1 14s 8d)	
To Julian Jenkins a poor woman weekly 6d		
with a house to dwell in of 7s yearly rent free	(yearly £1 13s 8d)	
To William Macy weekly 4d	(yearly 17s 4d)	
To William Hudd	yearly 4s*	
	total	£4 10s 8d.

Out rents:

To bailiff of city for landgavel	10s 5³/₄d	
To proctors of the commons for certain tenements	2s 6d	
To proctors of Stalls	8d	
To prior	6s 8d	
To priory sexton	2s	
To priory sexton 2lb of wax	1s	
To priory hosteler	2s	
To priory pittancer	2s	
	total	£1 7s 3³/₄d

Fee to John Talbot, rent collector:

wages	£1	
livery coat	10s	
board	£1 6s 8d	
	total	£2 16s 8d.

Obits or anniversaries	3s 2d

[Loss from] decay of tenements:

decayed tenement by the Cross Bath once held by David Horseman	7s	
tenement next to St Michael's church door, now a garden	7s	
2 tenements decayed beside the Cross Bath	14s	
tenement called the Crown	20s	
tenement besides Wotton	8s	
2 stables in St Michael's Lane	8s	
the corner** house decayed by St Michael's Church	4s	
3 tenements decayed, now gardens in Binbery Lane in John White's hands	15s	
corner** house now a void ground by Hot Bath	4s	
tenement decayed in Westgate Street	20s	
tenement that Hudd had	8s	
	total	£5 15s
	TOTAL	**£28 19s 5³/₄d**

From *Proceedings in the Court of Star Chamber*, SRS **27**, 157-59.

* The lower payment probably means that William Hudd died during the accounting year.
A common abbreviation for 'er' was overlooked by the editor of SRS **27, and has been added here.

Appendix 10

Contents of the Chapel of St Mary Magdalen c.1539

Thenventary of the ornamentes and goodes conveyed out of the Chapell of Mary Magdalene in Holleway nigh Bathe

In primis ii Chalices of silver oon gilt and thother parcell gilte	viiili vis	viiid
Item a childe of grace standing on the aulter with a silver ring tied in a lace		xiid
Item ii gilte peces Silver	vli	xiiis iiiid
Item iiii peces of silver ungilt	vili	
Item a bedestone gilt		viiid
Item a grete paire of beads of Jeate	[blank]	
Item x aulter clothes and ii towelles	xviiis iiiid	
Item iiii paire of Vestmentes	[blank]	
Item a Crosse	[blank]	
Item v candilstikkes of laten and oon of tynne		viis vid
Item a Senser, a pax, ii cruettes, and ii braunches of laten	[blank]	
Item a Cote of velivet on mary magdalene and a Cote of Tissue on saint John	[blank]	
Item a lent clothe and vii tapers	[blank]	
Item a pax with iii buttons of silver and gilte	[blank]	
Item a Cannapie with iiii buttons gilt	[blank]	
Item ii belles with stokkes and Iron	xxli	
Item vi Oxen	vili	
Item iiii beas		xls
Item lx Ewes	iiiili	
Item xxx [word missing in MS, although no gap]		lxs

Although E117 is largely made up of inventories of the goods of parish churches and guilds made in 1550, this undated single sheet does not belong to that series. The removal of stock was not warranted by the legislation of that year permitting the confiscation of church plate. Nor is it a detached part of E117/8/23(b), a book of inventories made in 1546 by the Commissioners for the Survey of Chantries in Somerset. The format is different. The fact that all the ornaments and stock were removed from St Mary Magdalen suggests that the inventory was made by Crown Commissioners at the suppression of Bath Priory in January 1539.

From PRO E117/8/23(d).

Abbreviations

BAFC	*Bath Antiquarian Field Club Proceedings*
BaRO	Bath and North Somerset Record Office
BaL	Bath Reference Library
BL	British Library
BMCA	Bath Municipal Charities Archive
BrL	Bristol Reference Library
BrRO	Bristol Record Office
BRS	Bristol Record Society
HL	Huntington Library, California
HMC	Historical Manuscripts Commission
MS(S)	Manuscript(s)
PRO	Public Record Office
PSANHS	*Proceedings of the Somerset Archaeology and Natural History Society*
Rolls Series	Chronicles and Memorials of Great Britain and Ireland during the Middle Ages, Published under the Direction of the Master of the Rolls
SANH	*Somerset Archaeology and Natural History*
SRO	Somerset Record Office
SRS	Somerset Record Society
TS	Typescript
VCH	*The Victoria History of the Counties of England*
WRS	Wiltshire Record Society

Format of references to published works and MS volumes:

x, y = volume and page number.

x/y = section and item number.

no.x = item number.

Bibliography

Abstracts of Somersetshire Wills ed. F. Brown 6 vols. (1887-90)

The Accounts of the Chamberlains of the City of Bath, 1568-1602, SRS **38**

An Act for Confirming a Scheme of the Charity Commissioners for Saint Mary Magdalen Hospital near Bath (1856)

Acts of the Privy Council of England, 46 vols. (London 1890-1964)

Ancient Deeds Belonging to the Corporation of Bath XIII-XVI Cent., trans. C. W. Shickle, Bath Records Society (Bath 1921)

Baker, C. H. C. and Baker, Muriel I., *The Life and Circumstances of James Brydges, First Duke of Chandos* (Oxford 1949)

The Barkers of Bath, Victoria Art Gallery (Bath 1986)

Bath Directory (1833-46)

Bellott's Hospital, Bath. Scheme for the Management and Regulation of the Hospital of Thomas Bellott at Bath in Somerset and the Application of the Income Thereof. Directed by the Court of Chancery, by order dated 27th November 1858 (London 1858)

Beresford-Smith, F. W., *A History of the Abbey Church House, Bath* (Bath 1954)

Bindoff, S. T. (ed.), *The History of Parliament: the House of Commons 1509-1558*, 3 vols. (London 1982)

Brooks, S., 'Bath and the Great Reform Bill' in J. Wroughton (ed), *Bath in the Age of Reform 1830-1841* (Bath 1972)

Bush, A. E. and Hatton, J., *Thomas Bellott* (Bath 1966)

Calendar of Bradford-on-Avon Examinations, Wiltshire Record Society **46**

Calendar of Charter Rolls, 6 vols. (London 1903-27)

Calendar of Entries in the Papal Registers relating to Great Britain and Ireland. Papal Letters. 18 vols. (London 1893-1994)

Calendar of Patent Rolls. Henry III, 6 vols. (London 1901-13)

Calendar of Patent Rolls. Edward III, 16 vols. (London 1891-1916)

Calendar of Patent Rolls. Edward VI, 6 vols. (London 1924-9)

Calendar of Patent Rolls. Elizabeth, 9 vols. (London 1939-1986)

Calendar of State Papers, Domestic Series of the Reign of Charles II, 28 vols. (London 1860-1939)

Calendar of Various Chancery Rolls ... 1277-1326 (London 1912)

The Camden Miscellany **9**, Camden Society New Series **53**

Carpenter, P. K., 'The Bath Idiot and Imbecile Institution' (forthcoming)

Carpenter, P. K., 'The Leper's Hospital at Bath', *Somerset and Dorset Notes and Queries* **34** (1997), no. 35

The Cartulary of Cirencester Abbey, Gloucestershire, ed. C. D. Ross (London 1964)

Cartulary of St Mark's Hospital, Bristol, BRS **21**

In Chancery. Cause between her majesties attorney general and the master, co-brethren and sisters of the hospital of St. John, and the chapel of St. Michael in Bath (privately printed 1864)

The Chronicle of Richard of Devizes of the Time of King Richard the First, ed. J. T. Appleby (London 1963)

Church, C. M., 'Reginald, bishop of Bath (1174-1191)', *Archaeologia* **50**, 295-360

Clark, L., Rawcliffe, C. and Roskell, J. S. (eds), *History of Parliament: The House of Commons 1386-1421*, 4 vols. (London 1992)

Clay, R. M. *The Medieval Hospitals of England* (London 1909)

Clews, S., 'Banking in Bath in the Reign of George III', *Bath History* **5**, 104-24

Collectanea I, SRS **39**

Collinson, J., *The History and Antiquities of the County of Somerset* (1791)

Colvin, H., *Biographical Dictionary of British Architects 1600-1840*, 3rd edn. (New Haven and London 1995)

The Complete Peerage by G. E. C[okayne], 2nd. edn ed. V. Gibbs, 13 vols. (London 1910-59)

Davenport, P., 'Abbey Church House' in P. Davenport (ed.), *Archaeology in Bath 1976-85* (Oxford 1991), 123-8

The Diary of John Evelyn ed. E. S. de Beer, 6 vols. (Oxford 1955)

The Dictionary of National Biography, 22 vols., reprinted (London 1967-8)

Diocese of Bristol: A catalogue of the Records of the Bishop and Archdeacon and of the Dean and Chapter (Bristol 1970)

A Directory for the City and Borough of Bath, Wells ... (1854)

Domesday Book (gen. ed.. J. Morris): **6** *Wiltshire* ed. C. and F. Thorn (Chichester 1979), **8** *Somerset* ed. C. and F. Thorn (Chichester 1980)

Ecclesiastical Documents, Camden Society **8**

Episcopal Registers, Diocese of Worcester. Register of Bishop Godfrey Giffard, September 23rd 1268 to August 15th 1301, Worcester Historical Society [15]

Epistolae Cantuarienses, Rolls Series

Falconer, R. W., *Bellott's Hospital: its incorporation with the General Hospital considered* (Bath 1857)

Feudal Aids = Inquisitions and Assessments Relating to Feudal Aids, 6 vols. (1899- 1920)

Foster, J., *Alumni Oxonienses 1715-1886*, (Oxford 1886)

Foster, J., *Alumni Oxonienses: the members of the University of Oxford 1500-1714*, (Oxford 1891)

Fuller, T., *The Church History of Britain* (London, 1837)

Gasquet, Abbot, 'Abbot Feckenham and Bath', *Downside Review*, **25**, 242-60

Gilchrist, R., *Contemplation and Action: the other monasticism* (London 1995)

Girouard, M., *Robert Smythson and the Elizabethan Country House* (New Haven and London 1983)

Goulstone, J., 'The Clements of Englishcombe' *Journal of the Bristol and Avon Family History Society* **51** (Spring 1988), 26-29

The Great Red Book of Bristol: Text, 4 vols., BRS, **4**, **8**, **16**, 18

Green, E., 'Bath lay subsidies Henry IV to Henry VIII', BAFC **6**, 379-411

Green, E., 'A Bath poll tax, 2 Richard II', BAFC **6**, 294-315

Green, M., *The Eighteenth Century Architecture of Bath* (Bath 1904)

Greene, J. P., 'Citizen House (Westgate Buildings) 1970' in B. Cunliffe (ed.), *Excavations in Bath 1950-1975* (Bristol 1979)

Greening, P., 'St Werburga's by Bath', in W. J. Wedlake *et al* (eds.), *North Somerset Miscellany* (Bath 1966), 20-4

Grenville, J., *Medieval Housing* (London and Washington 1997)

Guidott, T., *A Discourse of Bath and the Hot Waters There* (London 1676; 2nd edn 1725)

Hargood-Ash, J., *Looking Back at Weston 1535-1900* (Bath 1964)

Haskins, S., *Mary Magdalen* (London 1994)

Henderson, J., 'The hospitals of late medieval Florence', in L. Granshaw and R. Porter, *The Hospital in History* (London 1989), 63-92

Holland, E., 'The earliest Bath Guildhall', *Bath History* **2** (1988), 163-179

Itinerary of John Leland, ed. L. Toulmin Smith, 5 vols. (London 1907-10)

James, P. R., *The Baths of Bath* (Bristol 1938)

Jones, G., *History of the Law of Charity 1532-1827*, (Cambridge 1969)

Jones, W., *Bradford-on-Avon* (Bradford-on-Avon 1907)

Keevil, A. J., 'The Barton of Bath', *Bath History* **6** (1996), 25-53

King, A. J. and Watts, B. H., *The Municipal Records of Bath 1189-1604* (London n.d.)

Kiple, K. E. (ed), *The Cambridge World History of Human Disease* (Cambridge 1993)

Kolaczkowski, A., 'Jerom Murch and Bath Politics', *Bath History* **6** (1996), 155-73

The Law Reports. Chancery Division (London 1875-)

Le Neve, J. and Hardy, T. D., *Fasti Ecclesiae Anglicanae* (1854)

The Letters and Epigrams of Sir John Harington, ed. N. E. McClure (Philadelphia 1930)

Letters and Papers, Foreign and Domestic, of the Reign of Henry VIII, 23 vols (1862-1932)

Letters from Bath 1766-1767 by the Rev. John Penrose ed. B. Mitchell and H. Penrose (Gloucester 1983)

Manco, J., 'Bath and the Great Rebuilding', *Bath History* **4** (1992), 25-51

Manco, J., 'The buildings of Bath Priory', *SANH* **137** (for 1993), 75-109

Manco, J., 'The Cross Bath', *Bath History* **2** (1988), 49-84

Manco, J., 'Henry Savile's map of Bath', *SANH* **136** (for 1992), 127-39

Manco, J., 'The history of Binbury: medieval to modern' in P. Davenport (ed.), *Archaeology in Bath: excavations 1984-89* (forthcoming)

Manco, J., *The Parish of Englishcombe: a history* (Englishcombe 1995)

Materials for the History of Thomas Becket, Rolls Series

McLaughlin, D., 'Mowbray Green and the Old Bath Preservers', *Bath History* **4** (1992), 155-172

Medieval Deeds of Bath and District, SRS **73**

Miller, T., *The Birth of the Hospital in the Byzantine Empire* (Baltimore 1985)

Miller, T., 'The Knights of St John and the hospitals of the Latin West', *Speculum* **53**, 709-33

Mowl, T. and Earnshaw, B., *John Wood: Architect of Obsession* (Bath 1988)

MSS at Hatfield = HMC *Calendar of the Manuscripts of the Most Hon. the Marquis of Salisbury at Hatfield House*, 24 vols. (London 1883-1976)

MSS of Wells = HMC *Calendar of the Manuscripts of the Dean and Chapter of Wells*, 2 vols. (London 1907-14)

Nathan, H. L., Lord Nathan, *The Charities Act, 1960* (London 1962)

Neale, R. S., *Bath: A Social History 1680-1850* (London 1981)

Orderic Vitalis, *The Ecclesiastical History of England and Normandy* ed. and trans. M. Chibnall (Oxford 1978)

Orme, N. and Webster, M., *The English Hospital 1070-1570* (New Haven and London 1995)

Peach, R. E. M., *A Brief History of the Hospital of St. John Baptist, Bath* (Bath 1886)

Pedes Finum, Commonly Called Feet of Fines, for the County of Somerset, Richard I to Edward I, A.D. 1196 to A.D. 1307, SRS **6**; *1 Edward II to 20 Edward II, A.D. 1307 to A.D. 1346*, SRS **12**

Pleydell, J., *Sermon Preached at the Funeral of Mr Jos. Glanvill* (1681)

Plucknett, T. F. T., *The Legislation of Edward I* (Oxford 1949)

The Post Office Bath Directory (1858-1940)

Radulfi de Diceto decani Lundoniensis opera historica, Rolls Series

Rawcliffe, C., 'The Hospitals of Later Medieval London', *Medical History* **28**, 1-21

Rawcliffe, C., *Medicine and Society in Later Medieval England* (Stroud 1995)

Regista Regum Anglo-Normanum 1066-1154 ed. H. W. C. Davis *et al*, 3 vols. (Oxford 1915-68)

The Register of John de Drokensford, Bishop of Bath and Wells, A.D. 1309-1329, SRS **1**

The Register of John Stafford, Bishop of Bath and Wells, 1425-1443, SRS **31-2**

The Register of Nicholas Bubwith, Bishop of Bath and Wells, 1407-1424, SRS **29-30**

The Register of Ralph of Shrewsbury, Bishop of Bath and Wells, 1329-1363, SRS **9-10**

The Register of Thomas Bekynton, Bishop of Bath and Wells 1443-1465, SRS **49**

The Registers of the Abbey Church of SS Peter and Paul, Bath, 2 vols., Harleian Society Publications, Register Section, **27-8**

The Registers of Oliver King, Bishop of Bath and Wells, 1496-1503, and Hadrian de Castello, Bishop of Bath and Wells, 1503-1518, SRS **54**

The Registers of Thomas Wolsey, Bishop of Bath and Wells, 1518-1523, John Clerke, Bishop of Bath and Wells, 1523-1541, William Knight, Bishop of Bath and Wells, 1541-1547, and Gilbert Bourne, Bishop of Bath and Wells, 1554-1559, SRS **55**

'Reminiscences of John Louthe', *Narratives of the Days of the Reformation*, Camden Society **77**

Renfrew, J. M. and Robbins, M., 'Tobias Rustat and his monument', *Antiquaries Journal* **70** (1990), 416-23

Report of the Commissioners for Charities **4** (London 1820)

Report of the Commissioners for Charities, **6** (London 1822)

Richards, P., *The Medieval Leper and his Northern Heirs* (Cambridge 1977)

Riley-Smith, J., *The Knights of St John in Jerusalem c.1050-1310* (London 1967).

Rolls, R., *The Hospital of the Nation: The story of Spa medicine and the Mineral Water Hospital at Bath* (Bath 1988)

Rosenthal, J. T., *The Purchase of Paradise: gift giving and the aristocracy 1307-1485* (London 1972)

The Rule of Saint Augustine trans. R. Canning (Kalamazoo 1996)

St John's Hospital: Abstract of Surveyor's Report (Bath 1882)

St John's Hospital. Shall our Public Charities be Merely Church Charities? Report of a Public Meeting held at the Guildhall on Wednesday, December 7th 1859. Extracted from Keene's Bath Journal (Bath 1859)

The Scheme for the Future Government and Regulation of the Free Grammar School and Saint Catherine's Hospital or Black Alms at Bath in the County of Somerset (Bath 1849)

Scheme for the Management and Regulation of the Hospital of St John the Baptist with the Chapel of St Michael annexed, in the City of Bath (London 1877)

Scheme for the Management and Regulation of the Magdalen Hospital School and the application of the income thereof: Approved by the Queen's Most Excellent Majesty on the 29th of January, 1894 (Bath 1917)

Shum, F., *A Catalogue of Bath Books ... on the Hot Mineral Springs* (Bath 1913)

Smith, A. G. R., *The Emergence of a Nation State: the commonweath of England 1529-1660* (London 1984)

Somerset Incumbents ed. F. W. Weaver (Bristol 1889)

Somerset Medieval Wills 1383-1500, SRS **16**

Somerset Medieval Wills 1501-1530, SRS **19**

Somerset Medieval Wills 1531-1558, SRS **21**

Somersetshire Pleas ... from the Rolls of the Itinerant Justices, SRS **11**

Star Chamber = Proceedings in the Court of Star Chamber in the Reigns of Henry VII and Henry VIII, SRS **27**

Statutes of the Realm, 1278-1714, Record Commission, 11 vols. (1810-28)

Statutes of the United Kingdom 29 vols. (London 1804-69)

Stokes Shaw, W., 'Notes on the Chapel and Hospital of St Mary Magdalene, Bath', BAFC **2**, 98-111

The Survey and Rental of the Chantries ... in the County of Somerset as returned in ... 1548, SRS **2**

Symons, K. E. *The Grammar School of King Edward VI at Bath and its Ancient Foundation*, (Bath 1934)

Trollope, A., *The Warden*, with introduction by O. Chadwick (London 1995)

Tudor and Stuart Proclamations 1485-1715, 2 vols. (Oxford 1910)

Turner, W., *A Book of the Natures and Properties as well of the Bathes in England as of Other Bathes in Germany and Italy* (Cologne 1562)

Two Chartularies of the Priory of St Peter at Bath, SRS **7**

Valor Ecclesiasticus temp. Henr. VIII, Record Commission, 6 vols. (London 1810-34)

Venn, J. and J. A., *Alumni Cantabrigienses part 1: from earliest times to 1751*, 4 vols. (Cambridge 1922-27)

Venner, T., *Via Recta ad Vitam Longam* (1620)

Victoria History of Berkshire, 4 vols. (London 1906-27)

Victoria History of Somerset, 6 vols. (London 1911-78, Oxford 1985-92)

Visitation of Gloucestershire 1623, Harleian Society Publications **21**

Visitations of Berkshire 2, Harleian Society Publications **57**

Walker, E. W. A., *Skrine of Warleigh* (Somerset 1936)

Warner, R., *The History of Bath*, (1801)

Wedlake, W. J., 'St. John's Hospital Extensions, 1954', in B. Cunliffe (ed.), *Excavations in Bath 1950-1975* (Bristol 1979)

Willelmi Malmesbiriensis Monarchi de Gestis Pontificum Anglorum, Rolls Series

Williams, T. W., *Somerset Medieval Libraries* (Bristol 1897)

Wiltshire Returns to the Bishop's Visitation Queries 1783, WRS **27**

Wood, A. à, *Monumental Inscriptions in the Churches of Bath* (London 1881)

Wood, J., *The Description of the Hot-Bath at Bath ... together with the plans, elevation and section of the same* (Bath 1777)

Wood, J., *Essay Towards a Description of Bath* 2nd edn (Bath 1749)

Wood, M. E., *The English Medieval House* (London 1965)

Woodforde, C., *Stained Glass of Somerset* (Oxford 1946)

Wroughton, J., *A Community at War: the Civil War in Bath and North Somerset 1642- 1650*, (Bath 1992)

Youings, J., *The Dissolution of the Monasteries* (London 1971)

Young, R., *Mrs Chapman's Portrait: a beauty of Bath of the 18th century* (Bath 1926)

Index

Fox, Dr 146
Foxcote 35
Fraternity of St Catherine 42
Free Grammar School 134, 186 see also King
Edward's School
Freeman, Mr 72n
Frome 26, 34, 82
Fry, William 82
Fuge, Susan 179
Fulks (Fowkes), Mr 70
Fuller, Edward Newton 179
Fuller, Roy Carmichael Leedham 179

G

Galen 22, 38
gallery 26, 29, 46, 68, 69, 92
Gay, Mark 77
Gay, Richard 72
Genge, Dorothy 170
George Arthur Jones 178
George IV 126
George, Richard Francis 178
Gibbons, Grinling 88
Gibbs, Robert 24
Gibbs, Walter 98
Gilbert, Prior of Bath 40
Glanvill, Joseph 88
Glastonbury 23
Glastonbury, John of 36
Gory, Beatrice 82
Gosmale, Thomas 28, 177
Gossington 35, 82
Gournay, Sir Anselm de 24
Grand Chartreuse 16
Granville, Charles, 2nd Earl of Bath 72
Great House 70, 72, 97, 120 see also Abbey
Church House; Hetling House
Greenway, Thomas 61, 108, 177
Griffin, Katherine 82
Grigg, Revd, chaplain of St John's Hospital 122
guide 38, 58, 89 and see caretaker; nurse;
warden
Guild of St Catherine 42
Guildhall 42, 110, 136, 140, 141, 144
Gyll, Edmund 177

H

Haines, Roger 42
Hallatrow 34, 35, 82
Harbledown 15, 22, 23
Harding, Brother Peter 29
Harding, Walter 177
Harington, Dr Edward 118, 177
Harington, Dr Henry 177
Harington, Sir John 76
Harrison, Daniel 136
Harte, Frederick George 177
Hasting, John 177
Hatfield, Adam 177
Haycombe 80, 89
Henry, Master of St John's 177
Henry II 15, 16, 20
Henry VII 77, 187
Henry VIII 53
Hetling Court 120, 162, 165
  nos. 2-5 150
Hetling House 120, 136, 150 see also Abbey
Church House; Great House; Mrs Savile's
Lodging
Hetling Pump Room 120
Hetling Street 120
Heyford, William 177
High Street 78
Higman, Benjamin 178
Hill, Thomas 69, 74, 80

Hind, Arthur William Henry 179
Hobbs, John 108
Holloway 22, 23, 43, 53, 89, 110, 124, 125,
126, 128, 138, 152
Holloway House 108, **112**
Holloway, William, Prior of Bath 46, 48, 50, 53
Holme Pierrepont 86
Holy Roman Empire 72
Horner, Thomas 48
Horseman, David 180
Horton, James 46, 177
Horton, Jeremy 70
Horwood, Thomas Gilbert 177
Hosatus 22n see Hussey, Walter
hospitals
  Bath 115, 118 see also Bath General, Bath
  Mineral Water, Royal National Hospital
  for Rheumatic Diseases
  Bath General 140 see also Bath Hospital;
  Mineral Water; Royal National Hospital
  for Rheumatic Diseases
  Bellott's 74, **75**, 76, 77, 108n, **137**, **139**,
  140, 177
  Holy Cross and St Mary Magdalen 26
  Leper's 22, 60, 61, **62**, 120
  Mineral Water 142 see also Bath Hospital;
  Bath General; Royal National Hospital for
  Rheumatic Diseases
  Royal National Hospital for Rheumatic
  Diseases 115, 118 see also Bath Hospital;
  Bath General; Mineral Water
  Royal United 172 see also United
  Savoy, London 77
  SS John the Baptist and John the
  Evangelist, Sherborne 29
  St Bartholomew's, London 15n
  St Catherine, Bath 41, **42**, **45**, 56, 116,
  129, 130, **131**, 132, **133**, 134, 155, 162,
  167, 168, 169
  St Cross, Winchester 15n, 138
  St Giles, Wilton 15n
  St John the Baptist, Bath
    barn of 34, **35**
    cemetery of 34
    chaplain of 18, 20, 24, 26, 28, 42, 74, 86,
    122, 138, 140, 142, 144, 152
    gate of 30
    master's house 30
    masters of 35
      selection of 69, 88
    rooms over 68, 78, 80
  St John the Baptist, Bridgwater 20
  St John the Baptist, Canterbury 15n, 18
  St John the Baptist, Redcliffe 28
  St John the Baptist, Wells 20
  St John the Evangelist, Cirencester 15n
  St Margaret, Gloucester 15n
  St Mary Magdalen, Bath 15, 20, 22, 23, 24,
  26, 36, 43, **44**, 46, 47, 50, **51**, 52, 53, 54,
  56, 72, 88, 89, 90, 91, 108, 110, **114**, 120,
  124, 126, 127, 138, 161, 162, 163, 177
    capital messuage of 89, 110n
    farm of 23
    gardens of 23
    scheme for 138
  St Mary Magdalene, Exeter 24
  St Mary Magdalene, Gloucester 15n, 24
  St Nicholas, Harbledown, Canterbury 15n
  United 132 see also Royal United
Hot Bath 22, 30, 61, 62, 69, 70, 72, 106, 120,
122, 180
Hot Bath Pump Room 120
House of Lords, Clerk of 90
housekeeper 100, 124
housing association 166, 169

Housing Corporation 166, 169
Howse, Thomas 125
Hudd, William 180
Hugh of Wells 18, 23
Humphrey 74
Hungerford, Mary 72
Hungerford, Sir Giles 72
Hunt, William **134**, 142, 178
Hussey, Walter 22, 23, 24
Hutton Nichols Goodenough 172, 173

I

Iford, John de, Prior of Bath 28
Ilchester 35, 82, 110
Iles, Joan 81
Improvement Commission 120
infirmary 15, 20, 22, 23, 26, 28, 29, 30, 41,
48, 69
Ingram, Arthur Irvine 179
inmates 15, 24, 29, 36, 38, 40, 50, 54, 60, 89,
92, 114, 125, 138, 141, 142, 146, 156 see also
almsfolk
  rules for 76, 92, 146
  selection of 36 see also rules of admission
inns, pubs and taverns
  Bear Inn 81, 124
  Bell 25, 97, 116, 130
  Bunch of Grapes **72**, 92, **93**
  Catherine Wheel 78
  Chandos Arms 104, 156
  Chequers 104
  Crown 106, 120, 180
  George Inn 120
  Globe 108
  John Wissy's tavern 24
  Londonderry Inn 108
  Seven Dials 108
  Three Tuns 124
  White Hart 26, 80, 116, 130
Ireson, Nathaniel 108, 111
Ivy Bridge 80
Ivy, Ferdinando 72n
Ivy, Lettice 72n
Ivy, Sir George 72n
Ivy, Thomas 72n

J

Jackson, Arthur 77
Jackson, Reginald 177
James I 74
Jameson, William Luxmore 177
Jay, Edward 178
Jefferies, Richard 114
Jenkins, Julian 180
Jerusalem 18
Jessop, Gilbert 177
Jobbyn, Nicholas 54
Jocelyn of Wells 18
John, King 20
John Wood House 48, **100**, **101**, 165
Johnson, Samuel 122
Jolly, Thomas 136, 144, 178
Jolly, William Crucknell 178
Jones, Derek Morgan 166, 168, 179
Jones, Joseph 108n
Jones, Mrs 98, 104
Jones, Robert Preston 179
Judas tree 110, 127, 163

K

keeper 77, 89, 98 see also caretaker; guide;
nurse; warden
Kelly, Edward Peter Craig 179
Kemble, Revd Charles 178
Keynsham 24, 35, 84